MAKERS OF
WORLD
HISTORY

Volume I

MAKERS OF WORLD HISTORY

Volume I

J. Kelley Sowards, editor

Wichita State University

St. Martin's Press

New York

Editor: Louise Waller
Managing editor: Patricia Mansfield
Project editor: Erica Appel
Production supervisor: Katherine Battiste
Photo researcher: Inge King
Cover design: Nadia Furlan-Lorbek

For information, write:
St. Martin's Press, Inc.
175 Fifth Avenue
New York, NY 10010

ISBN: 0-312-06273-7

Acknowledgments

Akhenaton: Pritchard, J., ed. *Ancient Near Eastern Texts Relating to the Old Testament,* 3rd ed. with Supplement. Copyright © 1969 by Princeton University Press. "Hymn to Aton" reprinted by permission.

Reprinted with permission of Charles Scribner's Sons, an imprint of Macmillan Publishing Company from *The Dawn of Conscience* by James H. Breasted. Copyright 1933 James Henry Breasted; copyright © 1961 Charles Breasted, James Breasted, Jr. and Astrid Breasted Hormann.

Redford, D., *Akhenaton: The Heretic King.* Copyright © 1984 Princeton University Press. Excerpts from pp. 4, 57–60, 62–63, 137, 140–144, 166–167, 169–170, 175–178, 232–235. Reprinted with permission of Princeton University Press.

The Buddha: "The Buddha-Karita of Asvahosha" translated by E. B. Cowell from *Buddhist Mahayana,* "The Sacred Books of the East," Vol. 49, 1969. Reprinted by permission of Dover Publications, Inc.

"Buddha: What Did He Teach?" Extract taken from *The Buddha's Way* by H. Saddhatissa, reproduced by the kind permission of Unwin Hyman Ltd. Copyright © 1971 Unwin Hyman Ltd.

Acknowledgments and copyrights are continued at the back of the book on pages 301–302, which constitute an extension of the copyright page.

To Max and Carl, Jan and Jim,
Leona, and Anna Margaret

Preface

Are men and women able to force change upon history by their skill and wits, their nerve and daring? Are they capable of altering history's course by their actions? Or are they hopelessly caught in the grinding process of great, impersonal forces over which they have no real control?

Historians—like theologians, philosophers, and scientists—have long been fascinated by this question. People of every age have recognized great forces at work in their affairs, whether they perceived those forces as supernatural and divine, climatological, ecological, sociological, or economic. Yet obviously at least a few individuals—Alexander, Suleiman—were able to seize the opportunity their times offered and compel the great forces of history to change course. Still others—Confucius, Muhammad, Gandhi—were able, solely by the power of their thoughts or their visions, to shape the history of their periods and of all later times even more profoundly than conquerors or military heroes.

The purpose of this book is to examine the careers and the impact of a number of figures who have significantly influenced world history or embodied much that is significant about the periods in which they lived. At the same time the book introduces the student to the chief varieties of historical interpretation. Few personalities or events stand without comment in the historical record; contemporary accounts and documents, the so-called original sources, no less than later studies, are written by people with a distinct point of view and interpretation of what they see. Problems of interpretation are inseparable from the effort to achieve historical understanding.

The readings in this book have been chosen for their inherent interest and their particular way of treating their subject. Typically, three selections are devoted to each figure. The first selection is usually an autobiographical or contemporary biographical account; in a few instances, differing assessments by contemporaries are included. Next, a more or less orthodox interpretation is presented; it is often a selection from the "standard work" on the figure in question. The final selection offers a more recent view, which may reinforce the standard interpretation, revise it in light of new evidence, or dissent from it completely. In some cases, two very different recent views are set side by side.

A book of this size cannot hope to include full-length biographies of all the individuals studied. Instead, each chapter focuses on an important interpretive issue. In some chapters the figure's relative historical importance is at issue; in others the significance of a major point mooted in the sources; in still others the general meaning of the figure's career, as debated in a spread of interpretive positions. In every chapter, it is hoped, the question examined is interesting and basic to an understanding of the figure's place in history.

This book is an alternative edition of an earlier one, *Makers of the Western Tradition,* but adapted for use in World History, as opposed to Western Civilization, courses. The breakpoint between the two volumes lies in the late sixteenth/early seventeenth centuries—a fairly common dividing line between semester-long World History courses. Each volume contains fourteen chapters-figures; thus each fits into the fifteen weeks of a typical college semester. Each volume is also divided equally between Western and non-Western figures. This, I believe, reflects the usual subject emphasis of World History textbooks and courses. An effort was also made to represent a spread of regional civilizations among the non-Western figures—two Chinese, four Indian, two Japanese, three Near Eastern, two African, and one Native American. There is a similar spread among areas of emphasis—seventeen political leaders, seven philosophic-religious leaders, two literary-artistic figures, and three intellectuals.

Even in the selection of the Western figures every effort was made to choose figures or topics that reach out to the larger world. For example, the chapter on Alexander stresses his efforts to incorporate Asians in the management of his empire; the chapter on Cecil Rhodes deals with colonialism; and the chapter on Einstein addresses the worldwide implications of the threat of nuclear war.

For the convenience of both students and instructors, a series of Review and Study Questions has been added to each chapter. In addition, all the chapters conclude with Suggestions for Further Reading, listing in the format of the bibliographic note the best and most up-to-date books on their subjects.

J. K. S.

Contents

MAKERS OF
WORLD
HISTORY

Volume I

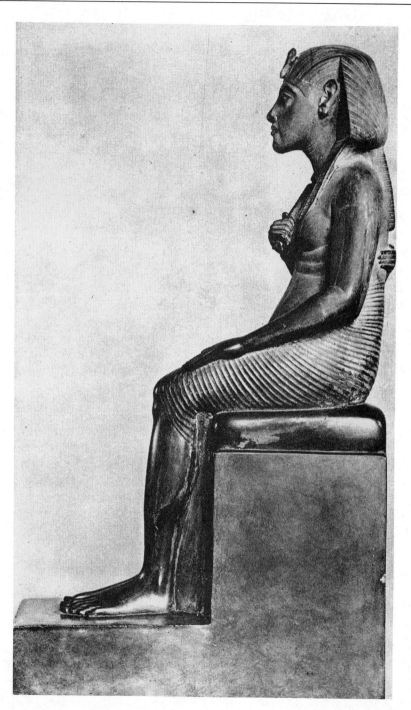

AKHENATON:
THE HERETIC KING

c. 1377 B.C.	Reign began
c. 1372 B.C.	Founded new capital of
	Akhetaton
c. 1360 B.C.	Died

With the enormous distance in time that separates us from ancient Egypt and the Near East, the scale of individual human size is reduced nearly to the point of oblivion. Even the greatest kings and conquerors, high priests, viziers, queens and "chief wives" tend to be reduced to lists of properties and exploits, names without substance or dimension.

For Egypt in particular the problem is compounded by the fact that the Egyptian culture tended to stress timelessness and eternity rather than history or individuals. The Egyptians had no continuous chronology. The names of successive pharaohs and their identifying epithets were often run together, overlapped, and sometimes blandly falsified in records and inscriptions or deliberately obliterated— probably for political purposes. The great modern British Egyptologist Sir Alan Gardiner, speaking of this maddening anonymity of Egyptian history, notes however that "in one case only, that of Akhenaten towards the end of Dyn. XVIII, do the inscriptions and reliefs bring us face to face with a personality markedly different from that of all his predecessors."[1]

This is the famous "heretic king," the most intriguing figure in Egyptian history.

---

[1]Sir Alan Gardiner, *Egypt of the Pharaohs* (Oxford: Oxford University Press; 1st ed., 1961; 1972), p. 55. The reader will note the first of several variations in the spelling of Akhenaton in this passage. Hieroglyphics did not write the vowels and there were consonant sounds we do not have. Hence considerable latitude in rendering names is to be expected.—ED.

A Hymn to Aton

There is no contemporary biographical account of this remarkable ruler, nor should we expect to find one. But what is more intriguing, conscious efforts apparently were made to obliterate every trace of him and of his reign. His name was systematically hacked out of official inscriptions and omitted from king lists. Even the genealogical lines, so important to Egyptian royal conti-nuity, were altered. But a handful of inscriptions did remain, the most sub-stantial being the Long Hymn to Aton, *from the tomb of one of Akhena-ton's successors, Eye. Part of this inscription follows below. Although the authorship of the hymn is not recorded it is quite possible that Akhenaton himself wrote it. Yet it is not about him. It is about the god Aton, the disk of the sun, to whom Akhenaton subordinated all the other myriad of Egyptian gods, "sole god, like whom there is no other!" This was the apostasy of "the heretic king." This was the offense that seems to have created the animus toward Akhenaton, nearly unique in Egyptian history.*

Thou appearest beautifully on the horizon of heaven
Thou living Aton, the beginning of life!
When thou art risen on the eastern horizon,
Thou hast filled every land with thy beauty.
Thou art gracious, great, glistening, and high over every land;
Thy rays encompass the lands to the limit of all that thou hast made:
As thou art Re, thou reachest to the end of them;
(Thou) subduest them (for) thy beloved son.
. . . .
When thou settest in the western horizon,
The land is in darkness, in the manner of death.
Every lion is come forth from his den;
All creeping things, they sting.
Darkness *is a shroud,* and the earth is in stillness,
For he who made them rests in his horizon.

At daybreak, when thou arisest on the horizon,
When thou shinest as the Aton by day,
Thou drivest away the darkness and givest thy rays.
. . . .
All the world, they do their work.
All beasts are content with their pasturage;

2

Trees and plants are flourishing.
The birds which fly from their nests,
Their wings are (stretched out) in praise to thy *ka*.
All beasts spring upon (their) feet.
Whatever flies and alights,
They live when thou hast risen (for) them.
The ships are sailing north and south as well,
For every way is open at thy appearance.
The fish in the river dart before thy face;
Thy rays are in the midst of the great green sea.

. . . .

How manifold it is, what thou hast made!
They are hidden from the face (of man).
O sole god, like whom there is no other!
Thou didst create the world according to thy desire,
Whilst thou wert alone:
All men, cattle, and wild beasts,
Whatever is on earth, going upon (its) feet,
And what is on high, flying with its wings.

The countries of Syria and Nubia, the *land* of Egypt,
Thou settest every man in his place,
Thou suppliest their necessities:
Everyone has his food, and his time of life is reckoned.
Their tongues are separate in speech,
And their natures as well;
Their skins are distinguished,
As thou distinguishest the foreign peoples.
Thou makest a Nile in the underworld,
Thou bringest it forth as thou desirest
To maintain the people (of Egypt)
According as thou madest them for thyself,
The lord of all of them, wearying (himself) with them,
The lord of every land, rising for them,
The Aton of the day, great of majesty.

. . . .

Thou art in my heart,
And there is no other that knows thee
Save thy son Nefer-kheperu-Re Wa-en-Re,
For thou hast made him well-versed in thy plans and in thy strength.

The world came into being by thy hand,
According as thou hast made them.
When thou hast risen they live,

When thou settest they die.
Thou art lifetime thy own self,
For one lives (only) through thee.
Eyes are (fixed) on beauty until thou settest.
All work is laid aside when thou settest in the west.
(But) when (thou) risest (again),
[*Everything is*] made to flourish for the king, . . .
Since thou didst found the earth
And raise them up for thy son,
Who came forth from thy body:
the King of Upper and Lower Egypt, . . . Akh-en-Aton. . . . and
the Chief Wife of the King . . . Nefert-iti, living and youthful forever
and ever.

The Dawn of Conscience

JAMES H. BREASTED

*The name of Akhenaton was scarcely known at all in Egyptian studies until
the beginning of this century and the excavations at Tell el-Amarna. The
documents and inscriptions that came to light—including the* Hymn to
Aton—*fascinated Egyptologists, and they began to reconstruct the history
of this king and his age. A leading role was taken by the American
Egyptologist James H. Breasted. Breasted created an engaging portrait of
the young pharaoh, hardly more than a boy, who turned his back upon the
militaristic aggressiveness of his father, Amenhotep III, in favor of a new
and revolutionary religious revelation. Breasted argued that Akhenaton
was not only the first clearly discernible individual in history but the first
person in history to conceive the worship of a single god, in his case Aton,
the disk of the sun. Further, Breasted argued, Akhenaton anticipated the
Hebrew monotheism of Moses and he adduced, as part of his case, the great*
Hymn to Aton *and its clear affinities with the Old Testament, in particular Psalm 104.*

*Breasted's account of Akhenaton and his religious revolution continues in
the following excerpt, taken from his most famous book,* The Dawn of
Conscience.

On a moment's reflection, such fundamental changes as these suggest
what an overwhelming tide of inherited thought, custom, and tradition had been diverted from its channel by the young king who was

guiding this revolution. It is only as this aspect of his movement is clearly discerned that we begin to appreciate the power of his remarkable personality. Before his time religious documents were commonly attributed to ancient kings and wise men, and the power of a belief lay chiefly in its claim to remote antiquity and the sanctity of immemorial custom. Until Ikhnaton the history of the world had largely been merely the irresistible drift of tradition. The outstanding exception was the great physician-architect, Imhotep, who introduced stone architecture and built the first stone masonry pyramidal tomb of the Thirtieth Century B.C. Otherwise men had been but drops of water in the great current. With the possible exception of Imhotep, Ikhnaton was the first individual in history. Consciously and deliberately, by intellectual process he gained his position, and then placed himself squarely in the face of tradition and swept it aside. He appeals to no myths, to no ancient and widely accepted versions of the dominion of the gods, to no customs sanctified by centuries—he appeals only to the present and visible evidences of his god's dominion, evidences open to all, and as for tradition wherever it had left material manifestations of other gods in records which could be reached, he endeavoured to annihilate it. A policy so destructive was doomed to encounter fatal opposition. . . .

Here had been a great people, the onward flow of whose life, in spite of its almost irresistible momentum, had been suddenly arrested and then diverted into a strange channel. Their holy places had been desecrated, the shrines sacred with the memories of thousands of years had been closed up, the priests driven away, the offerings and temple incomes confiscated, and the old order blotted out. Everywhere whole communities, moved by instincts flowing from untold centuries of habit and custom, returned to their holy places to find them no more, and stood dumfounded before the closed doors of the ancient sanctuaries. On feast days, sanctified by memories of earliest childhood, venerable halls that had resounded with the rejoicings of the multitudes, as we have recalled them at Siut, now stood silent and empty; and every day as the funeral processions wound across the desert margin and up the plateau to the cemetery, the great comforter and friend, Osiris, the champion of the dead in every danger, was banished, and no man dared so much as utter his name. Even in their oaths, absorbed from childhood with their mothers' milk, the involuntary names must not be suffered to escape the lips: and in the presence of the magistrate at court the ancient oath must now contain only the name of Aton. All this to them was as if the modern man were asked to worship X and swear by Y. Groups of muttering priests, nursing implacable hatred, must have mingled their curses with the execration of whole communities of discontented tradesmen—bakers who no longer drew a livelihood from the sale of ceremonial cakes at the temple feasts; craftsmen who no longer sold amulets of the old gods at the temple gateway; hack sculptors whose statues of Osiris lay under piles of dust in many a tumbled-down studio; cemetery stone-cutters who found their tawdry tombstones with scenes from the Book of the Dead banished from the necropolis; scribes whose rolls of the same book, filled with the names of the old gods, or even if they bore the word god in the plural, were anathema; actors and priestly mimes who were driven away from the sacred groves on the days when they should have presented to the people the "passion play," and murmuring groups of pilgrims at Abydos who would have taken part in this drama of the life and death and resurrection of Osiris; physicians deprived of their whole stock in trade of exorcising ceremonies, employed with success since the days of the earliest kings, two thousand years before; shepherds who no longer dared to place a loaf and a jar of water under yonder tree, hoping thus to escape the anger of the goddess who dwelt in it, and who might afflict the household with sickness in her wrath; peasants who feared to erect a rude image of Osiris in the field to drive away the typhonic demons of drought and famine; mothers soothing their babes at twilight and fearing to utter the old sacred names and prayers learned in childhood, to drive away from their little ones the lurking demons of the dark. In the midst of a whole land thus darkened by clouds of smouldering discontent, this marvellous young king, and the group of sympathisers who surrounded him, set up their tabernacle to the daily light, in serene unconsciousness of the fatal darkness that enveloped all around and grew daily darker and more threatening.

In placing the movement of Ikhnaton against a background of popular discontent like this, and adding to the picture also the far more immediately dangerous secret opposition of the ancient priesthoods, the still unconquered party of Amon, and the powerful military group, who were disaffected by the king's peace policy in Asia and his lack of interest in imperial administration and maintenance, we begin to discern something of the powerful individuality of this first intellectual leader in history. His reign was the earliest attempt at a rule of ideas, irrespective of the condition and willingness of the people upon whom they were to be forced. . . .

And so the fair city of the Amarna plain arose, a fatuous Island of the Blest in a sea of discontent, a vision of fond hopes, born in a mind fatally forgetful that the past cannot be annihilated. The marvel is that such a man should have first arisen in the East, and especially in Egypt, where no man except Ikhnaton possessed the ability to forget. Nor was the great Mediterranean World which Egypt now dominated any better prepared for an international religion than its Egyptian lords. The imperial imagination of Ikhnaton reminds one of that of Alexander the Great, a thousand years later, but it was many centuries in advance of his own age. . . .

The fall of the great revolutionary is shrouded in complete obscurity. The immediate result of his fall was the restoration of Amon and the old gods whom the Amonite priesthood forced upon Ikhnaton's youthful and feeble son-in-law, Tutenkhamon. The old régime returned. . . . In the great royal lists recording on the monuments the names of all the past kings of Egypt, the name of Ikhnaton never appears; and when under later Pharaohs, it was necessary in a state document to refer to him, he was called "the criminal of Akhetaton."

The Criminal of Akhetaton

DONALD B. REDFORD

It was inevitable that such an unequivocal and highly colored interpretation as Breasted's would attract critics. And it was not simply a matter of interpretation. The Amarna records continued to be studied and refined and new finds were made, there and elsewhere, including the dramatic discovery of the nearly intact tomb of Tutankhamen, Akhenaton's son-in-law. The continuing, patient work of Egyptologists, archaeologists, and historians has produced a rather more complicated story of Akhenaton than Breasted presented—and a considerably darker one. We now know, for example, that he actually reigned alone for only two and a half years at the most; the rest of his reign he shared with regents. This clearly implies that Akhenaton was somehow incompetent to rule, either because of physical or mental incapacity or because he chose not to exercise the powers of his office. We now know that the failure of his religious program was not a matter of the narrow jealousy of the priesthood of Amon, but a general rejection by the whole Egyptian society. It has even been argued that his monotheism may have been only a selfish celebration of his own religious totalitarianism and no true religious movement at all.

The materials for a radically revised assessment of Akhenaton and his reign have been accumulating for more than half a century and Akhenaton now stands revealed not as the clear-eyed visionary of Breasted but as the "heretic king." One of the leading figures in contemporary Akhenaton scholarship is the distinguished field Egyptologist Donald B. Redford. The following account is taken from Redford's book, Akhenaten: The Heretic King.

Possibly in the fifth month of the civil calendar in what had been his father's 38th year (January, 1377 B.C.), Amenophis IV[2] ascended the Horus throne of the living. If sculptors showed uncertainty as to how to treat the strange figure of their new sovereign in art, they but mirrored a general hesitancy and puzzlement about what to expect from this young and unknown ruler. In contrast to the frequent appearance of his brothers and sisters, Amenophis, the second son of Amenophis III—his older brother has died young—is conspicuous by his absence from the monuments of his father. It may well be that he was intentionally kept in the background because of a congenital ailment which made him hideous to behold. The repertoire of Amarna art has made us familiar with the effeminate appearance of the young man: elongated skull, fleshy lips, slanting eyes, lengthened ear lobes, prominent jaw, narrow shoulders, potbelly, enormous hips and thighs, and spindly legs. Of late the experts have tended to identify his problem with some sort of endocrine disorder in which secondary sex characteristics failed to develop, and eunuchoidism resulted.

Be that as it may, it is a fact that Amenophis does not appear on monuments during his father's reign. The only certain reference to him seems to be on a wine-jar seal from Malkata where his name appears in the expression, "the estate of the true(?) king's-son Amenophis." He was, then, old enough to have his own establishment during the last decade of his father's reign, and, as we should expect, was residing at that time with the rest of the court at Thebes. . . .

As we shall see, the changes in cultic iconography and, undoubtedly, the decision to build new structures for a new god belong to the very beginning of Akhenaten's reign. . . .

When Amenophis III died the great complex of Amun at Karnak seemed to have reached a stage of structural completion. . . .

For a few months into the new reign, or perhaps for as much as a single year, sculpting and architectural decoration of a traditional nature proceeded apace. . . . Sometime in the 5th year of his reign, the heretic pharaoh moved the court from Thebes to a new capital in Middle Egypt. Though the change seems to be sudden, it was in fact premeditated. It proved to be the major watershed in the Amarna period. At this point then, let us take stock of the earliest, "Theban" phase of this unusual reign, before moving on toward the denouement of the drama.

Though his intent may have crystalized in his 4th year, Amenophis IV appears to have made no move until his 5th. Then planners,

---

[2]This was the original regnal name assumed by Akhenaton.—ED.

surveyors, and builders appeared at the chosen site, and work began at a feverish pace.

But the king was not quite finished with Thebes. Before departing, and almost by way of a Parthian shot,[3] he unfurled his true iconoclastic colors. Amun was declared anathema. The king changed his name from "Amenophis, the Divine, the Ruler of Thebes" to Akhenaten, which means something like "He who is useful to the Sun-disc," or perhaps "Glorified Spirit of the Sun-disc." Everywhere at Thebes and other cities, in the sun-temples he had built, workmen laid coats of gypsum plaster over the second of the royal cartouches and recut the new name over the old. Undoubtedly it was at the same time that hatchetmen were dispatched to range throughout the temples of the land to desecrate the name "Amun" wherever it appeared on walls, steles, tombs, or objects d'art. Amun's congeners Mut, Osiris, and others suffered too, but to a lesser extent. . . . All efforts were now concentrated on building the new "dream city" of Akhetaten, the "Horizon of the Disc." Sometime during the 5th year, Amenophis IV, or Akhenaten as we shall now call him, arrived at the construction site with his court. No building was as yet complete, and most were probably but a marked layout on the ground; but the king was impatient to live with his father, the sun-disc, in his own special city, and was willing to put up with temporary quarters. The royal family for the rest of that year, and well into the 6th year, made do with a prefabricated dwelling, probably tentlike, which is called "tent (*imw psšt*) of apartments(?)" in the texts.

If people initially treated Amenophis IV with a certain wariness born of fear of an unknown quantity, they were soon to learn that the king lacked the fear-inspiring qualities of his father. The evenhanded policy Amenophis hoped to adopt toward Egypt's dependencies, and which in a moment of foolish candor he had made known even to his least trustworthy vassal, could easily be interpreted as weakness. Perhaps from the outset it was a weakness that the king was rationalizing as fairness. At any rate, Amenophis IV soon found it impossible to enforce his will in Egypt's Levantine sphere of influence. . . .

Even the casual observer will be struck first and foremost by the negative thrust of Akhenaten's reform of the cultus. He excised from the traditional religion much more than he added. The service of the gods was done away with, and their temples allowed to sit idle. In the wake of the desuetude of the cult, the myths of the gods, which provided the hypostasis of many cultic elements, simply disappeared.

---

[3]The Asiatic Parthians supposedly were adept at a backward bow shot when they seemed to be retreating.—ED.

The sun god Akhenaten championed, of course, enjoyed no mythology; after the early months of the reign he was not even permitted an anthropomorphic depiction. No archetypal symbolism informs the artistic style that celebrates the new god, and the very few names and accouterments the sun-disc borrows are entirely from the solar cult of Re and his divine congeners. The marvelously complex world of the Beyond is banished from the minds of men. No truth can come from anyone but the king, and his truth is entirely apodictic: no gods but the sun, no processional temples, no cultic acts but the rudimentary offering, no cult images, no anthropomorphisms, no myths, no concept of the ever-changing manifestation of a divine world. The Roman world might well have called Akhenaten an "atheist," for what he left to Egypt was not a "god" at all, but a disc in the heavens! . . . Roughly at about the same time that the king was laying firm plans for the move to the new site of Akhetaten, a drastic change overcame his cultic program. The decoration of the new temples was all but complete when the king openly broke with Amun. The "king of the gods," tolerated to this point, though his worship had probably languished through lack of priests, now witnessed the formal anathematization of his name and the closing of his temple. The program of defacement that followed was so thorough that we must postulate either a small army of hatchetmen dispatched throughout the realm, or parties of inspectors charged with seeing that local officials did the job. Everywhere, in temples, tombs, statuary, and casual inscriptions, the hieroglyphs for "Amun" and representations of the god were chiseled out; objects sacred to him were likewise defaced. People who bore names compounded with "Amun" were obliged to change them; and the king led the way by discarding the now unacceptable *Amenophis* ("Amun is satisfied") for *Akh-en-aten* ("Effective for the Sun-disc"). Osiris and his cycle of mortuary gods suffered a like anathematization. Funerary practices might be spared, but only if purged of all polytheistic elements. . . .

If any further proof is required of what the king was trying to do, let this one significant omission suffice: the plural word "gods" is never attested after year 5, and occasionally it is found erased in existing inscriptions. For Akhenaten's program, implicitly from the start, and now blatantly and universally, fostered a monotheism that would brook no divine manifestations. The Sun-disc was unique and supreme over all the universe, the only god there was. He did not change his shape or appear in other forms: he was always and only "the living Sun-disc—there is none other than he!"

At Akhetaten the major part of our knowledge about the character of the Disc comes from the great hymn inscribed in the tomb of Ay, quite likely a composition of the king himself. After Akhenaten's aversion to mythology and its symbolism had obliged him to expunge from the genre of hymns all such allusions, the only concepts that could be predicated of the deity were those of universalism, dependence of life on the sun, transcendence, creativity, cosmic regularity, and absolute power. . . .

The doctrine of the sun-disc constituted a strong reaffirmation of divine kingship, as the role Akhenaten assigned himself proves. In the first five years the fragmentary texts from the *talatat*[4] stress the paternity of the Disc and the sonship of the king: the latter is the son of the Sun-disc, the "beautiful child of the Disc" whose "beauty" was "created" by the heavenly luminary. Akhenaten has been granted the kingship by his father, and occupies his thone on earth: heaven and earth are his, his boundaries reach the limits of heaven, and all lands are beneath his feet.

Enough, I hope, has been brought forward in the preceding pages to show that the historical Akhenaten is markedly different from the figure popularists have created for us. Humanist he was not, and certainly no humanitarian romantic. To make of him a tragic "Christlike" figure is a sheer falsehood. Nor is he the mentor of Moses: a vast gulf is fixed between the rigid, coercive, rarified monotheism of the pharaoh and Hebrew henotheism,[5] which in any case we see through the distorted prism of texts written 700 years after Akhenaten's death. Certain affinities have long since been pointed out between the hymn to the sun-disc and Psalm 104, and the parallels are to be taken seriously. There is, however, no literary influence here, but rather a survival in the tradition of the northern centers of Egypt's once-great empire of the *themes* of that magnificent poetic creation.

If we pass in review the hard facts we have adduced above, and, in the absence of facts the circumstantial evidence, we then catch a glimpse of *this* pharaonic figure. A man deemed ugly by the accepted standards of the day, secluded in the palace in his minority, certainly close to his mother, possibly ignored by his father, outshone by his brother and sisters, unsure of himself, Akhenaten suffered the singular misfortune of acceding to the throne of Egypt and its empire. We have no idea who or what influenced him in his formative years; but he was not brought into contact with his father's court, nor is there any evidence that he spent time at Heliopolis. As a result he nurtured a fear

---

[4]*Talatat* are uniformly sized facing stones that were covered with texts and drawings. They were later removed from the site of El-Amarna and used as fill for other structures or scattered.—ED.

[5]The belief in one god as the specific tribal god of a particular people while not denying the existence of other gods of other peoples.—ED.

and aversion to his father's coterie of gifted administrators and the noble families from which they had sprung; and his apprehension was extended even to those foreign potentates with whom his father had been on intimate terms. There is evidence to suggest that he was a poor judge of character and a prey to sycophancy. Though he was apprehensive about his own lack of resolve, he nonetheless espoused a lenient policy toward his northern provinces which deterred him from acting unhesitatingly in the Asian sphere. Not being gifted as an administrator, Akhenaten was willing to leave the running of everyday affairs, both foreign and domestic, in the hands of military and civilian intermediaries, while he pursued his program of cultic reform.

Akhenaten, whatever else he may have been, was no intellectual heavyweight. He failed to comprehend (or if he did, to appreciate) the true role and potential of cultic mythology, possibly seeing in it a means of concealment rather than revelation of the deity. Maybe he was reacting to the sophisticated cynicism of the age, just as Luther did in the 16th century A.D.; but if so he was surely guilty of identifying the aberrations of the system with its essence. For myths are the building blocks of any religion, even Judeo-Christianity. Though they come to us as the often crass impedimenta from an early and slightly embarrassing stage in our intellectual development, myths nonetheless pose the challenge of reinterpretation on a higher plane and integration one with another to provide a new and consistent view of the supernatural. Ancient Egyptian, like modern, theologians rose to this challenge, and such documents as the Memphite Theology and the New Kingdom hymns to Ptah and Amun are philosophical treatises of the highest achievement. What did Akhenaten substitute for them, once he had declared them anathema? Nothing! If mythology (in the broadest application of the term) is the only means of divine revelation, apart from the vision of the mystic, then what Akhenaten championed was in the truest sense of the word, atheism.

For the icon he devised, that spiderlike disc, could never be viewed as "god." What it was Akhenaten tells us plainly enough: the Disc was his father, the universal king. Significant, it seems to me, is the fact that, on the eve of Amenophis III's passing, the king who sat upon Egypt's throne bore as his most popular sobriquet the title "The Dazzling Sun-disc"; on the morrow of the "revolution" the only object of veneration in the supernal realm is king Sun-disc, exalted in the heavens and ubiquitously termed by Akhenaten "my father." I will not pursue the implications of this, though they appear to me plain enough.

That Akhenaten possessed unusual ability as a poet is, I think, self-evident. For him nature itself, in all its forms, displayed sufficient fascination; the gratification to be had in ruminating on imponderables paled by comparison. Although many images are derivative, the great hymn to the Disc stands out as a major, almost "positivist," statement on the beauty of creation.

I strongly suspect Akhenaten also had a flair for art, sculpture, and design, although this might be harder to demonstrate. The startlingly new expressionism that bursts on the scene in the second year of the reign probably owes more to the monarch's tastes than to those of his artists; and in the light of the well-known drafting ability of Thutmosid kings, it would be difficult to deny that the king also had a hand in working out the details of the new canons. To me it is the art associated with his program that remains Akhenaten's single most important contribution.

Beautiful though they may be, the Amarna reliefs reveal one of the most displeasing characteristics of the way of life Akhenaten held up as a model, refined sloth. Can the king engage in no more strenuous activity than elevating offerings? True, he rides a chariot; how often does he walk? Time and again we glimpse him lounging, completely limp, in a chair or on a stool. He is seen eating and drinking at a table groaning with food, occasionally interrupting his indulgence to lean languidly from the balcony and smile weakly at some sniveling sycophant in the court beneath. Is this effete monarch, who could never hunt or do battle, a true descendant of the authors of Egypt's empire? The court over which he presides is nothing but an aggregation of voluptuaries, bent on personal gratification, and their opportunist followers.

If the king and his circle inspire me somewhat with contempt, it is apprehension I feel when I contemplate his "religion." In Egypt the sun may well be a reliable and beneficent power, but it is nonetheless destructive, and mankind seeks to hide from it. If Re must be worshipped, let there be a refuge of shade close at hand! Both Karnak and Akhetaten become infernos from March to November. Yet the monarch—with relish it would seem!—not only selected these unholy sites for his use, but insisted on the simple open shrine, with no roof and very little shade, in which to honor his father! As one stands on the baking sand of the vast Amarna amphitheater, one cannot help but sense a sinister quality in all of this.

Not content with the subjection of his own body to the rays of his father at every waking moment, the autocratic ruler demanded everyone else follow suit! A fascinating letter found in the Amarna Tablets from the king of Assyria tells us this, and thus opens a new vista on Akhenaten's mental state. Ashuruballit I, eager to open relations with Egypt now that Mitanni had been weakened, sent a delegation to Akhetaten; but they must have returned saying something like this: this pharaoh must be crazy! He holds his audiences, meetings, and ceremonies entirely in the sun, and keeps everyone standing in the heat! This occasioned the following remonstrance from the Assyrian sovereign to Akhenaten: "Why are my messengers kept standing in the open sun? They will die in the open sun. If it does the king good to stand in the open sun, then let the king stand there and die in the open sun. Then will there be profit for the king! But really, why should they die in the open sun? . . . They will be killed in the open sun!." The vignette here sketched is at once comical and outrageous. The regime was plainly, at this stage, intolerable.

For all that can be said in his favor, Akhenaten in spirit remains to the end totalitarian. The right of an individual freely to choose was wholly foreign to him. He was the champion of a universal, celestial power who demanded universal submission, claimed universal truth, and from whom no further revelation could be expected. I cannot conceive a more tiresome regime under which to be fated to live.

Review and Study Questions

1. Why was Akhenaton so hated and reviled by his own people in the centuries following his reign?
2. In your opinion, how important was the religious thought of Akhenaton, and how much influence did he have in the development of monotheism?
3. Was Akhenaton a heroic individual and intellectual pioneer, or was he a weak and incompetent dreamer? Give the reasons for your answer.

Suggestions for Further Reading

For all the antiquity of its subject, the Akhenaton controversy is essentially a modern one, a continuing dispute among Egyptologists about nearly everything connected with the so-called Amarna period of Eighteenth Dynasty Egyptian history and its central figure. The most extreme debunking interpretation of Akhenaton is F. J. Giles, *Ikhnaton: Legend and History* (London: Hutchinson, 1970). Very much in this tradition is Donald B. Redford, *Akhenaten: The Heretic King* (Princeton: Princeton University Press, 1984), excerpted for this chapter. Some of the studies in an earlier work by Redford, *History and Chronology of the Eighteenth Dynasty of Egypt: Seven Studies* (Toronto: University of Toronto Press, 1967) support his view. Dissenting from this view is Cyril Aldred, *Akhenaten: King of Egypt* (London: Thames and Hudson, 1988), a significant revision of Aldred's earlier *Akhenaten: A New Study.* Aldred's interpretation is popularized in Joy Collier, *King Sun: In Search of Akhenaten* (London: Ward Lock, 1970), also published under the title, *The Heretic Pharaoh* (New York: Day, 1970). The chapter on Akhenaton in P. H. Newby, *Warrior Pharaohs: The Rise and Fall of the Egyptian Empire* (London and Boston: Faber and Faber, 1980) is excellent and the final chapter in A. Rosalie David, *Cult of the Sun: Myth and Magic in Ancient Egypt* (London et al.: J. M. Dent, 1980) is a good survey of the controversy. Another source is James H. Breasted, *The Dawn of Conscience* (New York: Scribner, 1933), excerpted for this chapter. The inscription "A Hymn to Aton," also in this chapter, is taken from J. Pritchard, ed., *Ancient Near Eastern Texts Relating to the Old Testament,* 3rd edition with supplement (Princeton: Princeton University Press, 1969). The Pulitzer Prize–winning novelist Allen Drury has written a novel dealing with Akhenaton, *A God against the Gods* (New York: Doubleday, 1976) and one about his successor, Tutankhamun, *Return to Thebes* (New York: Doubleday, 1977). The most famous of all modern novels of ancient Egypt, Mika Waltari, *The Egyptian: A Novel,* tr. Naomi Walford (New York: Putnam, 1949), uses the revolution of Akhenaton as a backdrop for its plot.

For the larger setting of Egyptian history there are a number of excellent books. John A. Wilson, *The Burden of Egypt: An Interpretation of Ancient Egyptian Culture* (Chicago: University of Chicago Press, 1951), republished under the title *The Culture of Ancient Egypt* (Chicago: Phoenix, 1971), while somewhat dated in its research, is still valuable for its insights and is an eminently readable book. Equally readable is Sir Alan Gardiner, *Egypt of the Pharaohs: An Introduction* (London and New York: Oxford University Press, 1972). A somewhat more popularized book is Pierre Montet, *Lives of the Pharaohs* (Cleveland and New York: World, 1968). A good up-to-date historical survey of Egypt, including the Akhenaton period, is Cyril Aldred, *The Egyptians,* rev. and enlarged ed. (London: Thames and Hudson, 1984). John Romer, *People of the Nile: Everyday Life in Ancient Egypt* (New York: Crown, 1982) is lively and interesting as are T. G. H. James, *Pharaoh's People: Scenes from Life in Imperial Egypt* (Chicago: University of Chicago Press, 1984) and *Egypt's Golden Age: The Art of Living in the New Kingdom, 1558–1085 B.C.* (Boston: Museum of Fine Arts, 1982). Finally, to understand more fully the profound nature of Akhenaton's religious revolt, students should read Henri Frankfort, *Ancient Egyptian Religion: An Interpretation* (New York: Columbia University Press, 1948; republished by Harper Torchbooks, 1961), a popular but authoritative essay, and very readable. A more recent work of the same sort is A. Rosalie David, *The Ancient Egyptians: Religious Beliefs and Practices* (London: Routledge and Kegan Paul, 1982).

THE BUDDHA:
THE ENLIGHTENED ONE

c. 563 B.C.   Born
c. 547 B.C.   Married to Princess Yasodhara
c. 534 B.C.   Renounced princely life and be-
               gan his religious mission
c. 528 B.C.   Received the enlightenment
c. 483 B.C.   Died

Siddhartha Gautama was born about 563 B.C. in northeast India, in the city of Kapilavastua, near the border of Nepal. In midlife, after a long spiritual journey, he passed through the ultimate transcendental experience of self-awakening that made him the Buddha or "enlightened one." He went on from that experience through the next half-century of his long life to found one of the world's great religions, Buddhism.

The Buddha: Who Was He?

THE BUDDHA-KARITA OF ASVAGHOSHA

The traditional account of the Buddha's life, like those of other early religious leaders, is a blend of the historical and the legendary. Moreover, the biography of the Buddha became part of an enormous, pious accretion surrounding his teachings. These teachings, or "sayings," of the Buddha were supposed to have been put together in five collections or "baskets" by Ananda, a cousin and devoted early disciple, shortly after the Buddha's death. This is doubtful, however, since the opening words of the canon, "Thus have I heard," form a timeworn, formulaic phrase for reporting the Buddha's words within the framework of a long tradition of oral transmission. In fact, there is no trace of any authentic contemporary text; the texts all appear in later languages and dialects, and all bear the marks of an oral tradition.

The text from which the following selection is taken is one of several canonical or "official" biographical accounts, some written in Pali and some in Sanskrit. This one, the Buddha-Karita, *was written in Sanskrit by a Buddhist scholar named Asvaghosha, who probably lived in the first century of the Christian era. It takes the form of a long epic poem, thirteen books of which survive. The poem itself bears many of the marks of long oral transmission typical of epic literature: it repeats titles and epithets; it makes lavish use of omens and supernatural foreshadowing of events; and it endows its central figure with a range of divine and heroic attributes that virtually conceal the historic personality. It is, nevertheless, the best ancient version we have.*

The account begins by describing the Buddha's parents and his miraculous birth.

There was a city, the dwelling-place of the great saint Kapila, having its sides surrounded by the beauty of a lofty broad table-land as by a line of clouds, and itself, with its high-soaring palaces, immersed in the sky. . . .

A king, by name Suddhodana, of the kindred of the sun, anointed to stand at the head of earth's monarchs,—ruling over the city, adorned it, as a bee-inmate a full-blown lotus.

The very best of kings with his train ever near him,—intent on liberality yet devoid of pride; a sovereign, yet with an ever equal eye thrown on all,—of gentle nature and yet with wide-reaching majesty. . . .

To him there was a queen, named Mâyâ, as if free from all deceit (mâyâ)—an effulgence proceeding from his effulgence, like the splendour of the sun when it is free from all the influence of darkness,—a chief queen in the united assembly of all queens. . . .

Then falling from the host of beings in the Tushita heaven, and illumining the three worlds, the most excellent of Bodhisattvas suddenly entered at a thought into her womb, like the Nâga-king entering the cave of Nandâ.[1]

Assuming the form of a huge elephant white like Himâlaya, armed with six tusks, with his face perfumed with flowing ichor, he entered the womb of the queen of king Suddhodana, to destroy the evils of the world. . . .

Then one day by the king's permission the queen, having a great longing in her mind, went with the inmates of the gynaeceum[2] into the garden Lumbinî.

As the queen supported herself by a bough which hung laden with a weight of flowers, the Bodhisattva suddenly came forth, cleaving open her womb. . . .

Having thus in due time issued from the womb, he shone as if he had come down from heaven, he who had not been born in the natural way,—he who was born full of wisdom, not foolish,—as if his mind had been purified by countless aeons of contemplation. . . .

The wandering sage Asita appears and is entertained by the king.

Then the king, having duly honoured the sage, who was seated in his seat, with water for the feet and an arghya offering, invited him (to speak) with all ceremonies of respect. . . .

The sage, being thus invited by the king, filled with intense feeling as was due, uttered his deep and solemn words, having his large eyes opened wide with wonder: . . .

'But hear now the motive for my coming and rejoice thereat; a heavenly voice has been heard by me in the heavenly path, that thy son has been born for the sake of supreme knowledge. . . .

'Having forsaken his kingdom, indifferent to all worldly objects,

---

[1]The term *Bodhisattva* means "Buddha to be." It later came to mean all the previous lives of the Buddha. The other terms—*Tushita heaven, the three worlds,* and *the Nâga-king*—are later Hindu terms and concepts that came to permeate Buddhist literature.—ED.

[2]*Gynaeceum* is a term for women's quarters or harem.—ED.

and having attained the highest truth by strenuous efforts, he will shine forth as a sun of knowledge to destroy the darkness of illusion in the world.

'He will deliver by the boat of knowledge the distressed world, borne helplessly along, from the ocean of misery which throws up sickness as its foam, tossing with the waves of old age, and rushing with the dreadful onflow of death. . . .

Having heard these words, the king with his queen and his friends abandoned sorrow and rejoiced; thinking, 'such is this son of mine,' he considered that his excellence was his own.

But he let his heart be influenced by the thought, 'he will travel by the noble path,'—he was not in truth averse to religion, yet still he saw alarm at the prospect of losing his child. . . .

When he had passed the period of childhood and reached that of middle youth, the young prince learned in a few days the various sciences suitable to his race, which generally took many years to master.

But having heard before from the great seer Asita his destined future which was to embrace transcendental happiness, the anxious care of the king of the present Sâkya race turned the prince to sensual pleasures.

Then he sought for him from a family of unblemished moral excellence a bride possessed of beauty, modesty, and gentle bearing, of wide-spread glory, Yasodharâ by name, having a name well worthy of her, a very goddess of good fortune. . . .

In course of time to the fair-bosomed Yasodharâ,—who was truly glorious in accordance with her name,—there was born from the son of Suddhodana a son named Râhula, with a face like the enemy of Râhu.

Then the king who from regard to the welfare of his race had longed for a son and been exceedingly delighted [at his coming],—as he had rejoiced at the birth of his son, so did he now rejoice at the birth of his grandson. . . .

Having heard of the delightful appearance of the city groves beloved by the women, [the prince] resolved to go out of doors, like an elephant long shut up in a house.

The king, having learned the character of the wish thus expressed by his son, ordered a pleasure-party to be prepared, worthy of his own affection and his son's beauty and youth.

He prohibited the encounter of any afflicted common person in the highroad; 'heaven forbid that the prince with his tender nature should even imagine himself to be distressed.'

Then having removed out of the way with the greatest gentleness all those who had mutilated limbs or maimed senses, the decrepit and the sick and all squalid beggars, they made the highway assume its perfect beauty. . . .

But then the gods, dwelling in pure abodes, having beheld that city thus rejoicing like heaven itself, created an old man to walk along on purpose to stir the heart of the king's son.

The prince having beheld him thus overcome with decrepitude and different in form from other men, with his gaze intently fixed on him, thus addressed his driver with simple confidence:

'Who is this man that has come here, O charioteer, with white hair and his hand resting on a staff, his eyes hidden beneath his brows, his limbs bent down and hanging loose,—is this a change produced in him or his natural state or an accident?'

Thus addressed, the charioteer revealed to the king's son the secret that should have been kept so carefully, thinking no harm in his simplicity, for those same gods had bewildered his mind:

'That is old age by which he is broken down,—the ravisher of beauty, the ruin of vigour, the cause of sorrow, the destruction of delights, the bane of memories, the enemy of the senses.

'He too once drank milk in his childhood, and in course of time he learned to grope on the ground; having step by step become a vigorous youth, he has step by step in the same way reached old age.'

Being thus addressed, the prince, starting a little, spoke these words to the charioteer, 'What! will this evil come to me also?' and to him again spoke the charioteer:

'It will come without doubt by the force of time through multitude of years even to my long-lived lord; all the world knows thus that old age will destroy their comeliness and they are content to have it so.' . . .

Then the same deities created another man with his body all afflicted by disease; and on seeing him the son of Suddhodana addressed the charioteer, having his gaze fixed on the man:

'Yonder man with a swollen belly, his whole frame shaking as he pants, his arms and shoulders hanging loose, his body all pale and thin, uttering plaintively the word "mother," when he embraces a stranger,—who, pray, is this?'

Then his charioteer answered, 'Gentle Sir, it is a very great affliction called sickness, that has grown up, caused by the inflammation of the (three) humours, which has made even this strong man no longer master of himself.'

Then the prince again addressed him, looking upon the man compassionately, 'Is this evil peculiar to him or are all beings alike threatened by sickness?'

Then the charioteer answered, 'O prince, this evil is common to all;

thus pressed round by diseases men run to pleasure, though racked with pain.' . . .

But as the king's son was thus going on his way, the very same deities created a dead man, and only the charioteer and the prince, and none else, beheld him as he was carried dead along the road.

Then spoke the prince to the charioteer, 'Who is this borne by four men, followed by mournful companions, who is bewailed, adorned but no longer breathing?'

Then the driver,—having his mind overpowered by the gods who possess pure minds and pure dwellings,—himself knowing the truth, uttered to his lord this truth also which was not to be told:

'This is some poor man who, bereft of his intellect, senses, vital airs and qualities, lying asleep and unconscious, like mere wood or straw, is abandoned alike by friends and enemies after they have carefully swathed and guarded him.'

Having heard these words of the charioteer he was somewhat startled and said to him, 'Is this an accident peculiar to him alone, or is such the end of all living creatures?'

Then the charioteer replied to him, 'This is the final end of all living creatures; be it a mean man, a man of middle state, or a noble, destruction is fixed to all in this world.'

Then the king's son, sedate though he was, as soon as he heard of death, immediately sank down overwhelmed, and pressing the end of the chariot-pole with his shoulder spoke with a loud voice,

'Is this end appointed to all creatures, and yet the world throws off all fear and is infatuated! Hard indeed, I think, must the hearts of men be, who can be self-composed in such a road.

'Therefore, O charioteer, turn back our chariot, this is no time or place for a pleasure-excursion; how can a rational being, who knows what destruction is, stay heedless here, in the hour of calamity?' . . .

Later that same night

Having awakened his horse's attendant, the swift *Kham*daka, he thus addressed him: 'Bring me quickly my horse Ka*m*thaka, I wish to-day to go hence to attain immortality.

'Since such is the firm content which to-day is produced in my heart, and since my determination is settled in calm resolve, and since even in loneliness I seem to possess a guide,—verily the end which I desire is now before me. . . .

The city-roads which were closed with heavy gates and bars, and which could be with difficulty opened even by elephants, flew open of their own accord without noise, as the prince went through.

Firm in his resolve and leaving behind without hesitation his father who turned ever towards him, and his young son, his affectionate people and his unparalleled magnificence, he then went forth out of his father's city.

Then he with his eyes long and like a full-blown lotus, looking back on the city, uttered a sound like a lion, 'Till I have seen the further shore of birth and death I will never again enter the city called after Kapila.' . . .

For six years, vainly trying to attain merit, he practised self-mortification, performing many rules of abstinence, hard for a man to carry out. . . .

'Wearied with hunger, thirst, and fatigue, with his mind no longer self-possessed through fatigue, how should one who is not absolutely calm reach the end which is to be attained by his mind?

'True calm is properly obtained by the constant satisfaction of the senses; the mind's self-possession is only obtained by the senses being perfectly satisfied.

'True meditation is produced in him whose mind is self-possessed and at rest,—to him whose thoughts are engaged in meditation the exercise of perfect contemplation begins at once.

'By contemplation are obtained those conditions through which is eventually gained that supreme calm, undecaying, immortal state, which is so hard to be reached.' . . .

Then he sat down on his hams in a posture, immovably firm and with his limbs gathered into a mass like a sleeping serpent's hood, exclaiming, 'I will not rise from this position on the earth until I have obtained my utmost aim.'

Then the dwellers in heaven burst into unequalled joy; the herds of beasts and the birds uttered no cry; the trees moved by the wind made no sound, when the holy one took his seat firm in his resolve.

When the great sage, sprung from a line of royal sages, sat down there with his soul fully resolved to obtain the highest knowledge, the whole world rejoiced; but Mâra,[3] the enemy of the good law, was afraid.

Then, having conquered the hosts of Mâra by his firmness and calmness, he the great master of meditation set himself to meditate, longing to know the supreme end.

And having attained the highest mastery in all kinds of meditation, he remembered in the first watch the continuous series of all his former births. . . .

And having remembered each birth and each death in all those

---

[3]Mâra was the Hindu god of evil. He brought an assortment of threats and temptations to the Buddha at this time.—ED.

various transmigrations, the compassionate one then felt compassion for all living beings. . . .

When the second watch came, he, possessed of unequalled energy, received a pre-eminent divine sight, he the highest of all sight-gifted beings.

Then by that divine perfectly pure sight he beheld the whole world as in a spotless mirror.

As he saw the various transmigrations and rebirths of the various beings with their several lower or higher merits from their actions, compassion grew up more within him. . . .

The all-knowing Bodhisattva, the illuminated one, having thus determined, after again pondering and meditating thus came to his conclusion:

'This is pain, this also is the origin of pain in the world of living beings; this also is the stopping of pain; this is that course which leads to its stopping.' So having determined he knew all as it really was.

Thus he, the holy one, sitting there on his seat of grass at the root of the tree, pondering by his own efforts attained at last perfect knowledge.

The Buddha: What Did He Teach?

H. SADDHATISSA

Having thus attained "perfect knowledge," the Buddha had two choices. He could devote himself to contemplation or to teaching others how to attain the perfection he had achieved. While he pondered these choices the Brahman (Hindu) gods Indra and Brahma, according to legend, appeared to him and pleaded that he go out into the world and teach his doctrine. That was the decision he made, and the result was the creation of Buddhism.

Buddhism has been variously described as a form of meditation or yoga, a profound ethical system, a full-scale philosophy, and a salvationist religion. It is all these. Its origin, however, was relatively simple. It was a nontheistic religion, having no central god figure, although in later times the Buddha himself came to be worshipped as a god. Nor did it recognize the existence of an immortal soul. Rather, human beings as substantive creatures were seen as being caught up in an endless, miserable cycle of birth and death, re-birth and re-death. To free them from this cycle the Buddha formulated the Four Noble Truths: the truth of misery; the truth that misery comes from the desire for pleasure; the truth that this desire can be eliminated; and the truth that this elimination is the result of an Eightfold Path that people may follow to attain the ultimate goal of Nibbana, or Nirvana—an obscure condition that has been described by various terms such as enlightenment, non-being, and forgetfulness, although the Buddha himself never fully explained what he meant by it.

The following selection is a discussion of the Eightfold Path by a learned Indian Buddhist scholar, H. Saddhatissa, who is especially concerned to explain his religion in a way that westerners can understand. Saddhatissa's book has become a kind of standard "primer" of Buddhism.

The path leading to the release from suffering is said to be eight-fold. These are not consecutive steps. The eight factors are interdependent and must be perfected simultaneously, the fulfilment of one factor being unlikely without at least the partial development of the others. These eight factors are:

1. *sammā diṭṭhi*   right understanding or views
2. *sammā saṅkappa*   right thought or motives
3. *sammā vācā*   right speech
4. *sammā kammanta* right action
5. *sammā ājīva*   right means of livelihood
6. *sammā vāyāma*   right effort
7. *sammā sati*   right mindfulness
8. *sammā samādhi*   right concentration.

It is important to realize that the word *sammā* prefixing each of the eight factors has a wide range of meaning. In this context it can mean right as opposed to wrong, or it can, in the developed follower of the path, come to mean completed or perfected.

The initial task of one wishing to follow the eight-fold path is to observe oneself carefully and see which factors have already been developed to a certain extent and which are still in a very rudimentary condition. (Some people, for example, have developed their thinking faculty but their ability to communicate with other people is almost non-existent. Others, on the contrary, find it easy to form relationships but have an undeveloped reflective faculty.) The weak aspects of character or of life will then have to be brought into balance and harmony with the strong.

We shall proceed now to consider each factor of the path in turn.

1. *Sammā diṭṭhi* (right understanding or views) in the initial stages of one's practice of the path need mean little more than a vague recognition that 'all is not what it seems'. Right understanding implies in the first instance having seen through the delusion that material security automatically brings peace of mind, or that ceremonies and ritual can wipe out the effects of a past act. Gradually, as the path is perfected, right views, based on knowledge, replace the previous delusions or superstitions that were based on ignorance and lack of insight. . . .

2. *Sammā saṅkappa,* usually translated as right thought or right motives, seems to apply to the emotional basis of thought rather than to thinking itself. As the first factor of the path is concerned with the content and direction of thought, the second factor is concerned with the quality of the drive behind the thinking. . . .

This means that one's mind should be pure, free from carnal 'thirst' (*rāga*), malevolence (*vyāpāda*), cruelty (*vihiṃsā*) and the like. At the same time, one should be willing to relinquish anything that obstructs one's onward march.

3. *Sammā vācā* (right speech). By not indulging in, or listening to, lying, back-biting, harsh talk and idle gossip, we can establish a connecting link between 'right thought' and 'right action'. *Sammā vācā* is free from dogmatic assertions and from hypnotic suggestions; it is an instrument whereby one can learn and teach, comfort and be comforted. We are practising right speech when we use conversation as a means of coming to know people, to understand them and ourselves. . . .

4. *Sammā kammanta* (right action). . . . Right action is any action that proceeds from an unobstructed mind. Whereas morality, in the usual sense of the word, can be practised by one who is blind to the motives behind this behaviour right action is impossible without a clear and deep understanding.

The *path* of right action involves abstaining from unwholesome *kamma* and performing only those actions which will lead to beneficial results. The *goal* of right action, however, is to transcend even *kusala* (wholesome) *kamma*, for once the enlightenment experience has arisen in life, actions will cease to produce any *kammic* results, harmful or beneficial. . . .

5. *Sammā ājīva* (right means of livelihood). The simplest interpretation of this factor of the path is based on the five precepts. Conscientious observance of the five precepts automatically vetos certain trades and professions. The first precept—not to harm living things—requires that we do not earn our living by means of butchering cattle, dealing in flesh, fishing, hunting and so forth. Neither may one make or use weapons, nor engage in any form of warfare. Similarly the fifth precept—not to indulge in drinks or drugs that tend to cloud the

mind—prevents us not only from trafficking in drugs, but also from engaging in the manufacture or distribution of alcohol. . . .

Even if one manages more or less to avoid the wrong means of livelihood, the problems are not yet over. *Sammā ājīva* implies much more than the mere avoiding of wrong means of livelihood. It implies a careful weighing up of our attributes and potentialities, and the selecting of a job that will use the talents we have and at the same time help to develop our weak points. . . .

6. *Sammā vāyāma* (right effort). Although the canonical division of right effort into four categories seems at first sight to be rather pedantic and meaningless it has, if one studies it more closely, a sound practical and psychological validity. The four-fold division of right effort consists of:

1. the effort to cut off unwholesome states that have already arisen;
2. the effort to prevent the arising of unwholesome states that have not yet arisen;
3. the effort to preserve wholesome states that have already arisen;
4. the effort to encourage wholesome states that have not yet arisen.

Right effort requires the development of insight, intuition and will power. We need to develop insight in order to perceive which of the states of mind habitually present are to be preserved and which are to be weeded out. We need to develop intuition so that we can gauge when we are sailing close to a hitherto unknown state of mind and whether we should go ahead or withdraw from it. . . .

7. *Sammā sati* (right mindfulness) is the pivotal factor of the path. Without it none of the other factors can be brought to completion. Right mindfulness serves too as a control over the other factors, preventing the excessive development of one at the expense of the others. In Christian terminology *sammā sati* might be translated as 'the practice of the presence of God'; it implies gradually extending one's awareness until every action, thought and word is performed in the full light of consciousness. . . .

8. *Sammā samādhi.* Right concentration or meditation is the last factor of the path leading to the cessation of suffering. Meditation and its counterpart in daily life—mindfulness (*sati*)—form together the essence of the Buddha's teaching. . . .

It has been said of the mind that it is like a pool. Too often that pool is agitated and muddy, reflecting nothing but its own turbidity. Buddhist meditation is designed to quieten the mind until it becomes perfectly still. Then the deep recesses of the pool can be seen clearly, and it will reflect a true picture of whatever is presented to it. There are many hindrances in the way of one who seeks to quieten the mind in this way: violent emotions of desire or of hatred, restlessness and discontent, hesitation and doubt, laziness, weariness and sloth.

The Buddha in History

SIR PERCIVAL SPEAR

Neither the Buddha himself nor his followers thought very deeply about history. Buddhism is transcendental and hence oriented to the eternal rather than the historical. Nevertheless, the Buddha lived in historical time and acted upon historical events. Further, the Buddha and Buddhism are invariably treated in any history of India because of their immense historical importance.

The following selection is taken from probably the best one-volume survey of Indian history, India: A Modern History, *by Sir Percival Spear, an established scholar who spent most of his life and professional career in India. This survey, unlike many others of its kind, gives thorough coverage to the earlier history of "classical India." The selection deals with the setting of the Age of Buddha and with the revolutionary impact of the man and his ideas upon that age.*

Buddhism was one of several movements which arose in a period of unrest and ferment from about the year 600 B.C. Three causes may be hazarded for this ferment, one material, one moral, and one racial. On the material side there was the transition from a pastoral to an agricultural economy. The Indo-Aryan tribes were settling down, becoming tillers of the soil instead of shepherds of flocks. They were developing cities and becoming attached to the soil. Tribal groups were becoming territorial kingdoms. With crop-raising there began to be a surplus production which led to the development of arts and crafts, to exchange in the form of trade and commerce. Such a transition inevitably meant social tension. The merchant or *vaishya* class rose in importance and resented the privileges claimed by the upper two orders. To put it in modern terms, here was a situation which provided material for middle-class discontent with aristocratic privilege and priestly domination. Bourgeois aggressiveness bred anticlerical feelings.

The second force at work (in what proportions the two combined we cannot say at this distance of time) was a religious and intellectual ferment comparable with that of contemporary Greece. There was a striving after spiritual truth in a ferment of minds and much dissatisfaction with the current Brahminical order. In the thousand years or so since the Indo-Aryans had arrived the Brahmins or hereditary priests (worshipers of Brahma the creator) had seized the leadership of society from the nobles and had already established the most subtle and powerful domination of all, that of the mind. They had progressed, it is true, from the Vedic religion of hymns to the powers of nature and spells to secure boons and ward off dangers. They had developed the doctrine of *karma* or the law of consequences and the complementary doctrine of transmigration of souls from life to life. But the conditions governing the working of these laws were non-moral and ritualistic. Reliance was placed on *mantras* or spells, on sacrifice, and on priestly ritual. The law of consequences was not yet a law of *moral* consequences. The developing conscience of the age revolted against this mechanistic religiosity. There grew up a longing for *moksha* or freedom or release from rebirth, the conscience demanding something more than ritual and the mind something more than formulae. With these gropings schools of asceticism and moral discipline and schools of philosophy or intellectual apprehension developed. From the former came movements like Buddhism. . . .

Another element should be added to this ferment. It was the tension between the non-Aryans admitted to the Hindu fold, and the Brahmins. For example, the tribe in the Nepal hills from which the Buddha came is thought to have been of Mongolian stock. The nobles of such groups had little relish for the Brahmin superiority which they found established in the new society. To sum up, we may say that a period of heart-searching and change was introduced by class tension caused by the economic transition and the rise of a mercantile class, by intellectual and spiritual tension caused by the mechanistic character of the Brahmin ascendancy, and by race tension caused by the expansion of Hindu society to include non-Aryan groups. . . .

Siddhartha Gautama, the Buddha or Enlightened One, also known as Sakyamuni or Savior of the Sakyas, was born into a noble family of the Sakya tribe at Kapilavastu on the borders of Nepal. The date now most generally accepted is about 567 B.C., though the Buddhists of Ceylon put it as early as 623 B.C. He died around 487 B.C. at the age of eighty. Around his life there has grown a tangle of pious legend, through which it is very difficult to penetrate to the flowers of historic truth. On the main outline of the story, however, there is general agreement. Gautama grew up in an atmosphere of ease and luxury, married within his class, and had a son. In some way he became aware of the sorrow and suffering of the world and of the transitoriness of life. In his twenty-ninth year he left his palace and family, donned the yellow robe, and commenced to wander, a homeless ascetic. For six years he wandered, seeking wisdom and the secret of sorrow. He trod the well-worn path of asceticism and austerities without achieving his goal. He then gave up these practices, so that his disciples deserted him saying "the ascetic Gautama has become luxurious; he has ceased from striving and turned to a life of comfort." It was then that, sitting under a *bodhi* tree under a full moon at Gaya, he attained enlightenment or Buddhahood. The meaning of sorrow, the arising of sorrow, and the conquest of sorrow became clear to him. From Gaya he went to Sarnath near Banaras where, sitting in a deer park, he gave his first sermon. From that time he moved up and down north India, preaching the Path and organizing his followers.

The Buddha's teaching concerned the nature of sorrow, which for him was the manifestation of evil in the world. Sorrow arose from desire, and desire from attachment to the transitory features of an illusive world. Desire or attachment was the cause of rebirth in successive lives. Desire in its turn was fostered by illusion, the belief that the material, changing world was real. For the Buddha it was a dancing fantasm, tempting men with its glitter and movement to bind themselves to the ever-revolving wheel of life. Desire meant sorrow in life after life. The way of escape was to conquer desire. This would bring freedom from rebirth and absorption into the All, a state called Nirvana. Whether, in the Buddha's mind, this meant extinction or conscious bliss is uncertain; what is certain is that he considered this enlightenment infinitely preferable to the only alternative of enduring sorrow. It can thus be said that the doctrine of the Buddha amounted to a spiritual and mental discipline for the attainment of right views about life. About ultimates he was agnostic. There was no personal God in the original system. It would be a mistake, however, to picture the Buddha as a late-nineteenth-century rationalist, founding an Ethical Society and lecturing in rationalist halls. The accounts of his enlightenment have in them the marks of universal mystical experience, the feeling of oneness with the universe. It was this experience toward which the Buddha's doctrine and discipline led, and it was this experience which attracted his followers and dispensed with the need for theistic worship. Meditation took the place of prayer and inner peace of divine worship.

For a time the Buddha thought that his doctrine was "too profound and subtle" for "this race of mankind, who only seek and revel in pleasure." But he repented and persevered with his teaching. There developed during his life a double way. The first was the way of renunciation for those who aspired to Buddhahood and freedom or release from the wheel of life. These disciples were organized in the *Sangha* or order, containing both men and women. They renounced the world and donned the saffron robe, lived in communities of monks and nuns, and had no possessions but their robes, their staves, and begging bowls. The modern state name of Behar derives from the word *vihara,* a Buddhist monastery, for it was once famous for these establishments.

The second way was for the householder, who, while continuing to live in the world, sought, as it were, to improve his ultimate prospects by right living. This was the Middle Way of historic Buddhism, eschewing all extremes, whose code was the "noble eightfold path." This is the ethic of popular Buddhism, and consists of right views, right resolves, right speech, right action, right living, right effort, right recollectedness, and right meditation. Without going further into these rules we may note the spirit which underlay them. One thread was that of ahimsa or nonviolence. The spirit of life was in all creatures and all creatures were therefore akin. While the Christian prays for all men, the Buddhist prays for all sentient beings. There follow such practices as vegetarianism and the refusal to take life. Another thread was compassion, which may be called the characteristic and pervasive virtue of the original system. It is this feeling, together with that of abstraction, which irradiates the countenance of the Buddha in his Indian statues. It marked a distinction from the Brahmins of the time, for whom knowledge was the supreme gift. In the personality and message of the Buddha there is a serenity and spiritual calm which charms and subdues the student after two and a half millennia. Like the silver rays of a full moon on a calm night, the Buddha's words still shed their gentle light on the face of troubled humanity. "Now monks, I have nothing more to tell you than this; decay is inherent in all compounded things. Work out your salvation energetically." . . . The Buddha, on the other hand, while accepting some basic Hindu ideas such as *karma,* separated himself from current Hinduism in a number of ways. He discountenanced caste, the keystone of the Hindu social arch. He had no place for Brahmins, replacing them in his system with monks. Agnostic in ultimate belief, he could not support the gods of the populace. Like a later Protestant, he believed that the scriptures should be understood by the people. He taught in the current speech of the Gangetic plain, a dialect akin to the Pali which later became the Buddhist sacred language. He was an opponent of the priesthood, of magic and sacrifice, of privileges, and of hiding truth in the mystery of a strange language and unintelligible books. His message was for all equally. The Middle Path provided a way of life for all, the Discourses of the Buddha a holy book for all, and the life of renunciation a way of release for all. In some respects, Buddhism was a democratic protest against Brahmin supremacy. It had therefore to separate itself from Brahminism or perish. When and where it later reunited with Brahminism it did perish.

Review and Study Questions

1. In the account from the *Buddha-Karita of Asvaghosha* what elements suggest that Buddha was a supernatural being?
2. Do you consider the teachings of the Buddha primarily to be a salvationist religion or a moral philosophy? Why?
3. Why do you suppose Buddhism never gained a wide following in the Buddha's native India?
4. How reliable are essentially religious writings as historical sources?

Suggestions for Further Reading

As with most religions, there is an enormous literature of Buddhism, including a considerable amount of biographical material—though much of it legendary and unhistorical—on the Buddha himself. The rest of the *Buddha-Karita,* excerpted for this chapter, can be read with considerable profit. The version used here is the *Buddha-Karita of Asvaghosha,* tr. B. B. Cowell in *Buddhist Mahayara Texts,* "The Sacred Books of the East," vol. 49 (New York: Dover, 1969 [1894]). Also useful are such canonical works as the "Discourse on the Ariyan Quest," the "Greater Discourse to Saccaka," the "Great Discourse on the Lion's Roar," and "The Book of the Discipline," all in *Sacred Books of the Buddhists Series,* ed. F. Max Müller, 3 vols. (London: Luzac and Co., 1969 [1899]). Other useful works include *Buddhist Wisdom Books, Containing the Diamond Sutra and the Heart Sutra,* tr. and ed. Edward Conze (London: Allen and Unwin, 1958), *The Perfection of Wisdom in Eight Thousand Lines and Its Verse Summary,* tr. Edward Conze (Berkeley: Bolinas, 1973), *The Large Sutra on Perfect Wisdom,* tr. Edward Conze (Berkeley, Los Angeles, London: University of California Press, 1975), and H. Saddhatissa, *The Buddha's Way* (New York: Braziller, 1971), excerpted for this chapter. There are also a number of excellent anthologies: one of the best is *Buddhist Texts through the Ages,* ed. Edward Conze, in the Harper Torchbooks series (New York: Harper & Row, 1964). See also *Buddhism, a Religion of Infinite Compassion: Selections from Buddhist Literature,* ed. Clarence H. Hamilton (New

York: The Liberal Arts Press, 1952), and *The Buddhist Philosophy of Man: Early Indian Buddhist Dialogues,* ed. Trevor Ling (London et al.: Everyman's Library, 1981). An excellent interpretive guide to Buddhist sacred literature is Edward Conze, *Buddhist Thought in India* (London: Allen and Unwin, 1962), and a basic interpretive work is Helmuth von Glasenapp, *Buddhism: A Non-theistic Religion,* tr. Irmgard Schloegl (New York: Braziller, 1966). Edward Conze, *Buddhism: Its Essence and Development* (New York and Evanston: Harper, 1959) is a readable, understandable analysis.

Of the many biographies of the Buddha, most are conventional and pietistic, written by "true believers" such as H. Saddhatissa, *The Life of Buddha* (New York: Harper & Row, 1976). Of the more recent and critical, two brief biographies can be recommended: Betty Kelen, *Gautama Buddha: In Life and Legend* (New York: Lothrop, Lee and Shepart, 1967), simple, charming, and reliable, and Michael Carrithers, *The Buddha* (Oxford and New York: Oxford University Press, 1983), in the "Past Masters" series.

Of the interpretive studies of Buddhism the most important is probably Govind Chandra Pende, *Studies in the Origins of Buddhism* (Allahabad: University Allahabad, 1957). An old standard work is Edward J. Thomas, *The History of Buddhist Thought* (New York: Barnes and Noble, 1971 [1933]). A more recent and authoritative work is Richard H. Robinson and Willard L. Johnson, *The Buddhist Religion: A Historical Introduction,* 3rd ed., in "The Religious Life of Man Series" (Belmont, Cal.: Wadsworth, 1982). Two brief standard treatments are Edward Conze, *A Short History of Buddhism* (London: Allen and Unwin, 1980) and Christmas Humphreys, *Buddhism* (Baltimore: Penguin, 1969).

On the history of India the massive old standard *Cambridge History of India,* 6 vols. (Cambridge: Cambridge University Press, 1919–69), even with its supplementary volume on the Indus Civilization, is now seriously outdated. An essential work, though difficult and demanding, is A. L. Basham, *The Wonder That Was India: A Survey of the Culture of the Indian Sub-Continent Before the Coming of the Muslims* (New York: Grove Press, 1954). Of the briefer works that devote some attention to the age of the Buddha, one can recommend Percival Spear, *India: A Modern History,* excerpted for this chapter; the classic and still useful W. H. Moreland and Atul Chandra Chatterjee, *A Short History of India,* 4th ed. (London: Longmans, Green and Co., 1969 [1936]); and the excellent recent book by Stanley Wolpert, *A New History of India,* 3rd ed. (New York and Oxford: Oxford University Press, 1989).

CONFUCIUS:
THE MOST SAGELY
ANCIENT TEACHER

---

c. 551 B.C.	Born
c. 530 B.C.	Opened his school in Lu
c. 497 B.C.	Voluntary exile
c. 482 B.C.	Returned to Lu
c. 479 B.C.	Died

Chinese civilization was already more than a thousand years old by the time of Confucius. In the middle of the second millenium B.C. the first historical dynasty, the Shang, established itself in the basin of the Yellow River and its tributary system. It was united by common ancestry, a common language and script, and a common religion based on the cult of ancestors and carried on through elaborate state rituals. In the late twelfth century B.C. a new dynasty, the Chou, under King Wu and his brother Tan the Duke of Chou, came to dominate the Shang lands. They adopted the Shang political and religious systems and raised both to new heights. But by the time of Confucius in the mid-sixth century B.C., the Chou dynasty was in decline. A Chou king still reigned, but the concept of the dynastic state had been successfully challenged by regional political leaders, quarreling and fighting among themselves. This is the age known in Chinese tradition as the "Spring and Autumn Period."

Confucius looked back to the age of the early Chou as a kind of formative golden age—the Duke of Chou was his cultural hero—and he diligently studied the accumulated wisdom of that golden age, which had been handed down in poetry, history, customary law, and ritual. He hoped to find in the traditional wisdom the fundamental principles on which to organize the life of the state, the family, and the individual. He hoped also to find an administrative position in the

35

state that would permit him to apply those fundamental principles. But he never attained a sufficiently powerful position to realize this hope. Failing to become a political force himself, he became a teacher—the first private individual in Chinese history to do so. If he could not apply his principles himself then perhaps his students could. That is precisely what happened. Confucius's teachings became for his students the essential blueprint for good government, order, public welfare, and peace; and Confucius himself became "the most sagely ancient teacher," in the phrase of one of the Sung emperors of the twelfth century.

For more than two thousand years he has been regarded as China's great teacher, and his teachings have, for most of those two thousand years, been accepted as the orthodox way of life by both scholars and officials. One of his disciples wrote of him, "It would be as hard to equal our Master as to climb up on a ladder to the sky. Had our Master ever been put in control of a State or of a great Family it would have been described in the words: 'He raised them, and they stood, he led them and they went. He steadied them as with a rope, and they came. He stirred them, and they moved harmoniously. His life was glorious, his death bewailed. How can such a one ever be equalled?' "[1]

---

[1] *The Analects of Confucius,* tr. and ed. Arthur Waley (New York: Random House, 1938), 19:25, p. 230.

Who Confucius Was

SSU-MA CH'IEN

Despite the reverence for Confucius that has made him indisputably the most famous person in Chinese history, almost nothing is known about the man himself. His name has been Anglicized from the Chinese Kung fu-tzu, "Master Kung," but we do not know the family to which he actually belonged—the legendary account is entirely fictitious on this point. The traditional date and place of his birth, 551 B.C. in the minor state of Lu, are probably reasonably correct, as is the fact that he belonged to the lower nobility, the Shih or gentleman class. His own statement informs us that his father died shortly after Confucius's birth and that he was raised in relative poverty by his mother. Given these circumstances, it is not known how he received his education. Mencius (Meng-tzu), an important Confucian scholar of the fourth century B.C., tells us that, as a young man, Confucius served as a clerk of the state granaries of Lu and was later appointed to check on the pasture land belonging to the state. At nineteen he married, but nothing is known of his wife's family. He had a son and a daughter.

He continued to study to prepare himself for state service, but high office eluded him. His studies convinced him that good government could only be achieved by the application of the principles that were becoming clear in his own thinking—and those principles were unacceptable to the men of power who might have employed him. Moreover, it is likely that Confucius himself was too honest, blunt, and forthright to flatter them for the sake of a position.

He seems to have spent some time in the neighboring state of Ch'i but found no greater success there and returned to Lu. It was in this period that he established himself as a teacher. Between 501 and 495 B.C. he was employed by the government of Lu, though again not in a commanding position. He resigned in frustration and traveled in neighboring states for some ten years; virtually nothing is known of this period of his life. At the age of nearly seventy he returned to Lu, where he enjoyed some access to those in power because of his great reputation—though he still had no real authority. He continued to teach and to collate the ancient texts he had collected. Now old age was beginning to come upon him. He was grieved by the death of his son and several of his favorite disciples. There is no reliable account of his own death.

The foregoing sketchy account is gleaned from occasional personal refer-

ences in the Analects, *a collection of his sayings, and from the few credible details that can be sifted out of the legendary traditional account that is our only biographical source for Confucius. The following account is from a work entitled* The Historical Records, *written by Ssu-Ma Ch'ien about the turn of the second century* B.C., *some four hundred years after the time of Confucius. While it is called a work of history, it is far from our western notions of historical accuracy and relevancy. It does repeat most of the instances of personal reminiscence from the* Analects, *but it also reports as fact much of the miraculous lore and pure supposition that had already accumulated to obscure the historical character of Confucius. The English translators, George H. Danton and Annina Periam Danton, worked from an earlier German translation by the German scholar Richard Wilhelm, but collated it with an authoritative French translation by Edouard Chavanne, with the standard English text of the* Confucian Classics *by James Legge, and with the Chinese text itself.*

Confucius was born in the State of Lu, in the District of Ch'ang P'ing, in the city of Chou. His ancestor was from the State of Sung and was called K'ung Fang-shu. Fang-shu begat Po-hsia. Po-hsia begat Shu-Liang Ho. Late in life, Ho was united in matrimony with the daughter of the man, Yen, and begat Confucius. His mother prayed to the hill, Ni, and conceived Confucius.[2] It was in the twenty-second year of Duke Hsiang of Lu that Confucius was born (551 B.C.). At his birth, he had on his head a bulging of the skull, whence he is said to have received the name "Hill" (Ch'iu). His style or appellation was Chung Ni, his family name K'ung. When he was born, his father, Shu-Liang Ho, died. . . . Confucius was poor and of low estate, and when he grew older he served as a petty official of the family Chi, and while he was in office his accounts and the measures were always correct. Thereupon, he was made Chief Shepherd, then the beasts grew in numbers and multiplied.

Therefore he was appointed Minister of Public Works. Finally he left Lu, was abandoned in Ch'i, was driven out of Sung and Wei, suffered want between Ch'ên and Ts'ai. Thereupon he returned to Lu. Confucius was nine feet six inches tall. All the people called him a giant and marvelled at him. Lu again treated him well; so he returned to Lu. . . .

People of Ch'i spoke of him with praise; Duke Ching thereupon questioned him regarding the government. Confucius said: "Let the prince be prince, the servant servant, the father father, the son son." Duke Ching replied: "That is an excellent answer: if the prince be not

---

[2]This entire genealogy is fictitious.—ED.

prince, and the servant not servant; if the father be not father, and the son not son; even though I have my revenue, how could I enjoy it!"

On another day, he again questioned Confucius about the government. Confucius replied: "Governing consists in being sparing with the resources." Duke Ching rejoiced, and wished to grant Confucius the fields of Ni Ch'i as a fief. Then Yen Ying interfered and said: "Scholars are smooth and sophisticated; they cannot be taken as a norm; they are arrogant and conceited; they cannot be used to guide the lower classes. They attach a great importance to mourning; they emphasize the lamentations, and waste their substance on magnificent funerals; they cannot be used as regulators of manners. They travel about as advisers in order to enrich themselves; they cannot be used in the ruling of the state. Since the great sages have passed away and the House of Chou has degenerated, rites and music have become defective and incomplete. Now Confucius splendidly forms the rules of behaviour, increases the ceremonies of reception and departure, and the customs in walking and in bowing, so that many generations would not be enough to exhaust his teachings. Years would not suffice to plumb his rules of decorum. If you wish to use him to change the manners of Ch'i, this is not the correct way to lead the common people." After that time, Duke Ching continued to receive Confucius, always, to be sure, with great respect, but he no longer questioned him concerning decorum. . . .

After a while, Confucius departed from Lu and held a number of distinguished positions in neighboring states. These are recounted in great detail and are completely fabricated. Finally, hearing of the death of the ruler of Lu, Confucius decided to return.

Confucius gave instruction in four subjects: Literature, Conduct, Conscientiousness, and Loyalty. He was free from four things: he had "no foregone conclusions, no arbitrary predeterminations, no obstinacy, and no egoism." The matters in which he exercised the greatest caution were the periods of fasting, of warfare, of illness. The Master seldom spoke of fortune, of fate, of "perfect virtue."

He gave no help to him who was not zealous. If he presented one corner of a subject as an example, and the pupil could not transfer what he had learned to the other three corners, Confucius did not repeat.

In everyday life, Confucius was altogether modest, as though he were not able to speak. In the ancestral temple and at court, he was eloquent, yet his speeches were always cautious. At court, he conversed with the upper dignitaries in exact and definite terms; with the lower dignitaries he was free and open. Whenever he entered in at the duke's door, he walked as though bowed over, with quick steps; he approached as if on wings. Whenever the Prince commanded his presence at a reception of guests, his appearance was serious. Whenever a command of the Prince summoned him, he left his house without waiting for the horses to be put to his chariot. . . .

Confucius was ill. Tze Kung asked permission to visit him. Then Confucius walked back and forth in the courtyard, supporting himself on his staff, and said: "Tzu, why are you so late?" Then Confucius sighed and sang:

> "The Sacred Mountain caves in,
> The roof beam breaks,
> The Sage will vanish."

Then he shed tears and said to Tze Kung: "For a long time the world has been unregulated; no one understood how to follow me. The people of Hsia placed the coffin upon the east steps, the people of Chou placed it on the west steps, the people of Yin placed it between the two pillars. Last night I dreamed that I was sitting before the sacrificial offerings between the two pillars. Does that mean that I am a man of Yin?" Seven days later, Confucius died. Confucius had attained an age of seventy-three years, when he died, in the fourth month of the sixteenth year of Duke Ai of Lu (479 B.C.).

What Confucius Said

THE *ANALECTS* OF CONFUCIUS

There is no convincing evidence that Confucius wrote anything at all. Quite the contrary: he himself is reported to have said, "I have transmitted what was taught to me without making up anything of my own."[3] Nevertheless, stubborn tradition ascribes to his authorship or editorship a list of so-called Confucian Classics—the Classics of Poetry, History, Changes, Spring and Autumn Annals, and the Rites. This tradition holds that he wrote the Spring and Autumn Classic, that he selected the 305 poems in the Book

---

[3]*Analects*, 7:1–3, Waley ed. p. 123.

of Poetry *from some three thousand items, that he edited the* Book of History, *and that he perhaps collated the* Book of Rites. *But the book called the* Analects *of Confucius, Lun Yü, is probably closer to the authentic words of Confucius than any other. It is a collection of his "sayings" compiled many years after Confucius's death from the recollections of his disciples. The traditional books of the work contain material from very different periods, but books III–IX represent the oldest part of the work. It is from these books that the following excerpts are taken.*

The Analects—*or at least some of their contents—were known to Mencius in the fourth century* B.C., *but it was in the second century* A.D. *that they received something like their present form at the hands of the Confucian scholar Cheng Hsüan. By this time many of the sayings attributed to Confucius were actually much older proverbial maxims or those of his disciples that had a Confucian flavor to them. Some of the older traditional sayings, however, may actually have been appropriated by Confucius and thus may be attributed to him, as the sayings of his disciples may contain a kernel of what "the Master" said. But with all their faults and textual problems, the* Analects *preserve the words of Confucius better than any other source we have.*

Even if this is the case, we shall labor in vain in the Analects *to find a systematic statement of Confucius's philosophy. The* Analects *have neither unity nor logical order. They are a seemingly random collection of sayings. Some are autobiographical, some philosophical; some give practical advice, others relate trivial anecdotes. They often reflect genuine wisdom, insight, or compassion; almost as often they are perfectly ordinary in sentiment. Some are so cryptic as to be nearly incomprehensible. There are, to be sure, central themes, but the sayings that bear on them are scattered through the work and we are compelled to construct a system to set them in.*

The Confucian system is fundamentally a moral philosophy with almost no reference to religion. Confucius apparently did not believe in a personal deity. Of course, he honored the "will of Heaven," the traditional gods, and the rituals of their worship—but he had no concept of life after death and he contemptuously rejected traditional belief in ghosts and prodigies. Yet he did believe in transcendental values, in love and righteousness as cosmic virtues, and in "the way of Heaven" as directive of the way of humans. The tao *or "way" in its broadest implications refers to the entire sociopolitical order, with its public and familial roles, statuses, and ranks; the* tao *governs this order. But it also refers to the inner moral life of the individual. Confucius found that "the* tao *does not prevail in the world"[4] and saw himself as its restorer. It meant to him not only "the traditional" but "the*

---

[4]*Analects*, 12:2, Waley ed. p. 204.

good." A related concept is li, *which refers to all the rites, ceremonies, and forms of behavior that join people to each other. One of the most important Confucian principles is* jen, *"true manhood" or "perfect virtue"—the quality of a "gentleman" or a "superior person." This was also a traditional idea, but Confucius opened it up to ordinary people and attached to it a moral rather than a hierarchical meaning. One could achieve* jen *by study, zeal, and self-cultivation whatever one's status in society. In an ethical sense* jen *is inner serenity and indifference to fortune and misfortune. It is, in Confucius's own phrase, "human heartedness," and it brings a happiness that comes only from the possession of virtue. Probably the most influential of Confucius's principles was filial piety. It is in the family that* li *and* jen *are found. It is there that one learns how to exercize authority and submit to authority, and from the family these virtues are translated to the state. Though Confucius saw himself as a political reformer, his concept of government was quite simple. Government should exist to serve the needs of its people. Government should not unnecessarily interfere in the lives of its people; it should allow them scope for their own moral autonomy. A ruling class that does not enjoy the trust of its people will not endure.*

Most of these concepts and principles are represented in the following selection of the sayings of Confucius, from the Analects.

III.

3. The Master said, A man who is not Good, what can he have to do with ritual? A man who is not Good, what can he have to do with music?

4. Lin Fang asked for some main principles in connexion with ritual. The Master said, A very big question. In ritual at large it is a safe rule always to be too sparing rather than too lavish; and in the particular case of mourning-rites, they should be dictated by grief rather than by fear. . . .

18. The Master said, Were anyone to-day to serve his prince according to the full prescriptions of ritual, he would be thought a sycophant. . . .

26. The Master said, High office filled by men of narrow views, ritual performed without reverence, the forms of mourning observed without grief—these are things I cannot bear to see!

IV.

1. The Master said, It is Goodness that gives to a neighbourhood its beauty. One who is free to choose, yet does not prefer to dwell among the Good—how can he be accorded the name of wise?

2. The Master said, Without Goodness a man

> Cannot for long endure adversity,
> Cannot for long enjoy prosperity.

The Good Man rests content with Goodness; he that is merely wise pursues Goodness in the belief that it pays to do so.

3, 4. Of the adage 'Only a Good Man knows how to like people, knows how to dislike them,' the Master said, He whose heart is in the smallest degree set upon Goodness will dislike no one.

5. Wealth and rank are what every man desires; but if they can only be retained to the detriment of the Way he professes, he must relinquish them. Poverty and obscurity are what every man detests; but if they can only be avoided to the detriment of the Way he professes, he must accept them. The gentleman who ever parts company with Goodness does not fulfil that name. Never for a moment does a gentleman quit the way of Goodness. He is never so harried but that he cleaves to this; never so tottering but that he cleaves to this.

6. The Master said, I for my part have never yet seen one who really cared for Goodness, nor one who really abhorred wickedness. One who really cared for Goodness would never let any other consideration come first. One who abhorred wickedness would be so constantly doing Good that wickedness would never have a chance to get at him. Has anyone ever managed to do Good with his whole might even as long as the space of a single day? I think not. Yet I for my part have never seen anyone give up such an attempt because he had not the *strength* to go on. It may well have happened, but I for my part have never seen it. . . .

9. The Master said, A Knight[5] whose heart is set upon the Way, but who is ashamed of wearing shabby clothes and eating coarse food, is not worth calling into counsel.

10. The Master said, A gentleman in his dealings with the world has neither enmities nor affections; but wherever he sees Right he ranges himself beside it. . . .

14. The Master said, He does not mind not being in office; all he minds about is whether he has qualities that entitle him to office. He does not mind failing to get recognition; he is too busy doing the things that entitle him to recognition.

15. The Master said, Shên! My Way has one (thread) that runs right through it. Master Tsêng said, Yes. When the Master had gone out, the disciples asked, saying What did he mean? Master Tsêng said, Our Master's Way is simply this: Loyalty, consideration.

---

[5]This translates as *shih,* or "gentleman".—ED.

V.

5. The Master gave Ch'i-tiao K'ai leave to take office, but he replied, 'I have not yet sufficiently perfected myself in the virtue of good faith.' The Master was delighted. . . .

19. Chi Wên Tzu used to think thrice before acting. The Master hearing of it said, Twice is quite enough. . . .

27. The Master said, In an hamlet of ten houses you may be sure of finding someone quite as loyal and true to his word as I. But I doubt if you would find anyone with such a love of learning. . . .

VI.

16. The Master said, When natural substance prevails over ornamentation you get the boorishness of the rustic. When ornamentation prevails over natural substance, you get the pedantry of the scribe. Only when ornament and substance are duly blended do you get the true gentleman.

17. The Master said, Man's very life is *honesty*, in that without it he will be lucky indeed if he escapes with his life. . . .

20. Fan Ch'ih asked about wisdom. The Master said, He who devotes himself to securing for his subjects what it is right they should have, who by respect for the Spirits keeps them at a distance, may be termed wise. He asked about Goodness. The Master said, Goodness cannot be obtained till what is difficult has been duly done. He who has done this may be called Good. . . .

25. The Master said, A gentleman who is widely versed in letters and at the same time knows how to submit his learning to the restraints of ritual is not likely, I think, to go far wrong.

28. Tzu-kung said, If a ruler not only conferred wide benefits upon the common people, but also compassed the salvation of the whole State, what would you say of him? Surely, you would call him Good? The Master said, It would no longer be a matter of 'Good.' He would without doubt be a Divine Sage. Even Yao and Shun could hardly criticize him. . . .

VII.

6. The Master said, Set your heart upon the Way, support yourself by its power, lean upon Goodness, seek distraction in the arts.

7. The Master said, From the very poorest upwards—beginning even with the man who could bring no better present than a bundle of dried flesh—none has ever come to me without receiving instruction.

8. The Master said, Only one who bursts with eagerness do I in-

struct; only one who bubbles with excitement, do I enlighten. If I hold up one corner and a man cannot come back to me with the other three, I do not continue the lesson. . . .

11. The Master said, If any means of escaping poverty presented itself, that did not involve doing wrong, I would adopt it, even though my employment were only that of the gentleman who holds the whip. But so long as it is a question of illegitimate means, I shall continue to pursue the quests that I love. . . .

15. The Master said, He who seeks only coarse food to eat, water to drink and bent arm for pillow, will without looking for it find happiness to boot. Any thought of accepting wealth and rank by means that I know to be wrong is as remote from me as the clouds that float above. . . .

19. The Master said, I for my part am not one of those who have innate knowledge. I am simply one who loves the past and who is diligent in investigating it. . . .

21. The Master said, Even when walking in a party of no more than three I can always be certain of learning from those I am with. There will be good qualities that I can select for imitation and bad ones that will teach me what requires correction in myself. . . .

24. The Master took four subjects for his teaching: culture, conduct of affairs, loyalty to superiors and the keeping of promises.

25. The Master said, A Divine Sage I cannot hope ever to meet; the most I can hope for is to meet a true gentleman. The Master said, A faultless man I cannot hope ever to meet; the most I can hope for is to meet a man of fixed principles. Yet where all around I see Nothing pretending to be Something, Emptiness pretending to be Fullness, Penury pretending to be Affluence, even a man of fixed principles will be none too easy to find. . . .

27. The Master said, There may well be those who can do without knowledge; but I for my part am certainly not one of them. To hear much, pick out what is good and follow it, to see much and take due note of it, is the lower of the two kinds of knowledge. . . .

33. The Master said, As to being a Divine Sage or even a Good Man, far be it from me to make any such claim. As for unwearying effort to learn and unflagging patience in teaching others, those are merits that I do not hesitate to claim. Kung-hsi Hua said, The trouble is that we disciples cannot learn!

VIII.

8. The Master said, Let a man be first incited by the *Songs*, then given a firm footing by the study of ritual, and finally perfected by music. . . .

10. The Master said, One who is by nature daring and is suffering from poverty will not long be law-abiding. Indeed, any men, save those that are truly Good, if their sufferings are very great, will be likely to rebel. . . .

13. The Master said, Be of unwavering good faith, love learning, if attacked be ready to die for the good Way. Do not enter a State that pursues dangerous courses, nor stay in one where the people have rebelled. When the Way prevails under Heaven, then show yourself; when it does not prevail, then hide. When the Way prevails in your own land, count it a disgrace to be needy and obscure; when the Way does not prevail in your land, then count it a disgrace to be rich and honoured. . . .

IX.

24. The Master said, First and foremost, be faithful to your superiors, keep all promises, refuse the friendship of all who are not like you; and if you have made a mistake, do not be afraid of admitting the fact and amending your ways.

What Confucius Meant

H. G. CREEL

As we have already seen, there is no inherent thematic unity in the philosophy of Confucius. This, in combination with the enormous authority of his name and his sayings, has made it possible for Confucius to mean many things to many people over the centuries. He has been a sage, a prophet, a magician, a teacher, a philosopher, even a religious figure. To some extent, of course, he was a multifaceted thinker who truly did mean many things. But when we ask what his primary emphasis was, we can best answer that he was primarily a political reformer and that everything else in his thought stemmed from that emphasis. This view is reflected in the book, excerpted below, by H. G. Creel, Confucius the Man and the Myth. *Creel was a longtime professor at the University of Chicago and one of the most distinguished American Sinologists. This book, among many that he wrote, is one of the seminal works of twentieth-century Confucian interpretation. Indeed, John K. Fairbank, himself a distinguished Orientalist, wrote that "there is no doubt that we have in this book the most scholarly, vivid, and all-*

around view of Confucius the man now available."⁶ It is as authoritative now as when it was written a generation ago, to a large extent because it is a fundamental reinterpretation of Confucius. Creel rejects the entire Chinese Confucian tradition as historically unreliable, and goes back to contemporary records and to his own expert evaluation of them. In the selection below he begins with the political environment of Confucius's own age and his reaction to it.

The rulers and their powerful ministers were scions of hereditary noble houses. With rare exceptions, they were prey to the degeneration usually suffered by families in which power and luxury are bequeathed from father to son for many generations. They needed two virtues, prowess in war and skill in intrigue, and these they cultivated to the utmost. The result was a world that no man who cared for human dignity and human happiness could contemplate with equanimity.

Confucius was such a man, and he was profoundly disturbed. He dedicated his life to the attempt to make a better world. . . .

Confucius himself said that he was the intellectual heir of King Wên, the father of the founder of the Chou dynasty. He also implied, in a passage which is somewhat vague, that he looked upon the Duke of Chou, a son of Wên, as his inspiration. Chinese tradition, from a very early time, has regarded the Duke of Chou as a source of Confucian ideas and sometimes even as the founder of Confucianism, notwithstanding the fact that he lived more than five hundred years before Confucius. . . .

In China, the effect was to leave an ideal of kingship as a form of stewardship, in which the test of a good king was whether or not he brought about the welfare of the people. Since the Chou legitimized their title by the claim that they had replaced an oppressive sovereign, justice and kindness became the duty of every later ruler. The accepted theory was that every person in authority must regard his office as a sacred and difficult trust. As we have abundantly seen, it was almost universally honored in the breach rather than the observance. Yet the mere fact that such a code existed was of the highest importance. In it Confucius found ready to his hand much that was very useful for his undertaking. The fact that (like the teachings of Jesus) it was almost universally acknowledged to be right, though considered impracticable, gave to his doctrines a support they could have obtained in no other way. . . .

Since his own world was far from ideal, it is natural that he thought of the best state as one that had those things in which his own was

---

⁶*New York Times,* May 8, 1949, p. 7.

conspicuously lacking; in which, that is, the whole people should enjoy peace, security, and plenty. When we speak of peace, it is not to be supposed that Confucius was a pacifist; clearly he was not. But needless war was against his principles, and since most of the war in his day was internecine and an aspect of the general lawlessness, the governmental reforms he advocated would, if successful, have automatically eliminated it.

"Tzŭ-kung asked about government. The Master replied, 'An effective government must have sufficient food, sufficient weapons, and the confidence of the common people.' 'Suppose,' Tzŭ-kung said, 'that one of these three had to be dispensed with; which should it be?' The Master said, 'Weapons.' 'And what if one of the remaining two must be let go?' 'Then,' replied the Master, 'let the food go. For, from of old, death has been the lot of all men; but if the people have no confidence in the government, the state cannot stand.' ". . .

This last statement is extremely important. It does not mean that a government should starve its people to death in order to maintain itself; that would be absurd and very un-Confucian. What it does mean is that rulers should not drive and exploit their people unmercifully for the sake of economic gain, while giving the excuse that it is "for the people's own good" although they are too stupid to realize it. Even more important, it is an assertion that a state is a cooperative enterprise in which all, rulers and ruled alike, must share in the understanding of its purposes and the enjoyment of its benefits. . . .

"The Master said, 'If one tries to guide the people by means of rules, and keep order by means of punishments, the people will merely seek to avoid the penalties without having any sense of moral obligation. But if one leads them with virtue [both by precept and by example], and depends upon *li* to maintain order, the people will then feel their moral obligation and correct themselves.' " Here is the essence of Confucius' political philosophy. Not negative punishment but positive example; not tirades about what the people should not do but education as to what they should do. Not a police state dominated by fear but a cooperative commonwealth in which there is mutual understanding and good will between the rulers and the ruled. On this point he agreed with he most modern democratic theory. . . .

Once the people's poverty has been relieved, Confucius said, they should then be educated. We have already seen that he advocated at least some education for all the people. He once declared that if any man, no matter how humble, came to him seeking truth he was prepared to spend all the time that was necessary in helping him solve his problem. He boasted that he had never turned away a student, and in fact he seems to have accepted them, for training in the art of government, without regard to qualifications of birth or wealth, if only they were intelligent and industrious.

In thus advocating some education for all, and undertaking to make educated "gentlemen" out of ambitious commoners, Confucius was striking a blow that was ultimately fatal to the hereditary aristocratic order. . . . He undertook to take any intelligent student, of whatever background, and educate him to the point where he should be capable of making his own moral judgments. But he did not depend, to secure acceptance for his views, on any divine revelation or any claim of special authority for himself. Like the scientist, he believed that he could convince men through an appeal to their reason. This seems to be the sense of a somewhat obscure passage in the *Analects* in which he declares that the common people are the standard by which the justice of his actions may be tested.

Confucius conceived the highest political good to be the *happiness* of the people. This is of the utmost importance and is quite different from aiming merely at their welfare. . . .

The claim that a government brings about the welfare of the people may mean anything. But happiness is something else. "The Duke of Shê asked about government. The Master said, 'When there is good government, those who are near are made happy and those who are distant come.' " Another time he said that when the people of other states heard of a really good government they would be so eager to live under it that they would "come carrying their children on their backs." The important point about such statements is that they make the common people, and nobody else, the judges of what is good and what is bad government. Men can be forced to be orderly and to be productive, but they cannot be forced to be happy any more than a horse can be made to drink. They can be made happy only by a government that is good by their own standards. . . .

He appears to have believed that:

The proper aim of government is the welfare and happiness of the whole people.

This aim can be achieved only when the state is administered by those most capable of government.

Capacity to govern has no necessary connection with birth, wealth, or position; it depends solely on character and knowledge.

Character and knowledge are produced by proper education.

In order that the best talents may become available, education should be widely diffused.

It follows that the government should be administered by those persons, chosen from the whole population, who prove themselves to have profited most by the proper kind of education.

It is evident that this is not the same thing as saying that the people as a whole should control the government. But it does say that every man should have the opportunity to show whether he is capable of taking part in its control and its administration, and that if he proves himself so capable he should be not only permitted but urged to participate. This is in effect an aristocratic system, of government by an aristocracy not of birth or wealth but of virtue and ability.

Review and Study Questions

1. Why do you suppose the teachings of Confucius came to play so fundamental a role in Chinese civilization?
2. How does Confucius's emphasis on regulation and order translate into a political philosophy?
3. Why was the family so central to Confucius's philosophy? Why has it remained so central in Chinese life?
4. What elements of moral philosophy stand out in the precepts of Confucius?
5. Confucius was convinced that the character and knowledge necessary to rule are produced by proper education. To what extent has this basic Confucian conviction been adopted by the rulers of China?

Suggestions for Further Reading

The standard English text of Confucius's *Analects* as well as of the other so-called Confucian classics is the massive seven-volume *The Chinese Classics,* ed. and tr. James Legge (Oxford: Clarendon Press, 1893). This series also reproduces the Chinese text. There is a reprint of the first volume of this series, *The Four Books, Confucian Analects, the Great Learning, the Doctrine of the Mean, and the Works of Mencius,* ed. and tr. James Legge (New York: Paragon Books, 1966). *The Living Thoughts of Confucius,* ed. Alfred Doeblin (London et al.: Cassell, 1948) is a brief selection of translated passages from most of the important Confucian texts. *The Analects of Confucius,* ed. and tr. Arthur Waley (New York: Vintage Books, 1938), excerpted for this chapter, is a more modern and readable translation, the best available. The only English version of the Ssu-Ma Ch'ien historical biography is the one used in this chapter, Richard Wilhelm, *Confucius and Confucianism,* tr. George H. Danton and Annina Periam Danton (London: Routledge and Kegan Paul, 1972 [1931]).

On Confucius in Chinese literature, one of the most learned and readable works is Benjamin I. Schwartz, *The World of Thought in Ancient China* (Cambridge, Mass. and London: Harvard University Press, 1985). Burton Watson, *Early Chinese Literature* (New York and London: Columbia University Press, 1962) is one of the series "Companions to Asian Studies" and is an extremely useful handbook.

The best biography of Confucius is the one used in this chapter, H. G. Creel, *Confucius the Man and the Myth* (Westport, Conn.: Greenwood Press, 1972 [1949]), which is also available in the "Harper Torchbooks" series under the title *Confucius and the Chinese Way* (New York: Harper & Row, 1960). Two important interpretive works are Herbert Fingarette, *Confucius: The Secular as Sacred* (New York: Harper & Row, 1972) and Pierre Do-Dinh, *Confucius and Chinese Humanism*, tr. Charles Lam Markmann (New York: Funk and Wagnalls, 1969). D. Howard Smith, *Confucius* (New York: Scribner, 1973) and Liu Wu-Chi, *Confucius: His Life and Time* (New York: Philosophical Library, 1955) are competent standard biographies, as is the briefer Raymond Dawson, *Confucius* (New York: Hill and Wang, 1981) in the reliable "Past Masters" series. An interesting book is Kam Louie, *Critiques of Confucius in Contemporary China* (New York: St. Martin's Press, 1980), on how the Chinese Communists have dealt with the revered Confucian tradition. A book that goes to the other end of that tradition is John K. Shryock, *The Origins and Development of the State Cult of Confucius* (New York: Paragon Books, 1966 [1932]).

On the general history of the period, L. Carrington Goodrich, *A Short History of the Chinese People* (New York and London: Harper, 1943) is an excellent introduction to Chinese civilization and social history, largely based on original sources. Of the same sort is C. P. Fitzgerald and Norman Kotker, *The Horizon History of China* (New York: American Heritage Publishing Co., 1969). Charles O. Hucker, *China's Imperial Past* (Stanford: Stanford University Press, 1975) is a modern classic. John K. Fairbank, Edwin O. Reischauer, Albert M. Craig, *East Asia: Tradition and Transformation*, new impression (Boston et al.: Houghton Mifflin, 1978) is an authoritative and respected general survey.

THE IMAGE OF SOCRATES: MAN OR MYTH?

c. 470 B.C.	Born
c. 431–424 B.C.	Served in Peloponnesian War
406–405 B.C.	Served as a member of Athenian executive council
399 B.C.	Trial and death

By the lifetime of Socrates, in the late fifth century B.C., Greek civilization was almost at an end. This historic civilization was centered in Socrates' own city of Athens, which Pericles proudly called "the school of Hellas." But that magnificent city, which has so captivated our imagination, was widely regarded by its fellow city-states as a threat to their own independence—and with more than a little justification.

This threat led to the great Peloponnesian War, so vividly recounted in the pages of Socrates' contemporary, the historian Thucydides. Athens and its subject states were set against her arch-rival Sparta and Sparta's allies, the Peloponnesian League. It was a long, costly, and enervating war of almost thirty years' duration. And Athens finally lost it. Athens was humiliated, forced to accept its enemies' terms, and stripped of its subject states, its wealth, its navy. The buoyant optimism that had earlier characterized the city was one of the prime casualties of the war, along with confidence in its institutions and even in many of the presuppositions of its public life and private morality. It is in the backwash of these events that we must seek the life, and the death, of Socrates.

Socrates was surely the most famous Athenian of his age. Yet despite that fame, the facts of his life remain stubbornly vague. He was not a public official; hence we do not have archival records to rely on. And though he is a famous figure in literature, he actually wrote nothing himself to which we can refer. There are scattered references to him in Aristotle; a substantial (though prosaic) account in the works of Xenophon, who knew him; and, of course, the principal source of our information about him, the dialogues of the great philosopher Plato, who was Socrates' adoring pupil and disciple and made him the main character in most of his dialogues. And there are references and anecdotes from a considerable number of near contemporary accounts of Socrates that have been preserved, although the original sources are now lost.

What we know about Socrates is this. He was born an Athenian citizen about 470 B.C. His family belonged to the class of small artisans; his mother was a midwife and his father a stone mason. Socrates himself followed his father's trade. Rather late in life he married Xanthippe, and they had three sons, two of them still very young at the time of their father's death. Like most able-bodied Athenians of his time, Socrates was a veteran of the Peloponnesian War and even served with some distinction. On two occasions he seems to have held office on the large civic boards and commissions that carried on the business of the city. But generally he avoided public life. From a number of surviving descriptions and portrait busts we know what Socrates looked like—small and balding, anything but the lofty Greek ideal of physical beauty And we also know that he spent most of his time going about the city, trailed by a delighted and curious crowd of bright young aristocrats, asking often embarrassing questions of people who interested him, usually public officials and individuals of substance and position. This practice was to the detriment of his own family and his own trade. Socrates was a poor man.

The Clouds

ARISTOPHANES

The preceding bare account of Socrates is supplemented—one must almost say contradicted—by a single additional source, The Clouds *of Aristophanes. This work is of considerable value in that it is the only really substantial account of Socrates by a mature contemporary. Even Plato, our principal source of information, was forty years younger than Socrates, knew him only as an old man, and wrote* The Dialogues *many years after Socrates' death.* The Clouds *is, of course, not a biography. It is a play, by the greatest of Greek comic dramatists, in which Socrates is not only one of its chief characters but also the object of its satire.*

Aristophanes was a conservative, and his plays are a catalog of his objections to the management of the war and public policy, the state of literature and philosophy, the subversion of the stern old virtues "of our forefathers," and the "new morality" that he saw about him. In The Clouds *he accused Socrates of being a professional teacher who received, nay extracted, money for his "lessons"—which was not true. He denounced him as a cynical, opportunistic atheist—which was also apparently not the case. He attributed to him an expert competence in natural philosophy—which was highly unlikely. And in what was perhaps the most unfounded of all his charges, he portrayed Socrates as being the chief of the Sophists.*

The Sophists were a school of professional teachers, then very popular in Athens, who taught young men of wealth and position (usually for substantial fees) the techniques of public life, mostly logic and oratorical persuasion. The Sophists also tended to a flexible morality in which success was to be preferred to virtue, victory to either morality or philosophic consistency. It is a more than Socratic irony that Socrates should have been depicted as one of them, for it was squarely against the Sophists and their moral relativism that he had taken his stand. The whole point of his life, the reason he engaged other people in his famous questioning and endured their animosity, the entire "Socratic method" was an attempt to make people understand that there are moral absolutes, unchanging abstract principles of conduct to which they must ultimately resort.

Why Aristophanes portrayed Socrates in this fashion we do not know. Perhaps he genuinely believed that Socrates was a Sophist. Or perhaps he knew the truth but simply did not care, and made use of Socrates' notoriety in Athens to score his own point about the scandalous decline of education and what he regarded as philosophic quackery.

In any event, the play is cruel, mean, and malicious, but it is also out-rageously funny. And it gives us a view, however hostile, of the historic Socrates.

The Clouds *opens in the house of Strepsiades, a foolish old farmer, whose son Pheidippides' extravagant passion for racehorses has piled up so many debts that the old man is faced with ruin. One night, unable to sleep, Strepsiades decides to enroll the boy in the Sophist's school down the street. He calls it the "Thinkery." But Pheidippides will have nothing to do with "those filthy charlatans you mean—those frauds, those barefoot pedants with the look of death, Chairephon and that humbug, Sokrates."*

The old man then decides to go to the school himself. He kicks on the door, and a student-doorman answers. As they stand at the door, the student extols the wisdom of his master Socrates, citing a number of examples, not the least of which is Socrates' resolution of the problem of how the gnat hums. "According to him, the intestinal tract of the gnat is of puny propor-tions, and through this diminutive duct the gastric gas of the gnat is forced under pressure down to the rump. At that point the compressed gases, as through a narrow valve, escape with a whoosh, thereby causing the charac-teristic tootle or cry of the flatulent gnat."

Strepsiades is suitably impressed. "Why, Thales himself was an amateur compared to this! Throw open the Thinkery! Unbolt the door and let me see this wizard Sokrates in person. Open up! I'm MAD for education!" And Strepsiades enters the school.

STREPSIADES

    Look: who's that dangling up there in the basket?

STUDENT

Himself.

STREPSIADES

    Who's Himself?

STUDENT

        Sokrates.

STREPSIADES

          SOKRATES!
Then call him down. Go on. Give a great big shout.

STUDENT

Hastily and apprehensively taking his leave.

Er . . . *you* call him. I'm a busy man.

Exit Student.

STREPSIADES

O Sokrates!

No answer from the basket.

Yoohoo. Sokrates!

SOKRATES

From a vast philosophical height.

Well, creature of a day?

STREPSIADES

What in the world are you doing up there?

SOKRATES

Ah, sir,
I walk upon the air and look down upon the sun
from a superior standpoint.

STREPSIADES

Well, I suppose it's better
that you sneer at the gods from a basket up in the air
than do it down here on the ground.

SOKRATES

Precisely. You see,
only by being suspended aloft, by dangling
my mind in the heavens and mingling my rare thought
with the ethereal air, could I ever achieve strict
scientific accuracy in my survey of the vast empyrean.
Had I pursued my inquiries from down there on the ground,
my data would be worthless. The earth, you see, pulls down
the delicate essence of thought to its own gross level.

As an afterthought.

Much the same thing happens with watercress.

STREPSIADES

Ecstatically bewildered.

You don't say?
Thought draws down . . . delicate essence . . . into
watercress. O dear little Sokrates, please come down.
Lower away, and teach me what I need to know!

Sokrates is slowly lowered earthwards.

SOKRATES

What subject?

STREPSIADES

Your course on public speaking and debating techniques.
You see, my creditors have become absolutely ferocious.
You should see how they're hounding me. What's more,
Sokrates, they're about to seize my belongings.

SOKRATES

How in the
world could you fall so deeply in debt without realizing it?

STREPSIADES

How? A great, greedy horse-pox ate me up, that's how.
But that's why I want instruction in your second Logic,
you know the one—the get-away-without-paying argument.
I'll pay you *any* price you ask. I swear it.
By the gods.

SOKRATES

By the gods? The gods, my dear simple fellow,
are a mere expression coined by vulgar superstition.
We frown upon such coinage here.

STREPSIADES

What do *you* swear by?
Bars of iron, like the Byzantines?

SOKRATES

Tell me, old man,
would you honestly like to learn the truth, the *real* truth,
about the gods?

STREPSIADES

> By Zeus, I sure would. The *real* truth. . . .

[*At this point the chorus of clouds enters, singing.*]

STREPSIADES

Holy Zeus, Sokrates, who were those ladies that sang
that solemn hymn? Were they heroines of mythology?

SOKRATES

> No, old man.
Those were the Clouds of heaven, goddesses of men of
leisure and philosophers. To them we owe our repertoire of
verbal talents: our eloquence, intellect, fustian, casuistry,
force, wit, prodigious vocabulary, circumlocutory skill—

. . . .

[*The leader of the chorus greets them.*]

KORYPHAIOS

> Hail, superannuated man!
Hail, old birddog of culture!

To Sokrates.

> And hail to you, O Sokrates,
high priest of poppycock!
> Inform us what your wishes are.
For of all the polymaths on earth, it's you we most prefer—

. . . .

sir, for your swivel-eyes, your barefoot swagger down the
street, because you're poor on our account and terribly
affected.

STREPSIADES

Name of Earth, what a voice! Solemn and holy and awful!

SOKRATES

These are the only gods there are. The rest are but figments.

STREPSIADES

Holy name of Earth! Olympian Zeus is a figment?

SOKRATES

Zeus?
What Zeus?
Nonsense.
There is no Zeus.

STREPSIADES

No Zeus?
Then *who* makes it rain? Answer me that.

SOKRATES

Why, the Clouds,
of course.
What's more, the proof is incontrovertible.
For instance,
have you ever yet seen rain when you didn't see a cloud?
But if your hypothesis were correct, Zeus could drizzle
  from an empty sky
while the clouds were on vacation.

STREPSIADES

By Apollo, you're right. A pretty
  proof.
And to think I always used to believe the rain was just Zeus
pissing through a sieve.
All right, *who* makes it thunder?
Brrr. I get goosebumps just saying it.

SOKRATES

The Clouds again,
of course. A simple process of Convection.

STREPSIADES

I admire you,
but I don't follow you.

SOKRATES

Listen. The Clouds are a saturate water-solution.
Tumescence in motion, of necessity, produces precipitation.
When these distended masses collide—*boom!*
Fulmination.

STREPSIADES

But who makes them move before they collide? Isn't that
Zeus?

SOKRATES

Not Zeus, idiot. The Convection-principle!

STREPSIADES

                                        Convection? That's
a new one.
Just think. So Zeus is out and Convection-principle's in.
Tch, tch.

            But wait: you haven't told me who makes it thunder.

SOKRATES

But I just *finished* telling you! The Clouds are water-packed;
they collide with each other and explode because of the
pressure.

STREPSIADES

            Yeah?
And what's your proof for *that*?

SOKRATES

                            Why, take yourself as example.
You know that meat-stew the vendors sell at the Panathenaia?[1]
How it gives you the cramps and your stomach
starts to rumble?

STREPSIADES

                                        Yes,
by Apollo! I remember. What an awful feeling! You feel
sick and your belly churns and the fart rips loose like
thunder. First just a gurgle, *pappapax;* then louder,
pappaPAPAXapaX, and finally like thunder,
PAPAPAPAXAPAXAPPAPAXapap!

SOKRATES

Precisely.
First think of the tiny fart that your intestines make.

---

[1]The quadrennial festival of Athena, the patron goddess of Athens.—ED.

Then consider the heavens: their infinite farting is thunder.
For thunder and farting are, in principle, one and the same.

[*Strepsiades is convinced and is initiated into Socrates' school. But, alas, he is incapable of learning the subtleties Socrates sets out to teach him and is contemptuously dismissed from the school. Then the leader of the chorus suggests that he fetch his son to study in his place. A splendid idea! As Strepsiades drags his son on to the scene, Pheidippides protests.*]

PHEIDIPPIDES

But Father,
what's the matter with you? Are you out of your head?
Almighty Zeus, you must be mad!

STREPSIADES

"Almighty Zeus!"
What musty rubbish! Imagine, a boy your age
still believing in Zeus!

PHEIDIPPIDES

What's so damn funny?

STREPSIADES

It tickles me when the heads of toddlers like you
are still stuffed with such outdated notions. Now then,
listen to me and I'll tell you a secret or two
that might make an intelligent man of you yet.
But remember: you mustn't breathe a word of this.

PHEIDIPPIDES

A word of what?

STREPSIADES

Didn't you just swear by Zeus?

PHEIDIPPIDES

I did.

STREPSIADES

Now learn what Education can do for *you:*
Pheidippides, there is no Zeus.

PHEIDIPPIDES

There is no Zeus?

STREPSIADES

No Zeus. Convection-principle's in power now.
Zeus has been banished.

PHEIDIPPIDES

Drivel!

STREPSIADES

Take my word for it,
it's absolutely true.

PHEIDIPPIDES

Who says so?

STREPSIADES

Sokrates.
And Chairephon too. . . .

PHEIDIPPIDES

Are you so far gone on the road to complete insanity
you'd believe the word of those charlatans?

STREPSIADES

Hush, boy.
For shame. I won't hear you speaking disrespectfully
of such eminent scientists and geniuses. And, what's more,
men of such fantastic frugality and Spartan thrift,
they regard baths, haircuts, and personal cleanliness
generally as an utter waste of time and money—whereas
you, dear boy, have taken me to the cleaner's so many times,
I'm damn near washed up. Come on, for your father's sake,
go and learn.

[*Some time later*]
Enter Strepsiades from his house, counting on his fingers.

STREPSIADES

Five days, four days, three days, two days, and then
that one day of the days of the month
I dread the most that makes me fart with fear—
the last day of the month, Duedate for debts,
when every dun in town has solemnly sworn
to drag me into court and bankrupt me completely.

And when I plead with them to be more reasonable—
"But PLEASE, sir. Don't demand the whole sum now.
Take something on account. I'll pay you later."—
they snort they'll never see the day, curse me
for a filthy swindler and say they'll sue.

                              Well,
let them. If Pheidippides has learned to talk,
I don't give a damn for them and their suits.

                            Now then,
a little knock on the door and we'll have the answer.

He knocks on Sokrates' door and calls out.

Porter!
      Hey, porter!

Sokrates opens the door.

SOKRATES

                 Ah, Strepsiades. Salutations.

STREPSIADES

Same to you, Sokrates.

He hands Sokrates a bag of flour.

                 Here. A token of my esteem.
Call it an honorarium. Professors always get honorariums.

Snatching back the bag.

But wait: has Pheidippides learned his rhetoric yet—. . . .

SOKRATES

Taking the bag.

He has mastered it.

STREPSIADES

           O great goddess Bamboozle!

SOKRATES

Now, sir, you can evade any legal action you wish to.

[*But instead of help with his creditors, Strepsiades gets a very different kind of treatment from his son.*]

With a bellow of pain and terror, Strepsiades plunges out of his house, hotly pursued by Pheidippides with a murderous stick.

STREPSIADES

OOOUUUCH!!!
            HALP!
                  For god's sake, help me!

Appealing to the Audience.

                                    Friends!
Fellow-countrymen! Aunts! Uncles! Fathers! Brothers!
To the rescue!
            He's beating me!
                        Help me!
                              Ouuch!
O my poor head!
            Ooh, my jaw!

To Pheidippides.

                        —You great big bully,
Hit your own father, would you?

PHEIDIPPIDES

                        Gladly, Daddy.

STREPSIADES

You hear that? The big brute *admits* it.

PHEIDIPPIDES

                        Admit it? Hell,
I *proclaim* it. . . .
            Would a logical demonstration
convince you?

STREPSIADES

            A logical demonstration? You mean to tell me
you can *prove* a shocking thing like that?

PHEIDIPPIDES

                        Elementary, really.
What's more, you can choose the logic. Take your pick.
Either one.

STREPSIADES

            Either *which?*

PHEIDIPPIDES

Either *which?* Why,
Socratic logic or pre-Socratic logic. Either logic.
Take your pick.

STREPSIADES

Take my pick, damn you? Look,
who do you think paid for your shyster education anyway?
And now you propose to convince *me* that there's nothing
wrong in whipping your own father?

PHEIDIPPIDES

I not only propose it:
I propose to *prove* it. Irrefutably, in fact. Rebuttal
is utterly inconceivable. . . .

[*Pheidippides then "proves" that since his father beat him as a child "for your
own damn good" "because I loved you," then it is only "a fortiori" logic that
the father be beaten by the son, since "old men logically deserve to be beaten
more, since at their age they have clearly less excuse for the mischief that they
do."*]

*There is a long tense silence as the full force of this
crushing argument takes its effect upon Strepsiades.*

STREPSIADES

What?
But how. . . ?
Hmm,
by god, you're right!

To the Audience.

—Speaking for the older generation,
gentlemen, I'm compelled to admit defeat. The kids have
proved their point: naughty fathers should be flogged. . . .

[*But this arrogance is too much, logic or no logic, for Strepsiades.*]

STREPSIADES

O Horse's Ass, Blithering Imbecile,
Brainless Booby, Bonehead that I was to ditch the gods
for Sokrates!

He picks up Pheidippides' stick and savagely smashes the potbellied model of the Universe in front of the Thinkery. He then rushes to his own house and falls on his knees before the statue of Hermes.

—Great Hermes, I implore you!

[*Strepsiades and his slave set fire to the Thinkery and he beats the choking, sputtering Socrates and his pallid students off the stage.*]

The Apology

PLATO

In 399 B.C., twenty-five years after The Clouds, *Socrates stood before the great popular court of Athens. He was accused of much the same charges that had been leveled at him by Aristophanes, specifically "that Socrates is a doer of evil, who corrupts the youth; and who does not believe in the gods of the state, but has other new divinities of his own." The charges were brought by three fellow Athenians, Meletus, Lycon, and Anytus. Although only one of the accusers, Anytus, was a person of any importance, and he only a minor political figure, the charges carried the death penalty if the court so decided. Indeed, this was the intent of the accusers.*

Socrates, now seventy years old, rose to speak in his own defense; he was not the pettifogging buffoon of The Clouds. *Perhaps that man never really existed. By the same token, did the speaker at the trial ever exist? The trial is Socrates', but the account of it is Plato's.* The Apology, *from* The Dialogues of Plato, *is the "defense" of Socrates at his trial.*

How you, O Athenians, have been affected by my accusers, I cannot tell; but I know that they almost made me forget who I was—so persuasively did they speak; and yet they have hardly uttered a word of truth. But . . . first, I have to reply to the older charges and to my first accusers, and then I will go on to the later ones. For of old I have had many accusers, who have accused me falsely to you during many years; and I am more afraid of them than of Anytus and his associates, who are dangerous, too, in their own way. But far more dangerous are the others, who began when you were children, and took possession of your minds with their falsehoods, telling of one Socrates, a wise man, who speculated about the heaven above, and searched into the earth beneath, and made the worse appear the better cause. The disseminators of this tale are the accusers whom I dread; for their hearers are apt to fancy that such enquirers do not believe in the existence of the gods. And they are many, and their charges against me are of ancient date, and they were made by them in the days when you were more impressible than you are now—in childhood, or it may have been in youth—and the cause when heard went by default, for there was none to answer. And hardest of all, I do not know and cannot tell the names of my accusers; unless in the chance case of a Comic poet. . . .

I dare say, Athenians, that some one among you will reply, 'Yes, Socrates, but what is the origin of these accusations which are brought against you; there must have been something strange which you have been doing? All these rumours and this talk about you would never have arisen if you had been like other men: tell us, then, what is the cause of them, for we should be sorry to judge hastily of you.' Now I regard this as a fair challenge, and I will endeavour to explain to you the reason why I am called wise and have such an evil fame. . . .

. . . I will refer you to a witness who is worthy of credit; that witness shall be the God of Delphi—he will tell you about my wisdom, if I have any, and of what sort it is. You must have known Chaerephon; he was early a friend of mine. . . .Well, Chaerephon, as you know, was very impetuous in all his doings, and he went to Delphi and boldly asked the oracle to tell him whether—as I was saying, I must beg you not to interrupt—he asked the oracle to tell him whether any one was wiser than I was, and the Pythian prophetess answered, that there was no man wiser. Chaerephon is dead himself; but his brother, who is in court, will confirm the truth of what I am saying.

Why do I mention this? Because I am going to explain to you why I have such an evil name. When I heard the answer, I said to myself, What can the god mean? and what is the interpretation of his riddle? for I know that I have no wisdom, small or great. What then can he mean when he says that I am the wisest of men? And yet he is a god, and cannot lie; that would be against his nature. After long consideration, I thought of a method of trying the question. I reflected that if I could only find a man wiser than myself, then I might go to the god with a refutation in my hand. I should say to him, 'Here is a man who is wiser than I am; but you said that I was the wisest.' Accordingly I went to one who had the reputation of wisdom, and observed him—his name I need not mention; he was a politician whom I selected for examination—and the result was as follows: When I began to talk with him, I could not help thinking that he was not really wise, although he was thought wise by many, and still wiser by himself; and thereupon I tried to explain to him that he thought himself wise, but was not really wise; and the consequence was that he hated me, and his enmity was shared by several who were present and heard me. So I left him, saying to myself, as I went away: Well, although I do not suppose that either of us knows anything really beautiful and good, I am better off than he is,—for he knows nothing, and thinks that he knows; I neither know nor think that I know. In this latter particular, then, I seem to have slightly the advantage of him. Then I went to another who had still higher pretensions to wisdom, and my conclusion was exactly the same. Whereupon I made another enemy of him, and of many others besides him. . . .

This inquisition has led to my having many enemies of the worst and most dangerous kind, and has given occasion also to many calumnies. And I am called wise, for my hearers always imagine that I myself possess the wisdom which I find wanting in others: but the truth is, O men of Athens, that God only is wise, and by his answer he intends to show that the wisdom of men is worth little or nothing; he is not speaking of Socrates, he is only using my name by way of illustration, as if he said, He, O men, is the wisest, who, like Socrates, knows that his wisdom is in truth worth nothing. And so I go about the world, obedient to the god, and search and make enquiry into the wisdom of any one, whether citizen or stranger, who appears to be wise; and if he is not wise, then in vindication of the oracle I show him that he is not wise, and my occupation quite absorbs me, and I have no time to give either to any public matter of interest or to any concern of my own, but I am in utter poverty by reason of my devotion to the god.

There is another thing:—young men of the richer classes, who have not much to do, come about me of their own accord; they like to hear the pretenders examined, and they often imitate me, and proceed to examine others; there are plenty of persons, as they quickly discover, who think they know something, but really know little or nothing; and then those who are examined by them instead of being angry with themselves are angry with me: This confounded Socrates, they say; this villainous misleader of youth—and then if somebody asks them, Why, what evil does he practise or teach? they do not know, and cannot tell; but in order that they may not appear to be at a loss, they repeat the ready-made charges which are used against all philosophers about teaching things up in the clouds and under the earth, and having no gods and making the worse appear the better cause. . . .

Turning to the formal charges against him, Socrates dismisses them almost contemptuously, returning to the main charges as he sees them and his lifelong "argument" with his city and its citizenry.

And now, Athenians, I am not going to argue for my own sake, as you may think, but for yours, that you may not sin against the God by condemning me, who am his gift to you. For if you kill me you will not easily find a successor to me, who, if I may use such a ludicrous figure of speech, am a sort of gadfly, given to the state by God; and the state is a great and noble steed who is tardy in his motions owing to his very size, and requires to be stirred into life. I am that gadfly which God has attached to the state, and all day long and in all places am always fastening upon you, arousing and persuading and reproaching you. You will not easily find another like me, and therefore I would advise you to spare me. I dare say that you may feel out of temper (like a person who is suddenly awakened from sleep), and you think that you might easily strike me dead as Anytus advises, and then you would sleep on for the remainder of your lives, unless God in his care of you sent you another gadfly. When I say I am given to you by God, the proof of my mission is this:—if I had been like other men, I should not have neglected all my own concerns or patiently seen the neglect of them during all these years, and have been doing yours, coming to you individually like a father or elder brother, exhorting you to regard virtue; such conduct, I say, would be unlike human nature. If I had gained anything, or if my exhortations had been paid, there would have been some sense in my doing so; but now, as you will perceive, not even the impudence of my accusers dares to say that I have ever exacted or sought pay of any one; of that they have no witness. And I have a sufficient witness to the truth of what I say—my poverty. . . .

The jury returns the verdict of guilty.

There are many reasons why I am not grieved, O men of Athens, at the vote of condemnation. I expected it, and am only surprised that the votes are so nearly equal; for I had thought that the majority against me would have been far larger; but now, had thirty votes gone over to the other side, I should have been acquitted. And I may say, I think, that I have escaped Meletus. I may say more; for without the assistance of Anytus and Lycon, any one may see that he would not have had a fifth part of the votes, as the law requires, in which case he would have incurred a fine of a thousand drachmae.

And so he proposes death as the penalty. . . .

Some one will say: Yes, Socrates, but cannot you hold your tongue, and then you may go into a foreign city, and no one will interfere with you? Now I have great difficulty in making you understand my answer to this. For if I tell you that to do as you say would be a disobedience to the God, and therefore that I cannot hold my tongue, you will not believe that I am serious; and if I say again that daily to discourse about virtue, and of those other things about which you hear me examining myself and others, is the greatest good of man, and that the unexamined life is not worth living, you are still less likely to believe me. Yet I say what is true, although a thing of which it is hard for me to persuade you. Also, I have never been accustomed to think that I deserve to suffer any harm. Had I money I might have estimated the offence at what I was able to pay, and not have been much the worse. But I have none, and therefore I must ask you to proportion the fine to my means. Well, perhaps I could afford a mina, and therefore I propose that penalty: Plato, Crito, Critobulus, and Apollodorus, my friends here, bid me say thirty minae, and they will be the sureties. Let thirty minae be the penalty; for which sum they will be ample security to you. . . .

Socrates is condemned to death.

And now, O men who have condemned me, I would fain prophesy to you; for I am about to die, and in the hour of death men are gifted with prophetic power. And I prophesy to you who are my murderers, that immediately after my departure punishment far heavier than you have inflicted on me will surely await you. Me you have killed because you wanted to escape the accuser, and not to give an account of your lives. But that will not be as you suppose: far otherwise. For I say that there will be more accusers of you than there are now; accusers whom hitherto I have restrained: and as they are younger they will be more inconsiderate with you, and you will be more offended at them. If you think that by killing men you can prevent some one from censuring your evil lives, you are mistaken; that is not a way of escape which is either possible or honourable; the easiest and the noblest way is not to be disabling others, but to be improving yourselves. This is the prophecy which I utter before my departure to the judges who have condemned me.

Friends, who would have acquitted me, I would like also to talk with you about the thing which has come to pass, while the magistrates are busy, and before I go to the place at which I must die. Stay then a little, for we may as well talk with one another while there is time. You are my friends, and I should like to show you the meaning of this event which has happened to me. O my judges—for you I may truly call judges—I should like to tell you of a wonderful circumstance. Hitherto the divine faculty of which the internal oracle[2] is the source

---

[2] This was Socrates' famous "daimon," more than a conscience, less perhaps than a separate "in-dwelling" god, but, as he claimed, at least a guiding voice.—ED.

has constantly been in the habit of opposing me even about trifles, if I was going to make a slip or error in any matter; and now as you see there has come upon me that which may be thought, and is generally believed to be, the last and worst evil. But the oracle made no sign of opposition, either when I was leaving my house in the morning, or when I was on my way to the court, or while I was speaking, at anything which I was going to say; and yet I have often been stopped in the middle of a speech, but now in nothing I either said or did touching the matter in hand has the oracle opposed me. What do I take to be the explanation of this silence? I will tell you. It is an intimation that what has happened to me is a good, and that those of us who think that death is an evil are in error. For the customary sign would surely have opposed me had I been going to evil and not to good. . . .

Wherefore, O judges, be of good cheer about death, and know of a certainty, that no evil can happen to a good man, either in life or after death. He and his are not neglected by the gods; nor has my own approaching end happened by mere chance. But I see clearly that the time had arrived when it was better for me to die and be released from trouble wherefore the oracle gave no sign. For which reason, also, I am not angry with my condemners, or with my accusers; they have done me no harm, although they did not mean to do me any good; and for this I may gently blame them.

Still I have a favour to ask them. When my sons are grown up, I would ask you, O my friends, to punish them; and I would have you trouble them, as I have troubled you, if they seem to care about riches, or anything, more than about virtue; or if they pretend to be something when they are really nothing,—then reprove them, as I have reproved you, for not caring about that for which they ought to care, and thinking that they are something when they are really nothing. And if you do this, both I and my sons will have received justice at your hands.

The hour of departure has arrived, and we go our ways—I to die, and you to live. Which is better God only knows.

Socrates: A Modern Perspective

MOSES HADAS AND MORTON SMITH

Which Socrates are we to choose? Is it even possible to reconstruct the real man from either the idealized, "gospel"-like account of Plato or the malicious parody of Aristophanes, or from both together? Two distinguished American professors, Moses Hadas (d. 1966) and Morton Smith, do not think so. They state their case in the following selection from their book Heroes and Gods: Spiritual Biographies in Antiquity.

As surely as the figure of Achilles is the paradigm for heroic epic, so surely is Socrates the paradigm for aretalogy.[3] He is manifestly the point of departure for the development of the genre after his time, but he is also the culmination of antecedent development. It is likely that the historical Achilles (assuming there was one) was both more and less than Homer's image of him, but even if he was exactly as the image represents him, without it he could never have served posterity as a paradigm. Nor could Socrates have served posterity except through the image Plato fashioned. It is not, strictly speaking, a developed aretalogy that Plato presents; that is to say, he does not provide a single systematic account of a career that can be used as a sacred text. Indeed, Plato's treatment made it impossible for others to elaborate the image plausibly or to reduce it to a sacred text. But the whole image, full and consistent and unmistakable, is presupposed in every Platonic dialogue which contributes to it. Undoubtedly the historical Socrates was an extraordinarily gifted and devoted teacher, and his image does undoubtedly reflect the historical figure, but the image clearly transcends the man, and the image is the conscious product of Plato's art.

Because of Plato, and only Plato, Socrates' position in the tradition of western civilization is unique. Other fifth-century Greeks have won admiration bordering on adulation for high achievement in various fields, but only Socrates is completely without flaw; the perfect image leaves no opening for impugning his wisdom or temperance or courage or wholehearted devotion to his mission. We might expect that a

---

[3]The worship of, or reverence for, nobility or virtue; from the Greek *areté*, "virtue."—ED.

dim figure out of the imperfectly recorded past, an Orpheus or Pythagoras or even Empedocles, might be idealized, but Socrates lived in the bright and merciless light of a century that could ostracize Aristides, deny prizes to Sophocles, throw Pericles out of office. Perhaps the nearest approach to Plato's idealization of Socrates is Thucydides' idealization of Pericles; some critics have thought that Thucydides' main motive in writing his history was to glorify Pericles. But Thucydides never claimed for Pericles the kind of potency that Plato suggests for Socrates, and on the basis of Thucydides' own history the world has accepted Pericles as a farseeing but not preternaturally gifted or wholly successful statesman. Only in the case of Socrates has the idealized image effaced the reality.

What makes Plato's share in the idealization obvious is the existence of parallel accounts of Socrates that are less reverent. Plato's reports are indeed the fullest: the larger part of his extensive writings purports to be an exposition of Socrates' thought. But there are other witnesses. . . . In the *Clouds* of Aristophanes, Socrates is the central figure, and the boot is on a different foot, for it was produced in 423, when Socrates was not yet fifty and therefore in the prime of his career but not yet shielded by the extraordinary eminence later bestowed upon him. Nor was Aristophanes' comedy the only caricature of Socrates. Also in 423 a comic Socrates figures in a play of Amipsias and two years later in one of Eupolis. These poets, it must be remembered, were dealing with a personality that was familiar to them and also, perhaps more important, to their audiences.

The caricature, certainly Aristophanes' and presumably the others' also, is of course grossly unfair: Socrates did not meddle with natural science or receive pay for his teaching, as the *Clouds* alleges he did: the most carping critic could not question his probity. The very absurdity of the charges and the topsy-turvy carnival atmosphere of the festival eliminated the possibility of rancor; in the *Symposium,* of which the fictive date is a decade after the presentation of the *Clouds,* Plato represents Aristophanes and Socrates as consorting on the friendliest of terms. And yet it is plain that Aristophanes' large audience was not outraged by the frivolous treatment of a saint, and in the *Apology,* which Socrates is presumed to have pronounced at his defense twenty-five years later, the point is made that the caricature had seriously prejudiced the public against Socrates. To some degree, then, the caricature is a significant corrective to later idealization. . . .

Really to know where the truth lies, . . . we should have his actual words or a public record of his deeds, but Socrates wrote nothing and was not, like Pericles, a statesman. The image is therefore not subject to correction on the basis of his own works. Aristophanes also deals harshly with Euripides, but we have Euripides' own plays to read, so

that the caricature tells us more of Aristophanes than it does of Euripides. Isocrates wrote an encomium of Evagoras and Xenophon of
Agesilaus, but the praise of these statesmen carries its own corrective.
Of Socrates we know, or think we know, much more than of those
others—what he looked like, how he dressed and walked and talked,
and most of all, what he thought and taught. . . .

Actually the only significant datum in the inventory which is beyond dispute is that Socrates was condemned to death in 399 B.C. and
accepted his penalty when he might have evaded it. The magnanim-
ity of this act no one can belittle; it is enough to purify and enhance
even a questionable career, and it is certainly enough to sanctify a
Socrates. For Plato it clearly marked a decisive turn, as he himself
records in his autobiographical *Seventh Epistle*. For him it undoubtedly
crystallized the image of Socrates that fills the early dialogues. . . . All
of Plato's earlier dialogues, and the more plainly in the degree of
their earliness, are as much concerned with the personality of Socrates as with his teachings. His pre-eminence in reason, his devotion to
his mission, his selfless concern for the spiritual welfare of his fellow
men, the purity of his life, even his social gifts, are made prominent.
The *Apology*, quite possibly the earliest of the Socratic pieces, is concerned with the man and his personal program, not his doctrines.
Here he is made to present, without coyness or swagger or unction,
his own concept of his mission to sting men, like a gadfly, to self-
examination and to serve as midwife to their travail with ideas. The
Apology also illustrates the devotion of his disciples to Socrates and the
surprisingly large proportion of his jurors who were willing to acquit
him. Again, in the short early dialogues, which are mainly concerned
with questioning common misconceptions of such abstract nouns as
"piety" or "friendship," it is the man as defined by his program, not
the abstract doctrine, that is being presented. In the great central
group—*Protagoras, Gorgias, Symposium, Republic*—the proportion of
doctrinal content is larger, but the doctrine requires the personality of
Socrates to make it plausible. The moral significance of education
may emerge from the rather piratical dialectic in the *Protagoras*, but
the argument takes on special meaning from Socrates' wise and tender treatment of the eager and youthful disciple who is enamored of
Protagoras' reputation. That it is a worse thing for a man to inflict
than to receive an injury and that a good man is incapable of being
injured is the kind of doctrine which absolutely requires that its prom-
ulgator be a saint, as Socrates is pictured in the *Gorgias*; on the lips of
a lesser man it would be nothing more than a rhetorical paradox. A
great weight of individual prestige must similarly be built up to en-
able a man to enunciate the grand scheme of the *Republic*, and the
occasional playfulness of the tone only emphasizes the stature of the

individual who enunciates it. People too earth-bound to recognize such stature, like Thrasymachus in Book I, can only find the whole proceeding absurd. And only from a man whose special stature was recognized could the vision of Er be accepted as other than an old wives' tale.

In the *Symposium* more than in other dialogues the individuality of Socrates is underscored. It is not a trivial matter, for establishing the character of Socrates, that he could be welcome at a party of the fashionable wits of Athens, could get himself respectably groomed for the occasion, and engage in banter with his fellow guests without compromising his spiritual ascendancy one whit. We hear incidentally of his absolute bravery in battle and his disregard of self in the service of a friend, of his extraordinary physical vitality that enabled him to stand all night pondering some thought while his fellow soldiers bivouacked around him to watch the spectacle, of how he could lose himself in some doorway in a trance and so make himself late for his appointment until he had thought through whatever was on his mind. The subject of the *Symposium* is love, and love had been conceived of, in the series of speeches praising it, in a range from gross homosexuality to romantic attachment, to a cosmic principle of attraction and repulsion, to Socrates' own concept . . . of an ascent to union with the highest goodness and beauty. . . .

But it is in the *Phaedo* that Socrates comes nearest to being translated to a higher order of being. In prison, during the hours preceding his death, Socrates discourses to his devoted followers on the most timely and timeless of all questions, the immortality of the soul. The *Phaedo* is the most spiritual and the most eloquent of all dialogues; the account of Socrates' last moments is surely the second most compelling passion in all literature. If Plato's object was to inculcate a belief in immortality, there are of course sound practical reasons for giving the spokesman of the doctrine extraordinary prestige. In such an issue it is the personality of the teacher rather than the cogency of his arguments that is most persuasive. . . .

But the saintliness with which Socrates is endowed in the *Phaedo* seems more than a mere device to promote belief in the immortality of the soul. If belief is being inculcated, it is belief in Socrates, not in immortality. Only an occasional reader of the *Phaedo* could rehearse its arguments for immortality years or months after he had laid the book down; the saintliness of Socrates he can never forget. It is his image of Socrates rather than any specific doctrine that Plato wished to crystallize and perpetuate. From the tenor of all his writing it is clear that Plato believed that the welfare of society depended upon leadership by specially endowed and dedicated men. Ordinary men following a prescribed code would not do. Indeed, Plato conceived of his own effectiveness as teacher in much the same way; in the autobiographical *Seventh Epistle* he tells us that no one could claim to have apprehended his teachings merely from study of his writings: long personal contact with a master spirit is essential.

In the centuries after Plato the images of certain saintly figures who, like Socrates, had selflessly devoted themselves to the spiritual improvement of the community and had accepted the suffering, sometimes the martyrdom, these efforts entailed, played a considerable role in the development of religious ideas and practices. In some cases the image may have masked a character negligible or dishonest, and the men who created and exploited the image may have done so for selfish motives; but in some cases, surely, the man behind the image was a devoted teacher whose disciples embroidered his career in good faith into a kind of hagiology[4] that they then used for moral edification. Whatever the motivation, there can be little doubt that the prime model for the spiritual hero was Socrates. . . .

Review and Study Questions

1. How did Socrates respond to the charges brought against him at his trial?
2. By his conduct at his trial was Socrates seeking martyrdom? Explain your answer.
3. Is there any historical validity in the image of Socrates presented by Aristophanes in *The Clouds?*
4. Do you consider Plato's image of Socrates in *The Apology* more historically valid than Aristophanes' image of him in *The Clouds?* Why?
5. What part did the temper of the times play in the trial and execution of Socrates?
6. Was Socrates a spiritual hero? Give reasons for your answer.

Suggestions for Further Reading

Socrates is a maddeningly elusive historical figure: he exists only in the works of others. Luis E. Navia, *Socratic Testimonies* (Lanham, Md.: University Press of America, 1987), is a convenient outline of the sources of historical information we do have for Socrates and of the major critical

---

[4]Veneration of a saint or saints.—ED.

problems in Socratic studies. Because of the lack of historical sources there is a nearly irresistible urge to create a "historical Socrates," which has produced a number of biographical or semibiographical works on him. The preeminent modern account is A. E. Taylor, *Socrates* (New York: Anchor, 1953 [1933]), in which the great British Platonist argues that the striking figure of Socrates as derived from Plato's dialogues is essentially an accurate historical account. The book is clear and readable as well as authoritative. An almost equally good account is Jean Brun, *Socrates*, tr. Douglas Scott (New York: Walker, 1962), in which the author, writing for young people, simplifies and sorts out the leading elements in the traditional view of Socrates—i.e., the Delphic dictum "Know thyself," Socrates' "in-dwelling Daimon," and the Socratic irony. At the other extreme are Alban D. Winspear and Tom Silverberg, *Who Was Socrates?* (New York: Russell and Russell, 1960 [1939]), and Norman Gulley, *The Philosophy of Socrates* (London and New York: Macmillan and St. Martin's, 1968). Winspear and Silverberg argue—not entirely convincingly—for a complete revision of the tradition and make Socrates evolve in the course of his career from a democratic liberal to an aristocratic conservative. And Gulley argues for the rejection of Plato's view of Socrates as a skeptic and agnostic in favor of a more constructive role for Socrates in ancient philosophy. Laszlo Versényi, *Socratic Humanism* (New Haven, Conn.: Yale University Press, 1963), while not going as far as Gulley, does advocate a separation between the often paired Socrates and Plato in favor of tying Socrates more closely to the sophists, especially Protagoras and Gorgias. Students should find especially interesting Alexander Eliot, *Socrates: A Fresh Appraisal of the Most Celebrated Case in History* (New York: Crown, 1967). It is less a fresh appraisal than a popular and extremely readable review of Socrates' background, life, and the evidence brought to his trial. The second part of the book is what the author calls "a free synthesis" of all the Platonic dialogues touching on the trial and death of Socrates—essentially a new, dramatic dialogue account in fresh, modern English. On the matter of "the case" of Socrates—i.e., his trial and the evidence and testimony presented—two essays in Gregory Vlastos (ed.), *The Philosophy of Socrates: A Collection of Critical Essays* (South Bend, Ind.: University of Notre Dame Press, 1980 [1971]), Kenneth J. Dover, "Socrates in the *Clouds*" and A. D. Woozley, "Socrates on Disobeying the Law," are of considerable interest. On the two dialogues most pertinent to the trial and death of Socrates, *The Apology* and *The Crito*, two books are recommended. R. E. Allen, *Socrates and Legal Obligation* (Minneapolis, Minn.: University of Minnesota Press, 1980) is a clear and penetrating analysis of the dialogues as is Richard Kraut, *Socrates and the State* (Princeton, N.J.: Princeton University Press, 1984), which also makes the case for Socrates' conscious civil disobedience: it is the best modern treatment of Socrates before the law. Thomas C. Brickhouse and Nicholas D. Smith, *Socrates on Trial* (Princeton, N.J.: Princeton University Press, 1989) judiciously surveys all the evidence for the trial. On the other hand, I. F. Stone, *The Trial of Socrates* (New York: Anchor, 1989) is a muckraking attempt to portray Socrates as an antidemocratic reactionary—an outrageous book, but an interesting one. Mario Montuori, *Socrates: Physiology of a Myth*, tr. J. M. P. and M. Langdale (Amsterdam: J. C. Gieben, 1981) is an account paralleling that of Hadas and Smith in the chapter, but more detailed.

Of somewhat larger scope is the important scholarly work of Victor Ehrenberg, *The People of Aristophanes: A Sociology of Old Attic Comedy* (New York: Schocken, 1962 [1943]), a study not only of the characters in the plays but also of the audiences; see especially ch. 10, on religion and education, for Socrates. Of larger scope still is T. B. L. Webster, *Athenian Culture and Society* (Berkeley and Los Angeles: University of California Press, 1973), a superb analysis of the linkage between the culture of Athens and its society—the background to an understanding of the place of Socrates in that society and culture. For this sort of analysis, students may prefer Rex Warner, *Men of Athens* (New York: Viking, 1972), a brilliant popularization which sees Socrates as the end product as well as the victim of fifth-century Athenian culture. J. W. Roberts, *City of Sokrates: A Social History of Classical Athens* (London: Routledge and Kegan Paul, 1984), however, is the best modern historical treatment of Socrates' Athens.

The standard work on the system of Athenian government is A. H. M. Jones, *Athenian Democracy* (Oxford, England: Oxford University Press, 1957), which should be updated by reference to W. R. Connor, *The New Politicians of Fifth Century Athens* (Princeton, N.J.: Princeton University Press, 1971).

THE "PROBLEM" OF
ALEXANDER THE GREAT

356 B.C.	Born
336 B.C.	Became king of Macedonia
334 B.C.	Began conquest of Persia
333 B.C.	Battle of Issus
331 B.C.	Battle of Gaugamela and death of Darius, the Persian king
326 B.C.	Battle of Hydaspes in India
323 B.C.	Died

If Alexander had simply been a successful conqueror, no matter how stupefying his conquests, there would really be no "Alexander problem." But, from his own lifetime, there lingered about Alexander the sense that there was something more to him, that he was "up to something," that he had great, even revolutionary, plans. The conviction of manifest destiny that Alexander himself felt so strongly contributed to this, as did his instinct for the unusual, the cryptic, the dramatic in political and religious, as well as in strategic and military, decisions. But most of all, his death at age thirty-three, in the year 323 B.C.—his conquests barely completed and his schemes for the future only hinted at or imperfectly forecast—led the ancient writers to speculate about the questions, "What if Alexander had lived on?" "What plans would his imperial imagination have conceived?" and to sift and resift every scrap of information available—and to invent a few that were not!

The problem of the ancient sources themselves has added greatly to the difficulty of interpretation. And this is surely ironic. For Alexander's own sense of his destiny made him unusually sensitive to the need for keeping records of his deeds. A careful log or journal was maintained, but it exists today only in the most useless fragments, if indeed the "fragments" in question even came from that record. Alexander's staff included at least two scholar-secretaries to keep records.

81

One was Callisthenes, the nephew of Alexander's old friend and tutor Aristotle. The other was the scientist-philosopher Aristobulus. Callisthenes subsequently fell out with Alexander and was executed for complicity in a plot in 327 B.C. But, while nothing of his work remains it was clearly the basis for a strongly anti-Alexandrian tradition that flourished in Greece, especially in Athens. This hostile tradition is best represented in Cleitarchus, a Greek rhetorician of the generation following Alexander, who never knew him but who became "the most influential historian of Alexander."[1] The account of Aristobulus, who was apparently much closer and more favorable to Alexander than was Callisthenes or Cleitarchus, is also lost. Ptolemy, one of Alexander's most trusted generals and later founder of the Hellenistic monarchy in Egypt, wrote a detailed memoir based in part on Alexander's own *Journal*, but this did not survive either.

Later ancient writers like Diodorus, Plutarch, Curtius, and Justin did know these sources and used them. But of the accounts of Alexander surviving from antiquity, the best one is that of the Greek writer Arrian, of the second century—thus over four hundred years removed from his sources! Furthermore, while Arrian's account is our fullest and most detailed and is based scrupulously on his sources, it is terribly prosaic: we miss precisely what we most want to have, some sense of the "why" of Alexander. Despite Arrian's devotion to his subject, he tends to tell the story—mainly the military side of it at that—without significant comment. And where we would like to have him analyze, he moralizes instead.

Modern scholars have continued to be fascinated by the puzzle of what Alexander was "up to," and none more than William W. Tarn (d. 1957). Tarn was one of those brilliant English "amateurs" of independent means and equally independent views who have contributed so uniquely to scholarship in a score of fields. He was a lawyer by profession, but he devoted most of his scholarly life—more than half a century—to Greek history. Tarn practically invented Hellenistic scholarship, that is, the study of the post-Alexandrian period in the history of Greek civilization. He authored numerous books and studies, beginning with his "Notes on Hellenism in Bactria and India," which appeared in the *Journal of Hellenic Studies* for 1902, through his first important book, *Antigonos Gonatas* (1913), to *Hellenistic Civilization* (1928), *Hellenistic Military and Naval Developments* (1930), *The Greeks in Bactria and India* (1938), and chapters in the first edition of the *Cambridge Ancient History* (1924–1929).

---

[1]N. G. L. Hammond, *Alexander the Great: King, Commander and Statesman* (Park Ridge, N.J.: Noyes Press, 1980), p. 2.

Because the springboard of the Hellenistic age was Alexander, Tarn devoted special attention to him. He adopted the stance of a scholar-lawyer, in a sense, taking Alexander as his "client" and setting out to make a case for the defense. And Alexander was badly in need of such defense. The trend of modern scholarship before Tarn had been to view Alexander as an archtyrant, arbitrary and megalomaniac, a drunken murderer, and the oppressor of Greek political freedom and philosophic independence—a view derived ultimately from the Callisthenes-Cleitarchan tradition of antiquity.

Tarn was brilliantly successful in turning opinion around in his defense of Alexander, so much so that the "traditional" view of Alexander today is still essentially that created by Tarn. His authority has been so great that it has even affected the way in which we interpret the ancient sources themselves, whether they seem to be "for" or "against" Tarn's case.

The Ancient Sources:
Arrian, Eratosthenes, and Plutarch

In the first selection of this chapter, we present the five "proof texts" on which Tarn built his defense of Alexander: one from Arrian, one from Eratosthenes (preserved in Strabo), and three from Plutarch.

This passage, from The Life of Alexander the Great *by Arrian, took place near the end of Alexander's incredible journey of conquest. In 324 B.C. Alexander assembled his Macedonian troops at Opis in Mesopotamia and announced that he proposed to discharge and send home, with lavish rewards, all those who were disabled or overage. But, instead of gratitude, a smoldering resentment surfaced, and the entire Macedonian force began to clamor to be sent home. Arrian attributes the resentment to Alexander's "orientalizing," his adoption of Persian dress and customs, and his attempt to incorporate Persians and other peoples in his army. This had offended the Macedonians' stubborn pride and sense of exclusiveness, and they now threatened a mutiny. Alexander was furious. After having the ringleaders arrested, he addressed the Macedonians in a passionate, blistering speech, reminding them of their own accomplishments, as well as his, and of what he had done for them. Alexander's speech had a profound effect upon the Macedonians, as did the plans, immediately put into effect, for reorganizing the army in the event that they defected. But instead of deserting, the Macedonians repented.*

Alexander, the moment he heard of this change of heart, hastened out to meet them, and he was so touched by their grovelling repentance and their bitter lamentations that the tears came into his eyes. While they continued to beg for his pity, he stepped forward as if to speak, but was anticipated by one Callines, an officer of the mounted Hetaeri, distinguished both by age and rank. "My lord," he cried, "what hurts us is that you have made Persians your kinsmen— Persians are called 'Alexander's kinsmen'—Persians kiss you. But no Macedonian has yet had a taste of this honour."

"Every man of you," Alexander replied, "I regard as my kinsman, and from now on that is what I shall call you."

Thereupon Callines came up to him and kissed him, and all the others who wished to do so kissed him too. Then they picked up their weapons and returned to their quarters singing the song of victory at the top of their voices.

To mark the restoration of harmony, Alexander offered sacrifice to the gods he was accustomed to honour, and gave a public banquet which he himself attended, sitting among the Macedonians, all of whom were present. Next to them the Persians had their places, and next to the Persians distinguished foreigners of other nations; Alexander and his friends dipped their wine from the same bowl and poured the same libations, following the lead of the Greek seers and the Magi. The chief object of his prayers was that Persians and Macedonians might rule together in harmony as an imperial power. It is said that 9,000 people attended the banquet; they unanimously drank the same toast, and followed it by the paean of victory.

After this all Macedonians—about 10,000 all told—who were too old for service or in any way unfit, got their discharge at their own request.

Eratosthenes of Cyrene, who lived about 200 B.C., was head of the great Library of Alexandria and one of the most learned individuals of antiquity. But his works exist only in fragments and in citations in the writings of others, such as the following, from The Geography *by the Greek scientist Strabo, of the first century B.C.*

Now, towards the end of his treatise—after withholding praise from those who divide the whole multitude of mankind into two groups, namely, Greeks and Barbarians, and also from those who advised Alexander to treat the Greeks as friends but the Barbarians as enemies—Eratosthenes goes on to say that it would be better to make such divisions according to good qualities and bad qualities; for not only are many of the Greeks bad, but many of the Barbarians are refined—Indians and Arians, for example, and, further, Romans and Carthaginians, who carry on their governments so admirably. And this, he says, is the reason why Alexander, disregarding his advisers, welcomed as many as he could of the men of fair repute and did them favours—just as if those who have made such a division, placing some people in the category of censure, others in that of praise, did so for any other reason than that in some people there prevail the law-abiding and the political instinct, and the qualities associated with education and powers of speech, whereas in other people the opposite characteristics prevail! And so Alexander, not disregarding his advisers, but rather accepting their opinion, did what was consistent with, not contrary to, their advice; for he had regard to the real intent of those who gave him counsel.

Two of the Plutarch passages are from his essay "On the Fortune of Alexander," which is one of the pieces comprising the collection known as the Moralia.

Moreover, the much-admired *Republic* of Zeno, the founder of the Stoic sect, may be summed up in this one main principle: that all the inhabitants of this world of ours should not live differentiated by their respective rules of justice into separate cities and communities, but that we should consider all men to be of one community and one polity, and that we should have a common life and an order common to us all, even as a herd that feeds together and shares the pasturage of a common field. This Zeno wrote, giving shape to a dream or, as it were, shadowy picture of a well-ordered and philosophic commonwealth; but it was Alexander who gave effect to the idea. For Alexander did not follow Aristotle's advice to treat the Greeks as if he were their leader, and other peoples as if he were their master; to have regard for the Greeks as for friends and kindred, but to conduct himself toward other peoples as though they were plants or animals; for to do so would have been to cumber his leadership with numerous battles and banishments and festering seditions. But, as he believed that he came as a heaven-sent governor to all, and as a mediator for the whole world, those whom he could not persuade to unite with him, he conquered by force of arms, and he brought together into one body all men everywhere, uniting and mixing in one great loving-cup, as it were, men's lives, their characters, their marriages, their very habits of life. He bade them all consider as their fatherland the whole inhabited earth, as their stronghold and protection his camp, as akin to them all good men, and as foreigners only the wicked; they should not distinguish between Grecian and foreigner by Grecian cloak and targe, or scimitar and jacket; but the distinguishing mark of the Grecian should be seen in virtue, and that of the foreigner in iniquity; clothing and food, marriage and manner of life they should regard as common to all, being blended into one by ties of blood and children.

After dwelling on the wisdom of Alexander in affecting a mixed Graeco-Macedonian and Persian costume, Plutarch continues.

For he did not overrun Asia like a robber nor was he minded to tear and rend it, as if it were booty and plunder bestowed by unexpected good fortune. . . . But Alexander desired to render all upon earth subject to one law of reason and one form of government and to reveal all men as one people, and to this purpose he made himself conform. But if the deity that sent down Alexander's soul into this world of ours had not recalled him quickly, one law would govern all mankind, and they all would look toward one rule of justice as though toward a common source of light. But as it is, that part of the world which has not looked upon Alexander has remained without sunlight.

This passage from the famous "Life of Alexander" in Plutarch's Lives *deals with an incident early in Alexander's career, after his conquest of Egypt—his journey across the desert to the oracle of Ammon at Siwah.*

When Alexander had passed through the desert and was come to the place of the oracle, the prophet of Ammon gave him salutation from the god as from a father; whereupon Alexander asked him whether any of the murderers of his father had escaped him.[2] To this the prophet answered by bidding him be guarded in his speech, since his was not a mortal father. Alexander therefore changed the form of his question, and asked whether the murderers of Philip had all been punished; and then, regarding his own empire, he asked whether it was given to him to become lord and master of all mankind. The god gave answer that this was given to him, and that Philip was fully avenged. Then Alexander made splendid offerings to the god and gave his priests large gifts of money. . . . We are told, also, that he listened to the teachings of Psammon[3] the philosopher in Egypt, and accepted most readily this utterance of his, namely, that all mankind are under the kingship of God, since in every case that which gets the mastery and rules is divine. Still more philosophical, however, was his own opinion and utterance on this head, namely that although God was indeed a common father of all mankind, still, He made peculiarly His own the noblest and best of them.

Alexander the Great and the Unity of Mankind

W. W. TARN

We turn now to the thesis that W. W. Tarn built in defense of Alexander. He had begun to develop his characteristic view in a number of journal articles and anticipated it in fairly complete form in his contributions to the

---

[2]Alexander had come to the throne of Macedonia upon the murder of his father, Philip II, in 336 B.C.—ED.

[3]This is the only reference in antiquity to such a person.—ED.

1927 edition of the Cambridge Ancient History. *He was later to state it most completely in his monumental two-volume* Alexander the Great *(Cambridge: Cambridge University Press, 1948). But the most succinct statement of the Tarn thesis is that contained in his Raleigh Lecture on History, read before the British Academy in 1933. It is entitled "Alexander the Great and the Unity of Mankind."*

What I am going to talk about is one of the great revolutions in human thought. Greeks of the classical period, speaking very roughly, divided mankind into two classes, Greeks and non-Greeks; the latter they called barbarians and usually regarded as inferior people, though occasionally some one, like Herodotus or Xenophon, might suggest that certain barbarians possessed qualities which deserved consideration, like the wisdom of the Egyptians or the courage of the Persians. But in the third century B.C. and later we meet with a body of opinion which may be called universalist; all mankind was one and all men were brothers, or anyhow ought to be. Who was the pioneer who brought about this tremendous revolution in some men's way of thinking? Most writers have had no doubt on that point; the man to whom the credit was due was Zeno, the founder of the Stoic philosophy. But there are several passages in Greek writers which, *if* they are to be believed, show that the first man actually to think of it was not Zeno but Alexander. This matter has never really been examined; some writers just pass it over, which means, I suppose, that they do not consider the passages in question historical; others have definitely said that it is merely a case of our secondary authorities attributing to Alexander ideas taken from Stoicism. I want to consider to-day whether the passages in question are or are not historical and worthy of credence; that is, whether Alexander was or was not the first to believe in, and to contemplate, the unity of mankind. This will entail, among other things, some examination of the concept which Greeks called Homonoia, a word which meant more than its Latin translation, Concord, means to us; it is more like Unity and Concord, a being of one mind together, or if we like the phrase, a union of hearts; ultimately it was to become almost a symbol of the world's longing for something better than constant war. For convenience of discussion I shall keep the Greek term Homonoia.

Before coming to the ideas attributed to Alexander, I must sketch very briefly the background against which the new thought arose, whoever was its author; and I ought to say that I am primarily talking throughout of theory, not of practice. It may be possible to find, in the fifth century, or earlier, an occasional phrase which looks like a groping after something better than the hard-and-fast division of Greeks and barbarians; but this comes to very little and had no importance for history, because anything of the sort was strangled by the idealist philosophies. Plato and Aristotle left no doubt about their views. Plato said that all barbarians were enemies by nature; it was proper to wage war upon them, even to the point of enslaving or extirpating them. Aristotle said that all barbarians were slaves by nature, especially those of Asia; they had not the qualities which entitled them to be free men, and it was proper to treat them as slaves. His model State cared for nothing but its own citizens; it was a small aristocracy of Greek citizens ruling over a barbarian peasantry who cultivated the land for their masters and had no share in the State—a thing he had seen in some cities of Asia Minor. Certainly neither Plato nor Aristotle was quite consistent; Plato might treat an Egyptian priest as the repository of wisdom, Aristotle might suggest that the constitution of Carthage was worth studying; but their main position was clear enough, as was the impression Alexander would get from his tutor Aristotle.

There were, of course, other voices. Xenophon, when he wanted to portray an ideal shepherd of the people, chose a Persian king as shepherd of the Persian people. And there were the early Cynics. But the Cynics had no thought of any union or fellowship between Greek and barbarian; they were not constructive thinkers, but merely embodied protests against the vices and follies of civilization. When Diogenes called himself a cosmopolite, a horrible word which he coined and which was not used again for centuries, what he meant was, not that he was a citizen of some imaginary world-state—a thing he never thought about—but that he was not a citizen of any Greek city; it was pure negation. And the one piece of Cynic construction, the ideal figure of Heracles, labouring to free Greece from monsters, was merely shepherd of a *Greek* herd till after Alexander, when it took colour and content from the Stoics and became the ideal benefactor of humanity. All that Xenophon or the Cynics could supply was the figure of an ideal shepherd, not of the human herd, but of some national herd.

More important was Aristotle's older contemporary Isocrates, because of his conception of Homonoia. The Greek world, whatever its practice, never doubted that in theory unity in a city was very desirable; but though the word Homonoia was already in common use among Greeks, it chiefly meant absence of faction-fights, and this rather negative meaning lasted in the cities throughout the Hellenistic period, as can be seen in the numerous decrees in honour of the judicial commissions sent from one city to another, which are praised because they tried to compose internal discord. There was hardly a trace as yet of the more positive sense which Homonoia was to acquire later—a mental attitude which should make war or faction impossible because the parties were at one; and Isocrates extended the application of the word without changing its meaning. He took up a suggestion of the sophist Gorgias and proposed to treat the whole Greek world as one and the futile wars between city and city as faction fights—to apply Homonoia to the Greek race. For this purpose he utilized Plato's idea that the barbarian was a natural enemy, and decided that the way to unite Greeks was to attack Persia; "I come," he said, "to advocate two things: war against the barbarian, Homonoia between ourselves." But somebody had to do the uniting; and Isocrates bethought him of the Cynic Heracles, benefactor of the Greek race, and urged King Philip of Macedonia, a descendant of Heracles, to play the part. But if Philip was to be Heracles and bring about the Homonoia of the Greek world, the way was being prepared for two important ideas of a later time; the essential quality of the king must be that love of man, φιλανθρωπία,[4] which had led Heracles to perform his labours, and the essential business of the king was to promote Homonoia; so far this only applied to Greeks, but if its meaning were to deepen it would still be the king's business. The actual result of all this, the League of Corinth[5] under Philip's presidency, was not quite what Isocrates had dreamt of.

This then was the background against which Alexander appeared. The business of a Macedonian king was to be a benefactor of Greeks to the extent of preventing inter-city warfare; he was to promote Homonoia among Greeks and utilize their enmity to barbarians as a bond of union; but barbarians themselves were still enemies and slaves by nature, a view which Aristotle emphasized when he advised his pupil to treat Greeks as free men, but barbarians as slaves.

I now come to the things Alexander is supposed to have said or thought; and the gulf between them and the background I have sketched is so deep that one cannot blame those who have refused to believe that he ever said or thought anything of the sort. There are five passages which need consideration: one in Arrian; one from Eratosthenes, preserved by Strabo; and three from Plutarch, one of which, from its resemblance to the Strabo passage, has been supposed by one of the acutest critics of our time to be taken in substance from Eratosthenes,[6] and as such I shall treat it. The passage in Arrian says that, after the mutiny of the Macedonians at Opis and their reconciliation to Alexander, he gave a banquet to Macedonians and Persians, at which he prayed for Homonoia and partnership in rule between

---

[4]Literally "philanthropy."—Ed.

[5]The league Philip formed after defeating the Greek states at Chaeronea in 338 B.C.—Ed.

[6]The reference is to the German scholar E. Schwarz.—Ed.

these two peoples. What Eratosthenes says amounts to this. Aristotle told Alexander to treat Greeks as friends, but barbarians like animals; but Alexander knew better, and preferred to divide men into good and bad without regard to their race, and thus carried out Aristotle's real intention. For Alexander believed that he had a mission from the deity to harmonize men generally and be the reconciler of the world, mixing men's lives and customs as in a loving cup, and treating the good as his kin, the bad as strangers; for he thought that the good man was the real Greek and the bad man the real barbarian. Of the two Plutarch passages, the first says that his intention was to bring about, as between mankind generally, Homonoia and peace and fellowship and make them all one people; and the other, which for the moment I will quote without its context, makes him say that God is the common father of all men.

It is obvious that, wherever all this comes from, we are dealing with a great revolution in thought. It amounts to this, that there is a natural brotherhood of all men, though bad men do not share in it; that Homonoia is no longer to be confined to the relations between Greek and Greek, but is to unite Greek and barbarian; and that Alexander's aim was to substitute peace for war, and reconcile the enmities of mankind by bringing them all—all that is whom his arm could reach, the peoples of his empire—to be of one mind together: as men were one in blood, so they should become one in heart and spirit. That such a revolution in thought did happen is unquestioned; the question is, was Alexander really its author, or are the thoughts attributed to him those of Zeno or somebody else? . . .

"To try to answer that question," Tarn follows with a long and complex analysis of Homonoia and kingship in Graeco-Roman history, leading to the universalism of the late Roman empire.

The belief that it was the business of kings to promote Homonoia among their subjects without distinction of race thus travelled down the line of kingship for centuries; but the line, you will remember, had no beginning. . . . It must clearly have been connected with some particular king at the start, and that king has to be later than Isocrates and Philip and earlier than Diotogenes and Demetrius.[7] It would seem that only one king is possible; we should have to postulate Alexander at the beginning of the line, even if there were not a definite tradition that it *was* he. This means that Plutarch's statement,

---

[7]Isocrates (436–338 B.C.), the Athenian orator; Philip II of Macedonia (355–336 B.C.); Diotogenes, an early Hellenistic author of uncertain date; Demetrius (336–283 B.C.), an early Hellenistic ruler.—ED.

that Alexander's purpose was to bring about Homonoia between men generally—that is, those men whom his arm could reach—must be taken to be true, unless some explicit reason be found for disbelieving it; and I therefore now turn to the Stoics, in order to test the view that the ideas attributed to him were really taken from Stoicism. . . . We have seen that it was the business of kings to bring about Homonoia; but this was not the business of a Stoic, because to him Homonoia had already been brought about by the Deity, and it existed in all completeness; all that was necessary was that men should see it. . . .

This is the point I want to make, the irreconcilable opposition between Stoicism and the theory of kingship, between the belief that unity and concord existed and you must try and get men to see it, and the belief that unity and concord did not exist and that it was the business of the rulers of the earth to try and bring them to pass. . . . Consequently, when Eratosthenes says that Alexander aspired to be the harmonizer and reconciler of the world, and when Plutarch attributes to him the intention of bringing about fellowship and Homonoia between men generally—those men whom his arm reached— then, wherever these ideas came from, they were not Stoic; between them and Stoicism there was a gulf which nothing could bridge. This does not by itself prove that Alexander held these ideas; what it does do is to put out of court the only alternative which has ever been seriously proposed, and to leave the matter where I left it when considering the theory of kingship, that is, that there is a strong presumption that Alexander *was* their author. . . .

Before leaving Stoicism, I must return for a moment to Zeno's distinction of the worthy and the unworthy; for Alexander, as we saw, is said to have divided men into good and bad, and to have excluded the bad from the general kinship of mankind and called them the true barbarians. Might not *this* distinction, at any rate, have been taken from Stoicism and attributed to him? The reasons against this seem conclusive, apart from the difficulty of discarding a statement made by so sound and scientific a critic as Eratosthenes. First, no Stoic ever equated the unworthy class with barbarians; for to him there were no barbarians. . . . Secondly, while the unworthy in Zeno, as in Aristotle, are the majority of mankind, Alexander's "bad men" are not; they are, as Eratosthenes says, merely that small residue everywhere which cannot be civilized. One sees this clearly in a story never questioned, his prayer at Opis, when he prayed that the Macedonian and Persian races (without exceptions made) might be united in Homonoia. And thirdly, we know where the idea comes from: Aristotle had criticized some who said that good men were really free and bad men were really slaves (whom he himself equated with barbarians), and Alexander is in turn criticizing Aristotle; as indeed Eratosthenes says, though he does not quote this passage of Aristotle. The matter is not important, except for the general question of the credibility of Eratosthenes, and may conceivably only represent that period in Alexander's thought when he was outgrowing Aristotle; it does not conflict, as does Zeno's conception of the unworthy, with a general belief in the unity of mankind. . . .

There is just one question still to be asked; whence did Zeno get his universalism? Plutarch says that behind Zeno's dream lay Alexander's reality; and no one doubts that Alexander was Zeno's inspiration, but the question is, in what form? Most writers have taken Plutarch to mean Alexander's *empire;* but to me this explains nothing at all. One man conquers a large number of races and brings them under one despotic rule; how can another man deduce from this that distinctions of race are immaterial and that the universe is a harmony in which men are brothers? It would be like the fight between the polar bear and the parallelepiped. The Persian kings had conquered and ruled as large an empire as Alexander, including many Greek cities; why did Darius never inspire any one with similar theories? It does seem to me that what Plutarch really means is not Alexander's empire but Alexander's ideas; after all, the frequent references in antiquity to Alexander as a philosopher, one at least of which is contemporary, must mean *something*. Zeno's inspiration, then, was Alexander's idea of the unity of mankind; and what Zeno himself did was to carry this idea to one of its two logical conclusions. Judging by his prayer at Opis for the Homonoia of Macedonians and Persians, Alexander, had he lived, would have worked through national groups, as was inevitable in an empire like his, which comprised many different states and subject peoples; Theophrastus,[8] who followed him, included national groups in his chain of progress towards world-relationship. But Zeno abolished all distinctions of race, all the apparatus of national groups and particular states, and made his world-state a theoretic whole. His scheme was an inspiration to many; but in historical fact it was, and remained, unrealizable. But Alexander's way, or what I think was his way, led to the Roman Empire being called one people. I am not going to bring in modern examples of these two different lines of approach to world-unity, but I want to say one thing about the Roman Empire. It has been said that Stoic ideas came near to realization in the empire of Hadrian and the Antonines, but it is quite clear, the moment it be considered, that this was not the case; that empire was a huge national state, which stood in the line of kingship and was a partial realization of the ideas of Alexander. When a Stoic *did* sit on the imperial throne, he was at once compelled to make terms with the national state; to Marcus Aurelius, the Stoic world-state was no theoretic unity, but was to comprise the various particular states as a city comprises houses. And there is still a living reality in what he said about himself: "As a man I am a citizen of the world-state, but as the particular man Marcus Aurelius I am a citizen of Rome."

I may now sum up. We have followed down the line of kingship the theory that it was the business of a king to promote Homonoia among his subjects—all his subjects without distinction of race; and we have seen that this theory ought to be connected at the start with some king, who must be later than Philip and earlier than Demetrius; and there is a definite tradition which connects the origin of the theory with Alexander. We have further seen that the intention to promote Homonoia among mankind, attributed in the tradition to Alexander, is certainly not a projection backwards from Stoicism, or apparently from anything else, while it is needed to explain certain things said by Theophrastus and done by Alexarchus.[9] Lastly, we have seen the idea of the kinship or brotherhood of mankind appearing suddenly in Theophrastus and Alexarchus; their common source can be no one but Alexander, and again tradition supports this. Only one conclusion from all this seems possible: the things which, in the tradition, Alexander is supposed to have thought and said are, in substance, true. He did say that all men were sons of God, that is brothers, but that God made the best ones peculiarly his own; he did aspire to be the harmonizer and reconciler of the world—that part of the world which his arm reached; he did have the intention of uniting the peoples of his empire in fellowship and concord and making them of one mind together; and when, as a beginning, he prayed at Opis for partnership in rule and Homonoia between Macedonians and Persians, he meant what he said—not partnership in rule only, but true unity between them. I am only talking of theory, not of actions; but what this means is that he was the pioneer of one of the supreme revolutions in the world's outlook, the first man known to us who contemplated the brotherhood of man or the unity of mankind, whichever phrase we like to use. I do not claim to have given you exact proof of this; it is one of those difficult borderlands of history where one does not get proofs which could be put to a jury. But there is a very strong presumption indeed that it is true. Alexander, for the things he *did*, was called The Great; but if what I have said to-day be right, I do not think we shall doubt that this idea of his—call it a purpose, call it a dream, call it what you will—was the greatest thing about him.

---

[9]A minor Macedonian princeling, following Alexander, who set up his small state apparently on the model of Alexander's ideas.—ED.

The New Alexander

N. G. L. HAMMOND

Despite Tarn's enormous scholarly reputation and his lordly dismissal of critics, his own interpretive view of Alexander was bound to be challenged, and it has been. Tarn massively overstated his case. As Mary Renault put it, "the defence was pushed too far."[10] And Ernst Badian, probably Tarn's most effective critic among this generation of scholars, has called the Alexander of Tarn's vision a "phantom" that "has haunted the pages of scholarship" for "a quarter of a century."[11] In reaction against Tarn's view of Alexander not only as a stunning conqueror but as a conqueror of stunning philosophic profundity as well, scholars have again depicted him "as a ruthless murderer, an autocratic megalomaniac, even a bisexual profligate."[12] Even more careful and moderate scholars like R. D. Milns hold that such an idea as the kinship of mankind was quite beyond Alexander and must be attributed to "later thinkers and philosophers."[13]

Now the reaction seems to be moving back toward the Tarn view. The "new" Alexander is more anchored in his own times and mores, and none of the more recent authorities attribute to Alexander the "great revolution in thought" that Tarn did. But the Alexander we see today is considerably more cerebral and innovative both in thought and action. This new image of Alexander is nowhere better represented than in the work of the distinguished Cambridge classicist N. G. L. Hammond, Alexander the Great: King, Commander and Statesman, *from which the following excerpt is taken.*

We have the advantage of hindsight. We can see that it was Alexander's leadership and training which made the Macedonians incomparable in war and in administration and enabled them as rulers of the so-called Hellenistic kingdoms to control the greater part of the civilised world for a century or more. In a reign of thirteen years he

---

[10]Mary Renault, *The Nature of Alexander* (New York: Pantheon, 1975), p. 23.

[11]Ernst Badian, "Alexander the Great and the Unity of Mankind," *Historia* 7 (1958), 425.

[12]Hammond, *Alexander the Great,* p. 5.

[13]R. D. Milns, *Alexander the Great* (London: Robert Hale, 1968), p. 265.

brought to Macedonia and Macedonians the immense wealth which maintained their strength for generations. All this was and is an unparalleled achievement. Moreover, as king of Macedonia he did not drain his country unduly in his lifetime, since Antipater had enough men to defeat the Greeks in 331 B.C. and 322 B.C. Yet the system he was creating—quite apart from any further conquests he had in mind in 323 B.C.—was certain to put an immense strain on present and future Macedonians. They were spread dangerously thin at the time of his death, and the prolonged absence of so many Macedonians abroad was bound to cause a drop in the birth-rate in Macedonia itself. Of course Alexander expected his Macedonians to undertake almost superhuman dangers and labours, and it was their response to his challenge that made them great. But the dangers and labours were being demanded for the sake of a policy which was not Macedonian in a nationalistic sense, which the Macedonians did not wholly understand, and which they never fully implemented. Philip's singlemindedness made him the greatest king of Macedonia. Alexander's wider vision made him at the same time something more and something less than the greatest king of Macedonia. . . .

As constitutionally elected king, Alexander had sole right of command and an inherited authority. From the age of twenty onwards he appointed his deputies without let or hindrance, issued all orders, and controlled all payments, promotions, and discharges. His authority as a commander was almost absolute, his discipline unquestioned, and his position unchallenged. As religious head of the state, he interceded for his men and was seen daily to sacrifice on their behalf.

Unique in his descent from Zeus and Heracles, he was acclaimed "son of Zeus" by the oracle at Didyma, the Sibyl at Erythrae, and the oracle of Ammon (the last at least in the opinion of his men), and he fostered the idea of divine protection by having the sacred shield of Athena carried into battle by his senior Bodyguard (it saved his life against the Malli; [Arrian] 6.10.2). Before engaging at Gaugamela Alexander prayed in front of the army, raising his right hand towards the gods and saying, "If I am really descended from Zeus, protect and strengthen the Greeks." That prayer, apparently, was answered. In the eyes of most men—and most men then had faith in gods, oracles, and omens—Alexander was favoured by the supernatural powers. To those who were sceptical he had extraordinarily good luck.

The brilliance of Alexander's mind is seen most clearly in his major battles. . . . For example, he saw at once the advantages and disadvantages of Darius' position on the Pinarus river and he anticipated the effects of his own detailed dispositions and orders to a nicety. "He surpassed all others in the faculty of intuitively meeting an emergency," whether in besieging Tyre or facing Scythian tactics or storming an impregnable fortress. He excelled in speed and precision of thought, the calculation of risks, and the expectation of an enemy's reactions. Having himself engaged in every kind of action and having grappled with practical problems from a young age, he had a sure sense of the possible and extraordinary versatility in invention. Unlike many famous commanders, his mind was so flexible that at the time of his death he was creating an entirely new type of army.

A most remarkable quality of Alexander's was the concern for his men. No conqueror had so few casualties in battle, and the reason was that Alexander avoided "the battle of rats" by using his brains not just to win, but to win most economically. He made this his priority because he loved his Macedonians. He grew up among them and fought alongside them, both as a youth admiring his seniors and as a mature man competing with his companions. He honoured and rewarded courage and devotion to duty in them, paying a unique tribute to the first casualties by having bronze statues made by the leading sculptor, and he felt deeply with them in their sufferings and privations. He aroused in them an amazing response. He not only admired courage and devotion to duty in his own men but in his enemies, whom he treated with honour. In return he won the respect and loyalty of Asians of many races whom he had just defeated in battle. . . . Some commanders may have rivalled him in the handling of his own race. None have had such a capacity for leading a multiracial army. . . .

We have already touched upon his statesmanship in enhancing the prestige of the Macedonian monarchy and advancing the power of the Macedonian state. He reduced the harshness of customary law, (for instance, he no longer required the execution of the male relatives of a convicted traitor), and he was concerned for the welfare and the birth rate of Macedonia. He provided tax reliefs for the dependants of casualties, brought up war orphans at his own expense, and sought to avoid conflicts between the European and Asian families of his Macedonians by maintaining the latter in Asia. He increased the number of young Macedonians when he legitimised the soldiers' children by Asian women, and he sent the 10,000 veterans home in the expectation of their begetting more children in Macedonia. . . .

While Philip invented and inaugurated the Greek League, it was Alexander who demonstrated its efficacy as a *modus operandi* for the Macedonians and the Greeks and used their joint forces to overthrow the Persian Empire. By opening Asia to Greek enterprise and culture Alexander relieved many of the social and economic pressures which had been causing distress and anarchy in the Greek states. At the same time he was personally concerned with affairs in Greece, as we see from the large number of embassies which came to him in Asia rather than to his deputy, Antipater, in Macedonia. . . .

Alexander's originality is seen most clearly in Asia. He set himself an unparalleled task when he decided in advance not to make the Macedonians and the Greeks the masters of the conquered peoples but to create a self-sustaining Kingdom of Asia. Within his kingdom he intended the settled peoples to conduct their internal affairs in accordance with their own laws and customs, whether in a Greek city or a native village, in a Lydian or a Carian state, in a Cyprian or a Phoenician kingdom, in Egypt, Babylonia, or Persis, in an Indian principality or republic. As his power extended, he did not introduce European administrators at a level which would inhibit native self-rule (as so-called colonial powers have so often done); instead he continued native administrators in office and raised the best of them to the highest level in civil affairs by appointing them as his immediate deputies in the post of satrap (e.g., Mazaeus at Babylon) or nomarch (e.g., Doloaspis in Egypt). . . .

What is important is the effectiveness of Alexander's system: native civilians and armed forces alike lodged complaints with Alexander, the accused were tried legally and openly, and those found guilty were executed forthwith, in order "to deter the other satraps, governors, and civil officers" and to make it known that the rulers were not permitted to wrong the ruled in Alexander's kingdom. In the opinion of Arrian, who lived at the zenith of the Roman Empire and had a standard of comparison, it was this system which "more than anything else kept to an orderly way of life the innumerable, widely diffused peoples who had been subjugated in war or had of their own will joined him" (6.27.5). In the same way rebels, sometimes in the form of native pretenders, were put on trial; and, if found guilty, they were executed, often in the manner native to the particular area (Arrian 6.30.2). Where the rights of his subjects were at stake, he showed no mercy or favouritism for any Macedonian, Greek, Thracian, Persian, Median, or Indian. . . .

What Alexander sought in his senior administrators was summed up in the word "excellence" (*arete*). He assessed it by performance in his own army and in that of his enemy; for he approved courage and loyalty, wherever he found it. But a particular kind of excellence was needed where conquerors had to accept the conquered as their equals in administering the kingdom of Asia. The Macedonians justifiably regarded themselves as a military élite, superior to Greeks and barbarians, and closer to their king than any foreigner; and the Greeks despised all Asians as barbarians, fitted by nature only to be slaves. Yet here was Alexander according equal status, regardless of race, not only to all his administrators but also to all who served in his army! Resentment at this was the chief factor in the mutiny of the Macedo-

nians at Opis. On that occasion Alexander enforced his will. He celebrated the concept of equal status in an official banquet, at which the
Macedonians sat by their king, with whom they were not reconciled;
next were the Persians; and after them persons of "the other races."
All the guests were men who ranked first in reputation or in some
other form of excellence (*arete*). . . .

When Alexander encountered nomadic or marauding peoples, he
forced them, often by drastic methods of warfare, to accept his rule
and to adopt a settled way of life. Many of his new cities were founded
among these peoples so that "they should cease to be nomads," and
he encouraged the concentration of native villages to form new urban
centres. For he intended to promote peace, prosperity, and culture
within these parts of his kingdom too, and the cities and centres were
means to that end. Strongly fortified and well manned, they were
bastions of peace, and the young men in them were trained by Macedonian and Greek veterans to join Alexander's new army and maintain his peace. They were sited to become markets for agricultural
produce and interregional exchange, and their citizens, especially in
the new cities by the deltas of the Nile, the Euphrates, and the Indus,
learnt the capitalistic form of economy, which had brought such prosperity to the Greek states in the fifth and fourth centuries.

The cultural model for the new cities was the Macedonian town,
itself very strongly imbued with Greek ideas and practices. The ruling
element from the outset was formed by Macedonian and Greek veterans; and the Asians, although free to practise their own religion and
traditions, were encouraged to learn Greek and adopt some forms of
Greco-Macedonian life. According to Plutarch (*Mor.* 328e) Alexander
founded 70 new cities, which started their life with 10,000 adult male
citizens as the norm, and he must have envisaged a fusion of European and Asian cultures developing within and spreading out from
these arteries into the body of the kingdom. . . .

The effects of a statesman's ideas, especially if he dies at the age of
thirty-two, are rarely assessable within his lifetime. Yet before Alexander died his ideas bore fruit in the integration of Asians and Macedonians in cavalry and infantry units; the training of Asians in Macedonian weaponry; the association of Asians and Macedonians in each
file of the army; the settling of Macedonians, Greeks, and Asians in
the new cities; the spread of Greek as a common language in the army
and in the new cities; the development of Babylon as the "metropolis"
or capital of the kingdom of Asia; the honouring of interracial marriage; and the raising of Eurasian children to a privileged status.

Peace reigned in this kingdom of Asia, and its people now had little
to fear from their neighbours. Urbanisation, trade, water-borne com-

merce, agriculture, flood-control, land-reclamation, and irrigation were developing fast, and exchange was stimulated by the liberation of hoarded treasure. The gold and silver coinage of Alexander, uniform in types and weights, was universally accepted because it was of real, bullion value. In the eastern satrapies especially the gold darics and silver shekels of the Persian treasuries continued to circulate, and in the western satrapies local currencies were provided by the Greek, Cyprian, and Phoenician cities. . . .

The skill with which Alexander changed the economy of Asia into that system of commercial exchange which the Greeks had invented and we call capitalism, and at that within so few years, is one of the most striking signs of his genius. . . .

The fulfilment of Alexander's plans was impaired by his early death and by the strife between the generals which ensued. Yet even so, within the span of thirteen years, he changed the face of the world more decisively and with more longlasting effects than any other statesman has ever done. He first introduced into Asia the Greco-Macedonian city within the framework of a monarchical or autocratic state, and this form of city was to be the centre of ancient and medieval civilisation in the southern Balkans, the Aegean, and the Near East. For the city provided that continuity of Greek language, literature, and culture which enriched the Roman world, fostered Christianity, and affected Western Europe so profoundly. The outlook and the achievements of Alexander created an ideal image, an apotheosis of kingship which was to inspire the Hellenistic kings, some Roman emperors, and the Byzantine rulers. And his creation of a state which rose above nationalism and brought liberators and liberated, victors and defeated into collaboration and parity of esteem puts most of the expedients of the modern world to shame. . . .

That Alexander should grow up with a sense of mission was certainly to be expected. For he was descended from Zeus and Heracles, he was born to be king, he had the career of Philip as an exemplar, and he was advised by Isocrates, Aristotle, and others to be a benefactor of Macedonians and Greeks alike. His sense of mission was inevitably steeped in religious associations, because from an early age he had been associated with the king, his father, in conducting religious ceremonies, and he was imbued with many ideas of orthodox religion and of ecstatic mysteries. Thus two observations by Plutarch (*Mor.* 342 A and F) have the ring of truth. "This desire (to bring all men into an orderly system under a single leadership and to accustom them to one way of life) was implanted in Alexander from childhood and grew up with him"; and on crossing the Hellespont to the Troad Alexander's first asset was "his reverence towards the gods." Already by then he planned to found a Kingdom of Asia, in which he would rule over the peoples, as Odysseus had done, "like a kindly father" (*Odyssey* 5.11). He promoted the fulfilment of that plan "by founding Greek cities among savage peoples and by teaching the principles of law and peace to lawless, ignorant tribes." When he had completed the conquest of "Asia" through the favour of the gods and especially that of Zeus Ammon, he went on to establish for all men in his kingdom "concord and peace and partnership with one another" (*Mor.* 329 F).

This was a practical development, springing from a religious concept and not from a philosophical theory (though it led later to the philosophical theory of the Cynics, who substituted for Asia the whole inhabited world and talked of the brotherhood of all men), and it came to fruition in the banquet at Opis, when he prayed in the presence of men of various races for "concord and partnership in the ruling" of his kingdom "between Macedonians and Persians."

What distinguishes Alexander from all other conquerors is this divine mission. He had grown up with it, and he had to a great extent fulfilled it, before he gave expression to it at the banquet at Opis in such words as those reported by Plutarch (*Mor.* 329 C). "Alexander considered," wrote Plutarch, "that he had come from the gods to be a general governor and reconciler of the world. Using force of arms when he did not bring men together by the light of reason, he harnessed all resources to one and the same end, mixing the lives, manners, marriages and customs of men, as it were in a loving-cup." This is his true claim to be called "Alexander the Great": that he did not crush or dismember his enemies, as the conquering Romans crushed Carthage and Molossia and dismembered Macedonia into four parts; nor exploit, enslave or destroy the native peoples, as "the white man" has so often done in America, Africa, and Australasia; but that he created, albeit for only a few years, a supranational community capable of living internally at peace and of developing the concord and partnership which are so sadly lacking in the modern world.

Review and Study Questions

1. In your judgment, do the ancient sources quoted in this chapter support the interpretation of W. W. Tarn? Explain.

2. Is it credible that, given the nature and temperament of Alexander, he was responsible for such a sophisticated concept as "the natural brotherhood of all men"?

3. Is it justifiable to characterize Alexander as "the great"? Give your reasons.

Suggestions for Further Reading

As is often the case, the classical sources for the biography of Alexander are among the most lively and entertaining works about him, especially Plutarch and Arrian. Plutarch's "Life of Alexander" from his *Parallel Lives of Noble Greeks and Romans* (available in several editions) is, like the rest of the biographical sketches in this famous book, a gossipy and charming account, containing most of the familiar anecdotes associated with Alexander. Arrian's work, the most substantial of the ancient sources, despite a certain stuffiness and lack of analytical daring, is solidly based on more contemporary sources now long lost—particularly Ptolemy's journal and the work of Aristobulus. And it contains the best and most detailed account of Alexander's conquests. See the excellent modern translation by Aubrey de Sélincourt, *Arrian's Life of Alexander the Great* (Harmondsworth, England: Penguin, 1958).

The views of W. W. Tarn summarized in the excerpted passage above from his Raleigh Lecture on History, "Alexander the Great and the Unity of Mankind," are spelled out in greater detail in the chapters he wrote on Alexander and his age—chs. 12–15 of the *Cambridge Ancient History*, vol. 6 (Cambridge, England: Cambridge University Press, 1927), and in his larger *Alexander the Great*, 2 vols. (Cambridge, England: Cambridge University Press, 1948), based on the account in *Cambridge Ancient History* but expanded and updated.

Tarn's most bitter critic is Ernst Badian, who chose to challenge Tarn in particular for the views expressed in his Raleigh Lecture. Badian's article, with the same title, "Alexander the Great and the Unity of Mankind," appeared in *Historia*, 7 (1958), 425–444, and is reprinted in *Alexander the Great: The Main Problems*, ed. G. T. Griffith (New York: Barnes and Noble, 1966). This article is highly specialized, closely reasoned, and contains long passages in Greek; but it is very important and, despite the difficulties of the text, the argument can be clearly followed even by the nonspecialist. Peter Green, *Alexander the Great* (New York: Praeger, 1970), is a modern general account of Alexander's career in the same critical tradition as Badian. Two other modern works that deal more with the conquests than the conqueror are Peter Bamm, *Alexander the Great: Power as Destiny*, tr. J. M. Brownjohn (New York: McGraw-Hill, 1968), and Sir Mortimer Wheeler, *Flames over Persepolis: Turning Point in History* (New York: Morrow, 1968), the latter of particular interest because of Wheeler's expert knowledge of Near Eastern and Indian archaeology.

There is another relatively recent book that stresses the continuing work in archaeology, including the dramatic finds at Vergina in Macedonia: Robin Lane Fox, *The Search for Alexander* (Boston: Little,

Brown, 1980). The most balanced and readable modern general account, however, may still be A. R. Burn, *Alexander the Great and the Hellenistic Empire* (London: The English Universities Press, 1947), although the more recent R. D. Milns, *Alexander the Great* (London: Robert Hale, 1968) is also recommended.

Finally, Alexander is the subject of two first-rate historical novels by Mary Renault, *Fire from Heaven* (New York: Pantheon, 1969), and *The Persian Boy* (New York: Pantheon, 1972), the first carrying the story through Alexander's childhood to his accession to the throne of Macedonia, the second recounting his conquests as narrated by the Persian boy-eunuch Bagoas, Alexander's companion and lover. Renault has also produced a nonfiction account, fully as readable as her novels, and based on the meticulous research she prepared for them, *The Nature of Alexander* (New York: Pantheon, 1975).

ASOKA: BELOVED OF THE GODS

c. 292 B.C.	Born
c. 273 B.C.	Accession to the Mauryan throne
c. 269 B.C.	Coronation
c. 260 B.C.	Kalinga war
c. 258 B.C.	Conversion to Buddhism
c. 232 B.C.	Died

He was small, ugly, and rough-skinned—hardly likely to become "the beloved of the gods." Further, he was a younger son, out of the line of succession to the Indian Mauryan throne. But despite these obvious disadvantages, Asoka Maurya, in about 273 B.C., became the third king of the Mauryan dynasty, the greatest member of his house, and one of the great kings of all time.

It had been more than two centuries since the death of the Buddha, and the small, struggling kingdoms of his time in northeast India had been consolidated into the kingdom of Magadha. In the late fourth century B.C. the kingdom of Magadha was usurped by a young prince of the house of Maurya named Chandragupta, who met Alexander the Great when he was campaigning across the Indus. Chandragupta himself campaigned successfully against Seleucus I Nicator, one of Alexander's generals, who had seized the Asiatic portion of the Alexandrian empire. About 305 B.C. Chandragupta negotiated a treaty with Seleucus that ceded to him all the lands Seleucus had claimed east of the Indus. This was the beginning of a process of conquest that consolidated in the hands of the Mauryan kings nearly all of India to form the Mauryan empire, the first of India's imperial regimes.

Chandragupta was succeeded in about 297 B.C. by his son Bindusara, known by the Sanskrit epithet Amitraghata, "the slayer of foes." He carried the Mauryan conquest southward as far as Mysore and concluded favorable treaties with the handful of small independent kingdoms remaining in the south. All India was now dominated by the Mauryan empire. Little else is known about King Bindusara, except that the prowess of his loins was extraordinary—legend records that he fathered one hundred sons!

One of that hundred was Asoka, his successor. Asoka's mother was a masseuse or "barber girl" who charmed Bindusara and eventually was married to him, one of his sixteen wives. Her son, though tradition records that he was not one of his father's favorites, proved useful to Bindusara. He served capably as the governor of an important province and, on one occasion, was brought in as the emergency governor of another province, which had been mismanaged by one of his brothers. On the death of Bindusara there was apparently a struggle for the throne that lasted for some four years before Asoka emerged as his father's successor. Tradition has it that Asoka succeeded because he was cruel and ruthless: he is supposed to have murdered all ninety-nine of his brothers! But he was undeniably also experienced, capable, and effective as a ruler. He was formally crowned king in about 269 B.C.

In the ninth year of his reign an event occurred that transformed Asoka. It was the so-called Kalinga war. Kalinga was an important province on the eastern frontier of the empire, vital to the protection of both landward and coastal trade. It may have been partially conquered by Chandragupta. Hence, Asoka's war there may have been undertaken to complete its conquest or to suppress a rebellion. In any case it was a major military undertaking, carried on with all the bloodshed and cruelty of any war. When Asoka looked on the pain and devastation the war had caused, he was appalled by what he had done. It was the first and the last war he ever conducted. He committed himself instead to peace, kindness, and generosity. Within two years he converted to Buddhism and "Asoka's pilgrimage on the Noble Eightfold Path had begun."[1]

---

[1]Balkrishna Govind Gokhale, *Asoka Maurya* (New York: Twayne, 1966), p. 60.

The King of the Inscriptions

ASOKA MAURYA

We have the account of the Kalinga war and of Asoka's remarkable change of heart in the king's own words. It was one of a number of monumental inscriptions ordered carved into cliff faces by the king, probably suggested by the similar device used by the Persian kings of the Achaemenid dynasty. There survive sixteen major rock edicts along with a large number of minor rock edicts and seven edicts inscribed on pillars, from all parts of the empire. Although some of the inscriptions refer to years of Asoka's reign, they have been somewhat arbitrarily organized and numbered by modern scholars.

The passages excerpted below are taken from the thirteenth major rock edict (the Kalinga inscription), the twelfth, the fifth, the first, and the first minor rock edict, and two other unenumerated edicts. They not only tell the story of the Kalinga war but also recount the measures the king took to prevent the wholesale killing of animals for food and ritual sacrifice and his provisions for the welfare of people and animals. By far the greater number of the inscriptions, however, are not narrative but hortatory. They are posted "in order that the people may conform to them," for "all men are my children, and just as I desire for my children that they should obtain welfare and happiness both in this world and the next, the same do I desire for all men."[2]

Even more remarkable than the almost unprecedented public account of such a major royal repentance as that of Asoka's following the Kalinga war is the broad, humane spirit that invests the inscriptions. Even though the king came to embrace Buddhism as his personal religion, there is comparatively little in the inscriptions that pertains only to Buddhism. Rather, Asoka extends toleration to all religious sects and to their common "essential doctrine." That common doctrine he called "Dhamma," and by it he referred to a noble and moral ideal of toleration and kindness to all creatures, which he even extended to foreign policy. In the Kalinga inscription he states flatly that henceforth he will achieve "victory by Dhamma" rather than by war or conquest. Apparently he attempted to do precisely this.

---

[2]Romila Thapar, *Asoka and the Decline of the Mauryas* (Oxford: Oxford University Press, 1963), p. 257.

When he had been consecrated eight years the Beloved of the Gods, the king Piyadassi,[3] conquered Kaliṅga. A hundred and fifty thousand people were deported, a hundred thousand were killed and many times that number perished. Afterwards, now that Kaliṅga was annexed, the Beloved of the Gods very earnestly practised *Dhamma*, desired *Dhamma*, and taught *Dhamma*. On conquering Kaliṅga the Beloved of the Gods felt remorse, for, when an independent country is conquered the slaughter, death, and deportation of the people is extremely grievous to the Beloved of the Gods, and weighs heavily on his mind. What is even more deplorable to the Beloved of the Gods, is that those who dwell there, whether brahmans, *śramaṇas*,[4] or those of other sects, or householders who show obedience to their superiors, obedience to mother and father, obedience to their teachers and behave well and devotedly towards their friends, acquaintances, colleagues, relatives, slaves, and servants—all suffer violence, murder, and separation from their loved ones. Even those who are fortunate to have escaped, and whose love is undiminished [by the brutalizing effect of war], suffer from the misfortunes of their friends, acquaintances, colleagues, and relatives. This participation of all men in suffering, weighs heavily on the mind of the Beloved of the Gods. Except among the Greeks, there is no land where the religious orders of brahmans and *śramaṇas* are not to be found, and there is no land anywhere where men do not support one sect or another. Today if a hundredth or a thousandth part of those people who were killed or died or were deported when Kaliṅga was annexed were to suffer similarly, it would weigh heavily on the mind of the Beloved of the Gods.

The Beloved of the Gods believes that one who does wrong should be forgiven as far as it is possible to forgive him. And the Beloved of the Gods conciliates the forest tribes of his empire, but he warns them that he has power even in his remorse, and he asks them to repent, lest they be killed. For the Beloved of the Gods wishes that all beings should be unharmed, self-controlled, calm in mind, and gentle. . . .

The Beloved of the Gods, the king Piyadassi, honours all sects and both ascetics and laymen, with gifts and various forms of recognition. But the Beloved of the Gods does not consider gifts or honour to be as important as the advancement of the essential doctrine of all sects. This progress of the essential doctrine takes many forms, but its basis is the control of one's speech, so as not to extoll one's own sect or disparage another's on unsuitable occasions, or at least to do so only mildly on certain occasions. On each occasion one should honour

---

[3]Piyadassi is one of the throne names of Asoka meaning "of gracious mien."—ED.

[4]Another category of brahman priest.—ED.

another man's sect, for by doing so one increases the influence of one's own sect and benefits that of the other man; while by doing otherwise one diminishes the influence of one's own sect and harms the other man's. Again, whosoever honours his own sect or disparages that of another man, wholly out of devotion to his own, with a view to showing it in a favourable light, harms his own sect even more seriously. Therefore, concord is to be commended, so that men may hear one another's principles and obey them. This is the desire of the Beloved of the Gods, that all sects should be well-informed, and should teach that which is good, and that everywhere their adherents should be told, 'The Beloved of the Gods does not consider gifts or honour to be as important as the progress of the essential doctrine of all sects.' Many are concerned with this matter—the officers of *Dhamma,* the women's officers, the managers of the state farms, and other classes of officers. The result of this is the increased influence of one's own sect and glory to *Dhamma.* . . .

In the past there were no officers of *Dhamma.* It was I who first appointed them, when I had been consecrated for thirteen years. They are busy in all sects, establishing *Dhamma,* increasing the interest in *Dhamma,* and attending to the welfare and happiness of those who are devoted to *Dhamma,* among the Greeks, the Kambojas, the Gandhāras, the Riṣṭhikas, the Pitinikas, and the other peoples of the west. Among servants and nobles, brahmans and wealthy householders, among the poor and the aged, they [the officers of *Dhamma*], are working for the welfare and happiness of those devoted to *Dhamma* and for the removal of their troubles. They are busy in promoting the welfare of prisoners should they have behaved irresponsibly, or releasing those that have children, are afflicted, or are aged. They are busy everywhere, here [at Pāṭaliputra] and in all the women's residences, whether my own, those of my brothers and sisters, or those of other relatives. Everywhere throughout my empire the officers of *Dhamma* are busy in everything relating to *Dhamma,* in the establishment of *Dhamma* and in the administration of charities among those devoted to *Dhamma.* For this purpose has this inscription of *Dhamma* been engraved. May it endure long and may my descendants conform to it. . . .

The Beloved of the Gods, Piyadassi the king, has had this inscription on *Dhamma* engraved. Here, no living thing having been killed, is to be sacrificed; nor is the holding of a festival permitted. For the Beloved of the Gods, the king Piyadassi, sees much evil in festivals, though there are some of which the Beloved of the Gods, the king Piyadassi, approves.

Formerly in the kitchens of the Beloved of the Gods, the king Piyadassi, many hundreds of thousands of living animals were killed daily for meat. But now, at the time of writing this inscription on

Dhamma, only three animals are killed, two peacocks and a deer, and the deer not invariably. Even these three animals will not be killed in future. . . .

Everywhere in the empire of the Beloved of the Gods, the king Piyadassi, and even in the lands on its frontiers . . . the two medical services of the Beloved of the Gods, the king Piyadassi, have been provided. These consist of the medical care of man and the care of animals. Medicinal herbs whether useful to man or to beast, have been brought and planted wherever they did not grow; similarly, roots and fruit have been brought and planted wherever they did not grow. Along the roads wells have been dug and trees planted for the use of men and beasts.

The two following items are among the few pertaining specifically to Buddhism. The first asserts Asoka's membership in the sect. The second secures the position of monks and nuns in Buddhism.

Thus speaks the Beloved of the Gods, Asoka: I have been a Buddhist layman for more than two and a half years, but for a year I did not make much progress. Now for more than a year I have drawn closer to the Order and have become more ardent. The gods, who in India up to this time did not associate with men, now mingle with them, and this is the result of my efforts. Moreover this is not something to be obtained only by the great, but it is also open to the humble, if they are earnest and they can even reach heaven easily. This is the reason for this announcement—that both humble and great should make progress and that the neighbouring peoples also should know that the progress is lasting. And this investment will increase and increase abundantly, and increase to half as much again. . . .

No one is to cause dissention in the Order. The Order of monks and nuns has been united, and this unity should last for as long as my sons and great grandsons, and the moon and the sun. Whoever creates a schism in the Order, whether monk or nun, is to be dressed in white garments, and to be put in a place not inhabited by monks or nuns. For it is my wish that the Order should remain united and endure for long. This is to be made known to the Order of monks and the Order of nuns. Thus says the Beloved of the Gods: You must keep one copy of this document and place it in your meeting hall, and give one copy to the laity. The laymen must come on every *uposatha* day [day of confession and penance] to endorse this order. The same applies to special officers who must also regularly attend the *uposatha,* and endorse this order, and make it known. Throughout your district you must circulate it exactly according to this text. You must also have this precise text circulated in all the fortress districts [under military control].

The King of Buddhist Tradition

ASOKAVADANA

The rock and pillar edicts of Asoka had been written in the languages of the people in whose districts they were erected and in a popular script called Brahmi. But within half a century of Asoka's death, with the disintegration of the Mauryan empire, the Brahmi script had fallen out of usage. The edicts could no longer be read, and the inscriptions stood as mute monuments until the early nineteenth century, when modern scholarship began their decipherment once more—a process that is still far from complete.

In place of the image of Asoka revealed in the inscriptions there came to be another and more popular image, that of the great Buddhist king. This emphasis is understandable, for Asoka was indeed the archetype of the Buddhist king and was historically responsible for transforming Buddhism from a somewhat localized sect into a major religion. Most of the substance of this image of Asoka is legendary and exists in several overlapping versions, deriving from Sri Lanka, Tibet, and even China, as well as from India. But the most complete of the legendary accounts is the Indian Asokavadana, *which is excerpted below.*

The Asokavadana, *written in Sanskrit, was probably set down in the second century* B.C. *Already the king of the inscriptions had begun to fade into an altogether different figure. For this is not fundamentally a historical but a religious document. The Kalinga war is not even mentioned. Asoka is instead converted to Buddhism by the miracles of a Buddhist saint. The idea of* Dhamma, *which the inscriptions attribute to Asoka's reverence for the essence of all the religious sects he protected and tolerated—including Buddhism— becomes the exclusive Buddhist Dharma, the teachings of the Buddha. And finally, the king in the early part of his reign is depicted in the blackest and most evil terms, in order that his conversion can be seen as more miraculous and the benefactions of his later life more meritorious. Surely this is not very promising historical material. Yet it is a long and respected biographical tradition which, in the view of some scholars, preserves a genuine account of the life and activities of Asoka.[5] In the view of others it is, at best, "corrupted history."[6] In any case, at the very least, there seem to be some nuggets of*

---

[5]For example, Gokhale, *Asoka Maurya*, p. 172.

[6]John S. Strong, *The Legend of King Asoka: A Study and Translation of the Asokavadana* (Princeton: Princeton University Press, 1983), p. 12.

*undeniable historical fact preserved in the legendary account. The physical
description of Asoka may be authentic: there would seem to be no other ready
explanation for it. The work of Asoka and his brother Susima as provincial
governors has a ring of historicity to it. Perhaps the description—or at least the
existence—of the infamous prison and torture chamber is authentic. Certainly
Asoka's building of the 84,000 stupas is—although the number must surely be
reduced. Probably authentic as well is the later account of the king's pilgrimage to the thirty-two sites of the Buddha's earthly life and his founding of the
quinquennial festival to the Buddha.*

The account from the Asokavadana *is taken from the recent translation
of John S. Strong,* The Legend of King Asoka: A Study and Translation of the Asokavadana. *It begins with an incident in one of Asoka's
previous lives, when he was a boy named Jaya, who met the Buddha and
made him a humble, childish gift of dirt and of whom the Buddha prophe-
sied that one hundred years later "that boy will become a king named Asoka
in the city of Pataliputra. He will be a righteous dharmaraja, a cakravartin who rules over one of the four continents,[7] and he will distribute my
bodily relics far and wide and build the eighty-four thousand dharma-
rajikas.[8] This he will undertake for the well being of many people."[9]*

The account then proceeds to the events surrounding the birth of Asoka.

Now at that time, King Bimbisāra was reigning in the city of
Rājagṛha. . . .

Meanwhile, in the city of Campā, a certain Brahmin begot a fair,
good-looking, gracious daughter, the most beautiful girl in the country. The fortunetellers predicted she would marry a king and bear two
jewel-like sons: one would become a cakravartin ruling over one of
the four continents, the other would wander forth and fulfill his
religious vows.[10]

The Brahmin was excited by what the soothsayers said. (The whole
world desires good fortune.) He took his daughter to Pāṭaliputra.
There, he had her put on all of her jewels, and he offered her in
marriage to King Bindusāra, declaring her to be an auspicious and
praiseworthy celestial maiden. King Bindusāra had her introduced
into his harem.

---

[7]*Dharmaraja* means a king who rules according to Dharma and *cakravartin* means a
"wheel-turning" monarch who justly rules one of the four continents.—ED.

[8]A *dharmarajika* is a shrine, also called a *stupa*, in which are contained relics of the
Buddha.—ED.

[9]Strong, *The Legend of King Asoka*, pp. 203–4.

[10]This is a reference to Asoka's brother Vitasoka, who did become a Buddhist saint,
largely through the persuasion of Asoka.—ED.

Now the king's concubines were jealous of her. "This fair, gracious girl," they thought, "is the most beautiful woman in the country; if the king should ever make love to her, he would no longer pay any attention to us!" They instructed her therefore in the barber's art, and soon she became an expert at grooming the hair and the beard of the king. Indeed, whenever she started to do this, he [would relax so much that he] would quickly fall asleep. The king was very pleased with her and decided to grant her one wish.

"What would you most desire?" he asked.

"That your majesty should have intercourse with me," she answered.

"But you are a barber girl," said the king, "I am a monarch, a consecrated kṣatriya [member of the warrior caste]—how can I have intercourse with you?"

"Your majesty," she replied, "I am not a barber girl but the daughter of a Brahmin; my father gave me to your highness as a wife!"

"Who then taught you the barber's art?" asked the king.

"The harem women," was her answer.

"Well, then, you won't do the work of a barber any more," King Bindusāra declared, and he installed her as his chief queen. Together they dallied, enjoyed each other, and made love; she became pregnant and, after a period of eight or nine months, gave birth to a son. When the prince's full birth festival was being celebrated, she was asked what his name should be. "When this baby was born, I became 'without sorrow' (*a-śoka*)," the queen replied, and so the child was given the name Aśoka.

Subsequently, the queen gave birth to a second son, and since he was born "when sorrow had ceased" (*vigate śoke*), he was given the name Vītaśoka.

One day, Bindusāra decided to test his sons so as to determine which one would best be able to rule after his death. Accordingly he spoke to the wandering ascetic Piṅgalavatsājīva, asking him to examine the princes.

"Very well, your majesty," replied Piṅgalavatsājīva, "go with the princes to the Garden of the Golden Pavilion, and I will scrutinize them there." Bindusāra, therefore, summoned his sons and proceeded to that place.

Now Aśoka's body [had bad skin; it] was rough and unpleasant to the touch, and he was not at all liked by his father, King Bindusāra. His mother told him: "My son, the king wants to examine all the princes and has gone to the Garden of the Golden Pavilion to do so; you should go there as well."

But he retorted: "Why should I? The very sight of me is hateful to the king."

"Go nevertheless," she advised, and he finally consented. Asking his mother to send him some food later in the day, he departed forthwith.

As he was leaving Pāṭaliputra, Rādhagupta, the son of the prime minister, saw him and asked: "Aśoka, where are you going?"

"Today," he answered, "the king is going to examine the princes in the garden of the Golden Pavilion."

[When Rādhagupta heard this, he invited Aśoka to take] the old royal elephant on which he was mounted. It was a venerable beast, and Aśoka rode it out to the Garden of the Golden Pavilion. Once there, he got off and sat down on the ground in the midst of the other princes. Before long, food arrived for all of them; Aśoka's mother had sent him some boiled rice mixed with curds in a clay pot.

Then King Bindusāra said to the wanderer Piṅgalavatsājīva: "Master, please examine the princes; who will best be able to rule after my death?"

Piṅgalavatsājīva scrutinized the young men and realized that Aśoka would be king, but he thought: "Bindusāra does not like Aśoka; if I tell him he will be king, he will surely kill me!" So he said: "Your majesty, I will make my prediction without disclosing any names."

"Do so then," said the king, "predict without disclosure."

The wandering ascetic then declared: "He who has an excellent mount will become king."

All of the princes, of course, immediately thought that their mount was most excellent and they would become king, but Aśoka reflected: "I arrived on the back of an elephant; my mount is truly excellent! I shall be king."

Bindusāra then said: "Master, scrutinize the princes more than that!"

So Piṅgalavatsājīva declared: "Your majesty, he who has the best seat will become king."

And again, each of the princes thought his own seat was the best, but Aśoka reflected: "I am sitting on the ground; the earth is my seat! I shall be king."

In a similar fashion, Piṅgalavatsājīva examined the princes with regard to their vessels, food, and drink, and when he had finished he returned to Pāṭaliputra.

Later, Aśoka's mother asked him: "Who was predicted to become king?"

Aśoka responded: "The prediction was made without disclosure. The one who had the best mount, seat, drink, vessel, and food will become king. The back of an elephant was my mount, the earth was my seat, my vessel was made of clay, boiled rice with curds was my food, and water was my drink; therefore I know I shall be king."

Now the wanderer Piṅgalavatsājīva, knowing that Aśoka would ascend the throne, started honoring his mother. One day, she asked him which one of the princes would succeed her husband Bindusāra, and he told her it would be Aśoka.

"The king," she cautioned him, "may someday interrogate you on this matter and press you for an answer. You had better go and seek refuge in the borderlands. When you hear that Aśoka has become king, it will be safe to return." And so he went into exile in a neighboring country.

Now it happened that the city of Takṣaśilā rebelled against King Bindusāra. He therefore sent Aśoka there, saying: "Go, son, lay siege to the city of Takṣaśilā." He sent with him a fourfold army [consisting of cavalry, elephants, chariots, and infantry], but he denied it any arms. As Aśoka was about to leave Pāṭaliputra, his servants informed him of this: "Prince, we don't have any weapons of war; how and with what shall we do battle?"

Aśoka declared: "If my merit is such that I am to become king, may weapons of war appear before me!"

And as soon as he had spoken these words, the earth opened up and deities brought forth weapons. Before long, he was on his way to Takṣaśilā with his fourfold army of troops.

When the citizens of Takṣaśilā heard that Aśoka was coming, they bedecked the road for two and a half yojanas, and with their vases full of offerings, went out to welcome him.

"We did not want to rebel against the prince," they explained upon greeting him, "nor even against King Bindusāra; but evil ministers came and oppressed us." And with great hospitality, they escorted him into the city.

Sometime later, Aśoka was welcomed in a similar fashion in the kingdom of the Khaśas. There two great warriors entered his service; he provided for their livelihood, and they in return, marched ahead of him, cutting a path through the mountains. Everywhere they went the gods proclaimed: "Aśoka is to become a cakravartin ruler over one of the four continents; no one is to oppose him!" And eventually the whole earth, as far as the ocean, submitted to his rule. . . .

Shortly thereafter, it happened that the Takṣaśilans again rose in rebellion. This time the king sent Prince Susīma to quell the uprising; he, however, was not successful.

At the same time, King Bindusāra became very ill. He therefore recalled Susīma to Pāṭaliputra intending to install him as his successor, and ordered Aśoka to be sent to Takṣaśilā in his stead. The ministers, however, [thwarted his plan;] they smeared Prince Aśoka's body with turmeric, boiled some red lac in a spittoon, filled other bowls with the boiled juice, and put them aside, saying "See, Prince Aśoka has become ill, [he cannot go to Takṣaśilā]."

Now Bindusāra was on his deathbed and about to breathe his last. The ministers, therefore, brought Aśoka to him adorned with all his ornaments. "Consecrate him as king for now," they urged, "we will install Susīma on the throne later when he gets back." This, however, only made the king furious.

Aśoka, therefore, declared: "If the throne is rightfully mine, let the gods crown me with the royal diadem!" And instantly the gods did so. When King Bindusāra saw this, he vomited blood and passed away.

As soon as Aśoka became king, his authority extended to the yakṣas as far away as a yojana above the earth, and to the nāgas a yojana beneath it.[11] [As his first act] he appointed Rādhagupta prime minister.

Susīma too learned that Bindusāra had died and Aśoka had been installed on the throne. The news made him furious, and he hastened to return to the capital.

Meanwhile, in Pāṭaliputra, Aśoka posted his two great warriors at two of the city gates and Rādhagupta at a third. He himself stood at the eastern gate. In front of it, Rādhagupta set up an artificial elephant, on top of which he placed an image of Aśoka that he had fashioned. All around he dug a ditch, filled it with live coals of acacia wood, covered it with reeds, and camouflaged the whole with dirt. He then went and taunted Susīma: "If you are able to kill Aśoka, you will become king!"

Susīma immediately rushed to the eastern gate, intending to do battle with his half-brother, but he fell into the ditch full of charcoal, and came to an untimely and painful end. After he had been killed, his own great warrior, Bhadrāyuddha, was initiated into the Buddhist order and became an arhat[12] along with his retinue of several thousand men.

Once Aśoka had become king, many of his ministers began to look on him with contempt. In order to discipline them, he ordered them, [as a test of their loyalty], to chop down all the flower and fruit trees but to preserve the thorn trees.

"What is your majesty planning?" they asked, "should we not rather chop down the thorn trees and preserve the flower and fruit trees?" And three times they countermanded his order. Aśoka became furious at this; he unsheathed his sword and cut off the heads of five hundred ministers.

On another occasion, King Aśoka, together with his harem, went out to a park east of the city. It was springtime and the trees were in bloom or laden with fruit. Strolling through the park he came across an aśoka tree whose blossoms were at their peak, and thinking "this beautiful

---

[11]*Yakṣas* were supernatural beings who could be helpful or harmful. *Nāgas* were snakelike supernatural beings of the same sort who lived in the water or below ground.—ED.

[12]This is a term for Buddhist saint.—ED.

tree is my namesake," he became very affectionate. King Aśoka's body, however, was rough-skinned, and the young women of the harem did not enjoy caressing him. So after he had fallen asleep, they, out of spite chopped all the flowers and branches off the aśoka tree.

After some time the king awoke; his eyes immediately fell on his dismembered tree.

"Who did this?" he asked his servants who were standing nearby.

"Your majesty's concubines," they answered.

On learning this, Aśoka flew into a rage and burned the five hundred women alive. When the people saw all these vicious acts of the king, they concluded he was fearsome by temperament, and gave him the name "Aśoka the Fierce" (Caṇḍāśoka).

Rādhagupta, the prime minister, therefore, spoke to him: "Your majesty, it is not seemly for you yourself to do what is improper; why don't you appoint some royal executioners, men who will carry out the necessary killings for the king?" So Aśoka told his men to go and find him an executioner.

Now, not too far away, in a small village at the foot of the mountains, there lived a weaver who had a son named Girika. Fearsome and evil-minded, the boy reviled his mother and father, and beat up the other boys and girls. With nets and hooks, he caught and killed ants, flies, mice, and fish. He was a ferocious youth and so people called him "Girika the Fierce" (Caṇḍagirika).

When the king's men saw him engaged in these wicked deeds, they asked him: "Are you able to be King Aśoka's executioner?"

"I could execute the whole of Jambudvīpa!" was his answer. . . .

Then they took Girika to King Aśoka. The first thing he did was to ask the king to have a building made for his purposes. Aśoka had one built immediately; it was lovely from the outside as far as the gate, but inside it was actually a very frightful place, and people called it "the beautiful gaol."

Caṇḍagirika then said: "Your majesty, grant me this wish—that whosoever should enter this place should not come out alive." And the king agreed to his demand. . . .

Candagirika had arrested a Buddhist monk named Samudra—for no cause—and condemned him to torture and death. On the eve of his execution a transformation occurred.

And applying himself the whole night through to the Teaching of the Buddha, he broke the bonds of existence and attained supreme arhatship.

At dawn, Caṇḍagirika said: "Monk, the night has gone, the sun has risen, the time of your torture has come!"

And Samudra replied: "Indeed, my night has gone, and the sun that marks the time of highest favor has risen! You may do whatever you wish, my long-lived friend." . . .

Thereupon, that unmerciful monster, feeling no pity in his heart and indifferent to the other world, threw Samudra into an iron cauldron full of water, human blood, marrow, urine, and excrement. He lit a great fire underneath, but even after much firewood had been consumed, the cauldron did not get hot. Once more, he tried to light the fire, but again it would not blaze. He became puzzled, and looking into the pot, he saw the monk seated there, cross-legged on a lotus. Straightaway, he sent word to King Aśoka. Aśoka came to witness this marvel, and thousands of people gathered, and Samudra, seated in the cauldron, realized that the time for Aśoka's conversion was at hand.

He began to generate his supernatural powers. In the presence of the crowd of onlookers, he flew up to the firmament. . . .

At the sight of the sky-walker, the king's mouth hung open in astonishment. . . .

Now the king's faith in the Buddha was aroused and cupping his hands together out of respect, he implored the monk Samudra, saying:

> O son of the Daśabala,[13] please forgive me this evil deed.
> Today, I confess it to you and seek refuge
> in that Sage, the Buddha, in the best of sects,
> and in the Dharma that is taught by the Noble ones.

Furthermore:

> Because of my faith in the Blessed One,
> because of his venerability,
> I resolve today to adorn the earth
> with the chief of Jinas' caityas
> that are as white as the conch, the moon, and the crane.

Then Samudra departed from that place by means of his supernatural powers. [Aśoka too made ready to leave] but just as he was about to go, Caṇḍagirika, making an añjali,[14] said: "Your majesty, you granted me a wish—that no one at all should leave this place alive!"

"What?" said the king, "you want to put me to death too?"

"Just so," replied Caṇḍagirika.

"But which one of us," asked Aśoka, "entered this place first?"

---

[13]Another of the Buddha's epithets, "the ten-powered one."—ED.

[14]An *anjali* is a salutation of respect.—ED.

"I did," admitted Caṇḍagirika.

Aśoka therefore summoned his guard. They seized Caṇḍagirika and took him away to the torture chamber where he was burned to death. And the beautiful gaol was then torn down, and a guarantee of security extended to all beings.

Then King Aśoka, intending to distribute far and wide the bodily relics of the Blessed One, went together with a fourfold army to the droṇa stūpa that Ajātaśatru[15] had built. He broke it open, took out all the relics, and putting back a portion of them, set up a new stūpa. He did the same with the second droṇa stūpa and so on up to the seventh one, removing the relics from each of them and then setting up new stūpas as tokens of his devotion. . . .

Then Aśoka had eighty-four thousand boxes made of gold, silver, cat's eye, and crystal, and in them were placed the relics. Also, eighty-four thousand urns and eighty-four thousand inscription plates were prepared. All of this was given to the yakṣas for distribution in the [eighty-four thousand] dharmarājikās he ordered built throughout the earth as far as the surrounding ocean, in the small, great, and middle-sized towns, wherever there was a [population of] one hundred thousand [persons]. . . .

Now when King Aśoka had completed the eighty-four thousand dharmarājikās, he became a righteous dharmarāja, and thenceforth was known as "Dharmāśoka."

As it is said:

> For the benefit of beings throughout the world
> the noble Maurya built stūpas
> He had been known as "Aśoka the Fierce";
> by this act he became "Aśoka the Righteous."

A Modern Asoka

W. H. MORELAND AND ATUL CHANDRA CHATTERJEE

Given the two preceding divergent contemporary (or near-contemporary) views of the great king, how are we to choose between them or reconcile their differences? This is the central interpretive problem of Asokan scholar-

---

[15]The first Buddhist king, semimythical.—ED.

ship. A reasonably standard statement and resolution of the problem is to be found in one of the most widely respected general histories of India, W. H. Moreland and Atul Chandra Chatterjee's A Short History of India. *When this book was first published in 1936 the reviewer in* New Statesman *called it "a moderate, balanced, sensible work" and the* Times Literary Supplement *pointed out that it concentrates "on the evolution of Indian culture and its response to successive foreign contacts."[16] Each of its authors was an established authority, Moreland an academic and Sir Atul Chatterjee a distinguished public servant. The work has been republished in four editions, the last under the supervision of Sir Atul's daughter, and in a number of printings. It has never lost its authority.*

We now turn to Moreland and Chatterjee's judicious assessment of King Asoka.

Chandragupta was succeeded by his heir Bindusāra, who reigned for a quarter of a century, and of whom practically nothing is known; but in Bindusāra's son and successor, Asoka, we meet the first Indian ruler whose personality stands out clearly in history. His fame bulks largely in Buddhist literature, but the story there given has been coloured or distorted in the process of hagiography, and for the facts of his life we are indebted primarily to the edicts which, following an old Persian practice, he caused to be inscribed on rocks and pillars throughout his dominions. Many of these are still in existence, and in their simple, earnest language, marked by endless repetitions, there is no difficulty in recognising the man. We may question the extent to which his ideals were realised in practice, but there can be no question that we are in the presence of a great apostle of righteousness.

Asoka succeeded to the throne of Magadha about 274 B.C., the precise year being uncertain, and reigned, most probably, for thirty-seven years. For the first quarter of this period there is nothing to distinguish him from the ordinary Hindu ruler: apparently he had to fight for the succession, though it is safe to refuse credit to the legend that he killed ninety-nine of his brothers in the process; and, following the usual course of kingship, he conquered Kalinga, a region lying on the east coast between the Mahānadi and the Godāvarī rivers, corresponding to the modern Orissa with the most northerly portion of Madras. This was the turning-point of his life. Distressed by the suffering and misery caused by war, he resolved to abandon the traditional course, and turned to the teaching of the Buddha. The

---

[16]*New Statesman and Nation,* Jan. 9, 1937, p. 53, and *Times Literary Supplement,* Oct. 24, 1936, p. 852.

remainder of his life was spent in philanthropical administration, in promoting moral reform, and in propagating the doctrines which he had embraced.

For the administration of the empire Asoka employed three vice-roys, one at Taxila for the north-west, a second at Ujjain in Mālwa for the west and south-west, and a third for Kalinga on the south-east, apparently retaining direct control of the central region. It is impossi-ble to distinguish the tracts in this area which were held by vassal kings, but probably most of it was administered in this way, so that the empire may be regarded as a confederation of states. Its southern limits are not clearly defined, but the presence of inscriptions in the north of what is now the Mysore State indicates that Asoka's influence, if not his actual rule, extended well to the south of the river Kistna. The principles governing the administration were drawn from the Sacred Law, and accepted by Hindus and Jains as well as Buddhists; but Asoka laid particular stress on those which bear the names of *ahimsā* and *maitri*, or 'non-violence' and 'friendliness,' applied to all living creatures. In ac-cordance with these principles we find him insisting on the provision of shade and water along the roads, and of medical aid for animals as well as human beings; restricting the slaughter of animals; enjoining the just and humane treatment of prisoners; and appointing high officials, in addition to the existing administrative staff, charged specially with the organisation of charity, the redress of wrongs and the inculcation of moral principles.

The frontier policy of Asoka represented an entire breach with the Indian tradition of enlarging the borders of a kingdom by conquest. He desired that 'the unsubdued borderers should not be afraid of me, that they should trust me, and should receive from me happiness, not sorrow'; and he hoped that they too would accept the moral princi-ples which he preached to his own subjects. The extent to which his hopes were realised is not on record, but there is no reason to doubt that during his reign the frontiers were ordinarily peaceful.

As a moral reformer Asoka was essentially practical. If he cared anything about metaphysical speculations, the fact does not appear in his edicts; he laid stress on simple duties, which he considered had been too much neglected, obedience to parents, kind treatment of servants, slaves and animals, respect and generosity to priests and ascetics, toleration, friendliness, charity, simplicity of life—in a word, righteousness. In matters of religion he was no bigot: he discounte-nanced certain popular ceremonials, but he inculcated respect for Brāhmans among other classes, and he claimed as a merit that he had extended the knowledge of the gods of Hinduism among the jungle tribes. His activities in promoting Buddhism do not stand out as directed against the popular religion, and it is not possible to infer from the language of his edicts that he regarded himself as the champion of one creed against another; he was the champion of a life rather than a faith.

One side of these activities was the establishment of Buddhist shrines: tradition attributes to him an enormous number of such buildings, and, while the number is an obvious exaggeration, there is no doubt of the essential fact. Another side was the attempt to secure unity among the followers of the Buddha; a Council was held under his patronage at Patna, when the differences between various schools were composed, and the canon of authoritative scriptures was determined; and one of his edicts imposed penalties on schism. A third side was the despatch of missionaries throughout the empire and beyond its limits. There is nothing to show that his envoys achieved any success in the distant countries they are said to have visited, in Syria, Egypt or Greece; but nearer home, in north-west India, in Burma and elsewhere, the progress of Buddhism was marked. The most important results were secured in Ceylon, which may be described as the second home of the faith; here the doctrine laid down in Asoka's Council was preserved and codified; and when this school of Buddhism disappeared from India the authority of the Sinhalese canon was accepted in Burma and Siam.

No confident estimate can be made of the results of Asoka's efforts within the limits of his empire. So far as we know, his distinctive policy was not continued by his successors, under whom the empire fell to pieces; his edicts are more concerned with the future than the past; and there is no other source of information. We know only that a high ideal of righteousness was authoritatively set before the people; we can safely conclude that it was not realised in its entirety; we may be equally sure that it was not wholly without effect. The edicts stood for future generations to read; but the characters in which they were engraved became obsolete, and their decipherment belongs to the period of British rule. The survival of Asoka's fame in tradition shows at least that his figure struck the popular imagination; but his actual achievement cannot be determined.

Review and Study Questions

1. Is it possible to reconcile the two accounts of Asoka—the one from the inscriptions and the one in the *Asokavadana?* Explain.
2. What can you learn about Asoka from the inscriptions?
3. What are the most obvious distortions of truth in the *Asokavadana?* How do you account for them?

4. How do you interpret the story of "Girika the Fierce"? Why was it included in the *Asokavadana?*

Suggestions for Further Reading

In addition to the translation of the edicts excerpted for this chapter from Romila Thapar, *Asoka and the Decline of the Mauryas* (Oxford: Oxford University Press, 1963), there are also modern translations of them in Gokhale, *Asoka Maurya* (New York: Twayne, 1966) and R. K. Mookerji, *Asoka* (Delhi et al.: Motilal Banarsidass, 1962), and in K. A. Nikam and R. McKeon, *The Edicts of Asoka* (Chicago: University of Chicago Press, 1959). In contrast, the translation of the *Asokavadana,* also excerpted for this chapter, by John S. Strong, *The Legend of King Asoka: A Study and Translation of the Asokavadana* (Princeton: Princeton University Press, 1983), is the only available English translation.

There are a number of biographies of Asoka. The small, pioneering study by James M. Mcphail, *Asoka,* 2nd ed. (London: Oxford University Press, 1926), has been largely superseded, as has B. M. Barua, *Asoka and his Inscriptions* (Calcutta: New Age, 1948), a useful book for its time since it synthesized much of the scholarship of the previous two decades. An important technical study is P. H. L. Eggermont, *The Chronology of the Reign of Asoka Moriya* (Leiden: Brill, 1956). The two best biographies are Mookerji, *Asoka,* and Gokhale, *Asoka Maurya,* the latter especially good, by one of the most distinguished modern Indian historians.

Several of the works on Buddhism cited in the chapter on the Buddha are also valuable for Asoka. Robinson and Johnson, *The Buddhist Religion: A Historical Introduction* is good, as are Conze, *A Short History of Buddhism* and Humphreys, *Buddhism.* Also recommended is E. Zürcher, *Buddhism* (New York: St. Martin's Press, 1962).

The same is the case with the several histories of India cited for the chapter on the Buddha. In addition to W. H. Moreland and Atul Chandra Chatterjee, *A Short History of India,* 4th ed. (London: Longmans, Green and Co., 1969), excerpted for this chapter, see Basham, *The Wonder that Was India,* and Spear, *India: A Modern History.* Michael Edwardes, *A History of India From the Earliest Times to the Present Day* (New York: Farrar, Straus and Cudahy, 1961) is recommended, as is Stanley Wolpert, *A New History of India,* 3rd ed. (Oxford and New York: Oxford University Press, 1989), the latter being especially good for the Asokan period. Finally, Sir Mortimer Wheeler, *Early India and Pakistan to Asoka,* "Ancient Peoples and Places" (New York: Praeger, 1959) is good for its archaeological insights into the Asokan period and earlier.

JULIUS CAESAR: THE COLOSSUS THAT BESTRODE THE NARROW WORLD

C. 100 B.C.	Born
69 or 68 B.C.	Elected quaestor
62 B.C.	Elected praetor
59 B.C.	Elected consul; First Triumvirate with Crassus and Pompey
58–50 B.C.	Conquest of Gaul
49–45 B.C.	Civil war
44 B.C.	Assassinated

Unlike Alexander, who conquered the world "as a boy" and was dead at thirty-three, Julius Caesar reached a mature age without achieving astonishing success. He did have considerable experience as a political faction leader, but in the judgment of most of his contemporaries he was not likely to be a world conqueror of Alexander's stamp. And yet, in 49 B.C., when Caesar was fifty years old, a series of events began to unfold that would make him one of the great conquerors of world history and set him alongside Alexander in the estimation of scholar and schoolboy alike.

For ten years, Caesar had been building a military reputation with his successful campaigns in Gaul, Britain, and along the Rhine frontier, but always with an eye on events in the city of Rome and the Roman senate, where he had a personal interest in the fierce contest among cliques and factions that dominated senatorial politics in the last years of the Roman Republic. As the year 49 B.C. approached, Caesar's proconsular authority in Gaul was running out. He demanded that he be permitted to stand *in absentia* for the consulship for the following year—neither an unprecedented nor an unreasonable demand. Caesar attempted to negotiate with his old ally, the great general Pompey, perhaps to prolong their alliance. But Pompey,

125

his own military reputation threatened by Caesar's growing prestige, and relentlessly pressured by Caesar's enemies in the senate, refused him and joined with the senate in demanding that Caesar surrender his military command and return to Rome as a private citizen to stand for the consulship. But to do so would have meant his death or proscription. Thus, in January of 49 B.C., Caesar took the fateful step into open revolution, leading a token force across the Rubicon, the little stream that separated his Gallic province from peninsular Italy.

For nearly a century the Roman constitution had been progressively subverted by a succession of extralegal expedients to legitimize the authority of one strong man after another, one faction after another—whether the prolonged consulships of Marius, the perpetual dictatorship of Sulla, or the triumviral authority that Caesar himself had held with Pompey and Crassus. Such practices, as well as a pervasive disenchantment with the self-serving senatorial oligarchy, had created broad support in Rome and in Italy for a policy of change, even revolutionary change. Caesar's popular reputation attracted that support as he marched south toward Rome. Even Pompey's legions in Spain declared for Caesar. Pompey and his remaining allies fled to Greece, where they were pursued by Caesar under vast emergency authority readily granted by an overawed senate, and were defeated at Pharsalus. In the next four years, Caesar moved through Asia Minor and Syria, Egypt, North Africa, and Spain and encircled the Mediterranean with his conquests, giving the final rough form to the greatest empire of antiquity.

It was at this point that the plot to assassinate Caesar was formed. It was carried out on the Ides of March of the year 44 B.C.

Caesar and Alexander beg for comparison, despite the many dissimilarities in their lives. Plutarch, the greatest of ancient biographers, paired them in his *Parallel Lives of Noble Greeks and Romans,* and almost every other ancient writer who speculates upon the meaning of Caesar's career suggests comparison with Alexander. The obvious basis for the comparison is, of course, the military parallel and the fact that Caesar, like Alexander, seized his time and wrenched it so violently that the direction of world events was fundamentally changed. But equally important, both men were cut off before their schemes for a civil order could be realized. There was about Caesar, as about Alexander, an aura of things to come, of unfulfilled dreams even more astounding than his conquests. Thus the question again intrigues us, "What would Caesar have accomplished had he lived on?"

In one important respect Caesar differs radically from Alexander—in our sources of information about him. As we saw in the chapter on Alexander, all the contemporary works that dealt with his career have been lost, and the best surviving account of him was written some four hundred years after he died. Not so with Caesar. He lived during the most heavily documented period in ancient history, a time when we know more about the people and events at the center of the world's stage than we will know again for more than a thousand years. We have Caesar's own considerable volume of writings. We have the works of his great senatorial contemporary Cicero. We have the writings of poets and essayists and narrative historians. But despite the abundance of material and the wealth of detail about Julius Caesar, a clear and convincing picture of the man—what he was and what he might have become—eludes us, precisely because, as Shakespeare's Cassius says in *Julius Caesar,* ". . . he doth bestride the narrow world like a colossus," because his dominating personality, his overweening ambition, and his striking accomplishments made it nearly impossible for his contemporaries to be objective about him. His own writings are propagandistic, and the writings of Cicero, his often bitter and vindictive opponent, and Sallust, his partisan, are obviously biased. The accounts of both Pollio and Livy exist in epitomes or in traces in others' works. For our best account of Caesar, we must reach down into the imperial period that followed his own brilliant "golden age of Latin literature," to one of the writers of "the silver age," the biographer Suetonius.

The Life of Caesar

SUETONIUS

The choice of Suetonius is a good one on a number of counts. Although he has been charged with a journalistic style and mentality and with too great a fondness for scandal, rumor, and portent, the late imperial Historia Augusta, *for what it is worth, refers to him as having written* vere, *"truly," and a great modern Roman historian calls him "far and away the best authority" on Caesar.*[1] *Unlike his contemporary Plutarch, Suetonius was not a moralist using biography as a source of example. Nor was he a deliberate partisan: the factionalism of Caesar's age was long dead. Suetonius was interested only in writing a plain, straightforward account of the characters and events that were his subject. And, like Arrian, he turned to archival sources for his information. The book in which his biography of Caesar appears,* The Lives of the Twelve Caesars, *was begun when Suetonius was still in the imperial civil service of the Emperor Hadrian. It is clear that he had access to archival records, now long lost, as well as to literary sources, and that he followed his sources carefully. His biography of Caesar was apparently a part of the book done before Suetonius left the imperial service in about* A.D. *120 and thus is especially well documented with records and sources.*

And yet, in an important sense, Suetonius was the captive of those very sources he followed so scrupulously. For even though Suetonius was more than a century removed from his sources, the hostility toward Caesar that these records expressed is clearly reflected in Suetonius's writing. Despite his fascination and admiration for Caesar, Suetonius's basic assessment is that Caesar's arrogance and his flaunting of the republican tradition led to his murder: "He abused his power and was justly slain."

Even after the Civil War and the furious activity of the years 48–44 B.C., *Suetonius tells us, Caesar was full of plans for beautifying the city of Rome, opening libraries, draining the Pomptine marshes, building new highways, constructing a canal through the Isthmus of Corinth, and waging war against both the Dacians and the Parthians.*

---

[1]Sir Ronald Syme, in a review of Matthias Gelzer's "Caesar der Politiker und Staatsmann" in *Journal of Roman Studies*, 34 (1944), 95.

All these enterprises and plans were cut short by his death. But before I speak of that, it will not be amiss to describe briefly his personal appearance, his dress, his mode of life, and his character, as well as his conduct in civil and military life.

He is said to have been tall of stature, with a fair complexion, shapely limbs, a somewhat full face, and keen black eyes; sound of health, except that towards the end he was subject to sudden fainting fits and to nightmare as well. He was twice attacked by the falling sickness during his campaigns. He was somewhat overnice in the care of his person, not only keeping the hair of his head closely cut and his face smoothly shaved, but as some have charged, even having superfluous hair plucked out. His baldness was a disfigurement which troubled him greatly, since he found that it was often the subject of the gibes of his detractors. Because of it he used to comb forward his scanty locks from the crown of his head, and of all the honors voted him by the Senate and people there was none which he received or made use of more gladly than the privilege of wearing a laurel wreath at all times. . . .

It is admitted by all that he was much addicted to women, as well as very extravagant in his intrigues with them, and that he seduced many illustrious women, among them Postumia, wife of Servius Sulpicius, Lollia, wife of Aulus Gabinius, Tertulla, wife of Marcus Crassus, and even Gnaeus Pompey's wife Mucia. . . .

He had love affairs with Queens, too, including Eunoe the Moor, wife of Bogudes, on whom, as well as on her husband, he bestowed many splendid presents, as Naso writes. But his greatest favorite was Cleopatra, with whom he often feasted until daybreak, and he would have gone through Egypt with her in her state-barge almost to Aethiopia, had not his soldiers refused to follow him. Finally he called her to Rome and did not let her leave until he had laden her with high honors and rich gifts, and he allowed her to give his name to the child which she bore. . . .

That he drank very little wine not even his enemies denied. There is a saying of Marcus Cato that Caesar was the only man who undertook to overthrow the state when sober. Even in the matter of food Gaius Oppius tells us that he was so indifferent, that once when his host served stale oil instead of fresh, and the other guests would have none of it, Caesar partook even more plentifully than usual, that he might not seem to charge his host with carelessness or lack of manners.

But his abstinence did not extend to pecuniary advantages, either when in command of armies or when in civil office. For we have the testimony of some writers that when he was Proconsul in Spain, he not only begged money from the allies, to help pay his debts, but also attacked and sacked some towns of the Lusitanians, although they did not refuse his terms and opened their gates to him on his arrival. In Gaul he pillaged shrines and temples of the Gods filled with offerings, and oftener sacked towns for the sake of plunder than for any fault. . . .

He was highly skilled in arms and horsemanship, and of incredible powers of endurance. On the march he headed his army, sometimes on horseback, but oftener on foot, bareheaded both in the heat of the sun and in rain. He covered great distances with incredible speed, making a hundred miles a day in a hired carriage and with little baggage, swimming the rivers which barred his path or crossing them on inflated skins, and very often arriving before the messengers sent to announce his coming. . . .

He joined battle, not only after planning his movements in advance but on a sudden opportunity, often immediately at the end of a march, and sometimes in the foulest weather, when one would least expect him to make a move. It was not until his later years that he became slower to engage, through a conviction that the oftener he had been victor, the less he ought to tempt fate, and that he could not possibly gain as much by success as he might lose by a defeat. He never put his enemy to flight without also driving him from his camp, thus giving him no respite in his panic. When the issue was doubtful, he used to send away the horses, and his own among the first, to impose upon his troops the greater necessity of standing their ground by taking away that aid to flight. . . .

When his army gave way, he often rallied it single-handed, planting himself in the way of the fleeing men, laying hold of them one by one, even seizing them by the throat and turning them to face the enemy; that, too, when they were in such a panic that an eagle-bearer made a pass at him with the point as he tried to stop him, while another left the standard in Caesar's hand when he would hold him back. . . .

At Alexandria, while assaulting a bridge, he was forced by a sudden sally of the enemy to take to a small skiff. When many others threw themselves into the same boat, he plunged into the sea, and after swimming for two hundred paces, got away to the nearest ship, holding up his left hand all the way, so as not to wet some papers which he was carrying, and dragging his cloak after him with his teeth, to keep the enemy from getting it as a trophy.

He valued his soldiers neither for their personal character nor their fortune, but solely for their prowess, and he treated them with equal strictness and indulgence. . . .

He certainly showed admirable self-restraint and mercy, both in his conduct of the civil war and in the hour of victory. While Pompey threatened to treat as enemies those who did not take up arms for the government, Caesar gave out that those who were neutral and of neither party should be numbered with his friends. He freely allowed all those whom he had made Centurions[2] on Pompey's recommendation to go over to his rival. . . . At the battle of Pharsalus he cried out, "Spare your fellow citizens," and afterwards allowed each of his men to save any one man he pleased of the opposite party. . . .

Yet after all, his other actions and words so far outweigh all his good qualities that it is thought he abused his power and was justly slain. For not only did he accept excessive honors, such as an uninterrupted consulship, the dictatorship for life, and the censorship of public morals, as well as the forename Imperator,[3] the surname of Father of his Country, a statue among those of the Kings,[4] and a raised couch in the orchestra of the theater. He also allowed honors to be bestowed on him which were too great for mortal man: a golden throne in the House and on the judgment seat; a chariot and litter in the procession at the circus; temples, altars, and statues beside those of the Gods; a special priest, an additional college of the Luperci, and the calling of one of the months by his name. In fact, there were no honors which he did not receive or confer at pleasure.

He held his third and fourth consulships in name only, content with the power of the dictatorship conferred on him at the same time as the consulships. Moreover, in both years he substituted two Consuls for himself for the last three months, in the meantime holding no elections except for Tribunes and plebeian Aediles, and appointing Praefects instead of the Praetors, to manage the affairs of the city during his absence. When one of the Consuls suddenly died the day before the Kalends of January, he gave the vacant office for a few hours to a man who asked for it. With the same disregard of law and precedent he named magistrates for several years to come, bestowed the emblems of consular rank on ten ex-Praetors, and admitted to the House men who had been given citizenship, and in some cases even half-civilized Gauls. He assigned the charge of the mint and of the public revenues to his own slaves, and gave the oversight and command of the three legions which he had left at Alexandria to a favorite boy of his called Rufio, son of one of his freedmen.

No less arrogant were his public utterances, which Titus Ampius records: that the Republic was a name only, without substance or reality; that Sulla did not know his A. B. C. when he laid down his

---

[2]Centurions were "company grade" officers in the Roman legion.—ED.

[3]The title *Imperator*, synonymous with conqueror, was that by which troops would hail a victorious commander. It first assumed a permanent and royal character through Caesar's use of it as a praenomen.—ED.

[4]Statues of each of the seven Kings of Rome were in the Capitol, to which an eighth was added in honor of Brutus, who expelled the last of the Kings. The statue of Julius was afterward raised near them.—ED.

dictatorship; that men ought now to be more circumspect in address-
ing him, and to regard his word as law. So far did he go in his
presumption, that when a soothsayer once announced to him the
direful omen that a victim offered for sacrifice was without a heart, he
said: "The entrails will be more favorable when I please. It ought not
to be taken as a miracle if a beast have no heart."

But it was the following action in particular that roused deadly
hatred against him. When the Senate approached him in a body with
many highly honorary decrees, he received them before the temple of
Venus Genetrix without rising. Some think that when he attempted to
get up, he was held back by Cornelius Balbus; others, that he made
no such move at all, but on the contrary frowned angrily on Gaius
Trebatius when he suggested that he should rise. This action of his
seemed the more intolerable, because when he himself in one of his
triumphal processions rode past the benches of the Tribunes, he was
so incensed because one of their number, Pontius Aquila by name, did
not rise, that he cried: "Come then, Aquila, mighty Tribune, and take
from me the Republic," and for several days afterwards, he would
promise a favor to no one without adding, "That is, if Pontius Aquila
will give me leave."

To an insult which so plainly showed his contempt for the Senate he
added an act of even greater insolence. After the sacred rites of the
Latin Festival, as he was returning to the city, amid the extravagant
and unprecedented demonstrations of the populace, some one in the
press placed on his statue a laurel wreath with a white fillet tied to it.
When Epidius Marullus and Caesetius Flavus, Tribunes of the Commons, gave orders that the ribbon be removed from the crown and
the man taken off to prison, Caesar sharply rebuked and deposed
them, either offended that the hint at regal power had been received
with so little favor, or, as was said, that he had been robbed of the
glory of refusing it. But from that time on he could not rid himself of
the odium of having aspired to the title of monarch, although he
replied to the Commons, when they hailed him as King, "I am Caesar
and not King." At the Lupercalia, when the Consul Antony several
times attempted to place a crown upon his head as he spoke from the
rostra, he put it aside and at last sent it to the Capitol, to be offered to
Jupiter Optimus Maximus. Nay, more, the report had spread in various quarters that he intended to move to Ilium or Alexandria, taking
with him the resources of the state, draining Italy by levies, and
leaving it and the charge of the city to his friends; also that at the next
meeting of the Senate Lucius Cotta would announce as the decision
of the Fifteen,[5] that inasmuch as it was written in the books of fate

---

[5]The college of fifteen priests who inspected and expounded the Sybilline books.—
Ed.

that the Parthians could be conquered only by a King, Caesar should be given that title. . . .

More than sixty joined the conspiracy against him, led by Gaius Cassius and Marcus and Decimus Brutus. At first they hesitated whether to form two divisions at the elections in the Campus Martius, so that while some hurled him from the bridge as he summoned the tribes to vote, the rest might wait below and slay him; or to set upon him in the Sacred Way or at the entrance to the theater. When, however, a meeting of the Senate was called for the Ides of March in the Hall of Pompey, they readily gave that time and place the preference.

Now Caesar's approaching murder was foretold to him by unmistakable signs: . . . when he was offering sacrifice, the soothsayer Spurinna warned him to beware of danger, which would come not later than the Ides of March. . . .

Both for these reasons and because of poor health he hesitated for a long time whether to stay at home and put off what he had planned to do in the Senate. But at last, urged by Decimus Brutus not to disappoint the full meeting, which had for some time been waiting for him, he went forth almost at the end of the fifth hour. When a note revealing the plot was handed him by some one on the way, he put it with others which he held in his left hand, intending to read them presently. Then, after many victims had been slain, and he could not get favorable omens, he entered the House in defiance of portents, laughing at Spurinna and calling him a false prophet, because the Ides of March were come without bringing him harm. Spurinna replied that they had of a truth come, but they had not gone.

As he took his seat, the conspirators gathered about him as if to pay their respects, and straightway Tillius Cimber, who had assumed the lead, came nearer as though to ask something. When Caesar with a gesture put him off to another time, Cimber caught his toga by both shoulders. As Caesar cried, "Why, this is violence!" one of the Cascas stabbed him from one side just below the throat. Caesar caught Casca's arm and ran it through with his stylus, but as he tried to leap to his feet, he was stopped by another wound. When he saw that he was beset on every side by drawn daggers, he muffled his head in his robe, and at the same time drew down its lap to his feet with his left hand, in order to fall more decently, with the lower part of his body also covered. And in this wise he was stabbed with three and twenty wounds, uttering not a word, but merely a groan at the first stroke, though some have written that when Marcus Brutus rushed at him, he said in Greek, "You too, my child?" All the conspirators made off, and he lay there lifeless for some time, until finally three common slaves put him on a litter and carried him home, with one arm hanging down.

The Heroic Image of Caesar

THEODOR MOMMSEN

Theodor Mommsen (1817–1903) was awarded the Nobel Prize for Literature in 1902, largely for the literary achievement of his monumental, multivolume The History of Rome. *The Nobel citation called him the "greatest . . . master of historical narrative" of his age—a considerable claim in an era that had produced Ranke and Burckhardt, Guizot, Grote, Carlyle, and Macaulay. Still, the assertion may be true. Mommsen, a prolific writer, had gained an immense and well-deserved authority, and his massive* The History of Rome *was profoundly influential. It was Mommsen who at last placed the study of ancient history on a scientific and critical foundation. And he began and directed the first great critical collection of ancient Latin inscriptions.*

Like W. W. Tarn, Theodor Mommsen was trained both in classics and in law. His first academic appointment was as professor of law at Leipzig. Then in 1858 he was appointed to the chair of ancient history at the University of Berlin. Throughout his long life, Mommsen was not only a professor but a passionate political activist. He was involved in the Revolution of 1848 and lost his academic post at Leipzig because of it. In the 1870s he was a prominent member of the Prussian Parliament, frequently clashing with Otto von Bismarck. Like many great historians, Mommsen read the past in terms of present politics. Thus his view of Caesar and the late Roman Republic was colored by his profound disillusionment with German political liberalism and an equally profound hatred for Junker conservatism. Julius Caesar became for Mommsen the archetypal strong man who had swept away the broken pieces of a ruined oligarchy and set the rule of the beneficent Roman Empire firmly on its base. While Mommsen has been rightly criticized for the extravagance of his opinions both on Caesar and on the late Roman Republic, his views, though never quite accepted as the "standard" interpretation, did exert a strong influence on modern scholarship until fairly recently.

Here, from The History of Rome, *is Mommsen's evaluation of Julius Caesar. The prose is old fashioned and florid and the judgments are dated, but there is still some power left in the sweep of Mommsen's portrayal of his "perfect man."*

The new monarch of Rome, the first ruler over the whole domain of Romano-Hellenic civilization, Gaius Julius Caesar, was in his fifty-sixth year . . . when the battle at Thapsus [46 B.C.], the last link in a long chain of momentous victories, placed the decision as to the future of the world in his hands. Few men have had their elasticity so thoroughly put to the proof as Caesar—the sole creative genius produced by Rome, and the last produced by the ancient world, which accordingly moved on in the path that he marked out for it until its sun went down. Sprung from one of the oldest noble families of Latium—which traced back its lineage to the heroes of the Iliad and the kings of Rome, and in fact to the Venus-Aphrodite common to both nations—he spent the years of his boyhood and early manhood as the genteel youth of that epoch were wont to spend them. He had tasted the sweetness as well as the bitterness of the cup of fashionable life, had recited and declaimed, had practised literature and made verses in his idle hours, had prosecuted love-intrigues of every sort, and got himself initiated into all the mysteries of shaving, curls, and ruffles pertaining to the toilette-wisdom of the day, as well as into the still more mysterious art of always borrowing and never paying. But the flexible steel of that nature was proof against even these dissipated and flighty courses; Caesar retained both his bodily vigour and his elasticity of mind and of heart unimpaired. In fencing and in riding he was a match for any of his soldiers, and his swimming saved his life at Alexandria; the incredible rapidity of his journeys, which usually for the sake of gaining time were performed by night—a thorough contrast to the procession-like slowness with which Pompeius moved from one place to another—was the astonishment of his contemporaries and not the least among the causes of his success. The mind was like the body. His remarkable power of intuition revealed itself in the precision and practicability of all his arrangements, even where he gave orders without having seen with his own eyes. His memory was matchless, and it was easy for him to carry on several occupations simultaneously with equal self-possession. . . .

Caesar was thoroughly a realist and a man of sense; and whatever he undertook and achieved was pervaded and guided by the cool sobriety which constitutes the most marked peculiarity of his genius. To this he owed the power of living energetically in the present, undisturbed either by recollection or by expectation; to this he owed the capacity of acting at any moment with collected vigour, and of applying his whole genius even to the smallest and most incidental enterprise; to this he owed the many-sided power with which he grasped and mastered whatever understanding can comprehend and will can compel; to this he owed the self-possessed ease with which he arranged his periods as well as projected his campaigns; to this he owed the "marvellous serenity" which remained steadily with him through good and evil days; to this he owed the complete independence, which admitted of no control by favourite or by mistress, or even by friend. It resulted, moreover, from this clearness of judgment that Caesar never formed to himself illusions regarding the power of fate and the ability of man; in his case the friendly veil was lifted up, which conceals from man the inadequacy of his working. Prudently as he laid his plans and considered all possibilities, the feeling was never absent from his breast that in all things fortune, that is to say accident, must bestow success; and with this may be connected the circumstance that he so often played a desperate game with destiny, and in particular again and again hazarded his person with daring indifference. As indeed occasionally men of predominant sagacity betake themselves to a pure game of hazard, so there was in Caesar's rationalism a point at which it came in some measure into contact with mysticism.

Gifts such as these could not fail to produce a statesman. From early youth, accordingly, Caesar was a statesman in the deepest sense of the term, and his aim was the highest which man is allowed to propose to himself—the political, military, intellectual, and moral regeneration of his own deeply decayed nation, and of the still more deeply decayed Hellenic nation intimately akin to his own. The hard school of thirty years' experience changed his views as to the means by which this aim was to be reached; his aim itself remained the same in the times of his hopeless humiliation and of his unlimited plenitude of power, in the times when as demagogue and conspirator he stole towards it by paths of darkness, and in those when, as joint possessor of the supreme power and then as monarch, he worked at his task in the full light of day before the eyes of the world. . . . According to his original plan he had purposed to reach his object, like Pericles and Gaius Gracchus, without force of arms, and throughout eighteen years he had as leader of the popular party moved exclusively amid political plans and intrigues—until, reluctantly convinced of the necessity for a military support, he, when already forty years of age, put himself at the head of an army [59 B.C.]. . . .

The most remarkable peculiarity of his action as a statesman was its perfect harmony. In reality all the conditions for this most difficult of all human functions were united in Caesar. A thorough realist, he never allowed the images of the past or venerable tradition to disturb him; for him nothing was of value in politics but the living present and the law of reason, just as in his character of grammarian he set aside historical and antiquarian research and recognized nothing but on the one hand the living *usus loquendi* and on the other hand the rule of symmetry. A born ruler, he governed the minds of men as the wind drives the clouds, and compelled the most heterogeneous natures to place themselves at his service—the plain citizen and the rough subaltern, the genteel matrons of Rome and the fair princesses of Egypt and Mauretania, the brilliant cavalry-officer and the calculating banker. His talent for organization was marvellous; no statesman has ever compelled alliances, no general has ever collected an army out of unyielding and refractory elements with such decision, and kept them together with such firmness, as Caesar displayed in constraining and upholding his coalitions and his legions; never did regent judge his instruments and assign each to the place appropriate for him with so acute an eye.

He was monarch; but he never played the king. Even when absolute lord of Rome, he retained the deportment of the party-leader; perfectly pliant and smooth, easy and charming in conversation, complaisant towards every one, it seemed as if he wished to be nothing but the first among his peers. Caesar entirely avoided the blunder into which so many men otherwise on an equality with him have fallen, of carrying into politics the military tone of command; however much occasion his disagreeable relations with the senate gave for it, he never resorted to outrages. . . . Caesar was monarch; but he was never seized with the giddiness of the tyrant. He is perhaps the only one among the mighty ones of the earth, who in great matters and little never acted according to inclination or caprice, but always without exception according to his duty as ruler, and who, when he looked back on his life, found doubtless erroneous calculations to deplore, but no false step of passion to regret. There is nothing in the history of Caesar's life, which even on a small scale can be compared with those poetico-sensual ebullitions—such as the murder of Kleitos or the burning of Persepolis—which the history of his great predecessor in the east records. He is, in fine, perhaps the only one of those mighty ones, who has preserved to the end of his career the statesman's tact of discriminating between the possible and the impossible, and has not broken down in the task which for greatly gifted natures is the most difficult of all—the task of recognizing, when on the pinnacle of success, its natural limits. What was possible he performed, and never left the possible good undone for the sake of the impossible better, never disdained at least to mitigate by palliatives evils that were incurable. But where he recognized that fate had spoken, he always obeyed. . . .

Such was this unique man, whom it seems so easy and yet is so infinitely difficult to describe. His whole nature is transparent clearness; and tradition preserves more copious and more vivid information about him than about any of his peers in the ancient world. Of such a personage our conceptions may well vary in point of shallowness or depth, but they cannot be, strictly speaking, different; to every not utterly perverted inquirer the grand figure has exhibited the same essential features, and yet no one has succeeded in reproducing it to the life. The secret lies in its perfection. In his character as a man as well as in his place in history, Caesar occupies a position where the great contrasts of existence meet and balance each other. Of mighty creative power and yet at the same time of the most penetrating judgment; no longer a youth and not yet an old man; of the highest energy of will and the highest capacity of execution; filled with republican ideals and at the same time born to be a king; a Roman in the deepest essence of his nature, and yet called to reconcile and combine in himself as well as in the outer world the Roman and the Hellenic types of culture—Caesar was the entire and perfect man.

Caesar the Politician

RONALD SYME

The long-time Oxford professor Sir Ronald Syme is probably our leading ancient historian today. His most important book, and possibly the outstanding work in Roman history in this generation,[6] is The Roman Revolution. *Syme worked on this book through the late 1930s, against the backdrop of events taking place in Mommsen's Germany, but the vision of one-person rule was not quite as alluring to him as it had been to Mommsen. Syme's view of Caesar, however, was not only affected by the rise of Hitler and the political drift toward World War II. He had before him an impressive accumulation of scholarly research on the darker side of the Caesarian monarchy. Eduard Meyer's* Caesars Monarchie und das Principat des Pompejus *(1919) argues that Caesar aspired to the establishment of a Hellenistic monarchy in Rome. The second volume of Jerome Carcopino's* Histoire Romaine *(1936) deals with Caesar and maintains that, since his youth, Caesar's ambition was directed toward monarchy.*

Syme also read the important work of Matthias Gelzer—Die Nobilität der Römischen Republik (1912) and Caesar der Politiker und Staatsmann (1921)—which prompted him to examine some of the same ground, the social and political setting in which Caesar lived and died. Syme, like Gelzer, was especially interested in the senatorial oligarchy. The "Roman Revolution" of his title, he argues, occurred when this oligarchy lost its power to a new social group composed of people from all parts of Italy, even the provinces. And he saw Caesar as the political genius who began the revolution that he could not then control.

---

[6]Cf. the review, for example, of Michael Ginsburg in *American Historical Review,* 46 (1940), 108.

Syme insists that Caesar be judged—as he was murdered—"for what he was, not for what he might become," be that an oriental despot or a Hellenistic monarch. What Caesar was was a Roman aristocrat whose brilliance and luck enabled him to surpass his fellow aristocrats. The key event leading to his assassination was not his arrogance, which was common to his class and station, and not even his high-handedness in subverting the republic; it was the Caesarian dictatorship, prolonged first for ten years and then, in January of 44 B.C., for life, that was intolerable to the senatorial nobility and the cause of his murder.

The following, from The Roman Revolution, *is Syme's analysis of Caesar.*

The conquest of Gaul, the war against Pompeius and the establishment of the Dictatorship of Caesar are events that move in a harmony so swift and sure as to appear pre-ordained; and history has sometimes been written as though Caesar set the tune from the beginning, in the knowledge that monarchy was the panacea for the world's ills, and with the design to achieve it by armed force. Such a view is too simple to be historical.

Caesar strove to avert any resort to open war. Both before and after the outbreak of hostilities he sought to negotiate with Pompeius. Had Pompeius listened and consented to an interview, their old *amicitia* might have been repaired. With the nominal primacy of Pompeius recognized, Caesar and his adherents would capture the government—and perhaps reform the State. Caesar's enemies were afraid of that—and so was Pompeius. After long wavering Pompeius chose at last to save the oligarchy. Further, the proconsul's proposals as conveyed to the State were moderate and may not be dismissed as mere manoeuvres for position or for time to bring up his armies. Caesar knew how small was the party willing to provoke a war. As the artful motion of a Caesarian tribune had revealed, an overwhelming majority in the Senate, nearly four hundred against twenty-two, wished both dynasts to lay down their extraordinary commands. A rash and factious minority prevailed.

The precise legal points at issue in Caesar's claim to stand for the consulate in absence and retain his province until the end of the year 49 B.C. are still matters of controversy. If they were ever clear, debate and misrepresentation soon clouded truth and equity. The nature of the political crisis is less obscure. Caesar and his associates in power had thwarted or suspended the constitution for their own ends many times in the past. Exceptions had been made before in favour of other dynasts; and Caesar asserted both legal and moral rights to preferential treatment. In the last resort his rank, prestige and honour, summed up in the Latin word *dignitas*, were all at stake: to Caesar, as he claimed, "his *dignitas* had ever been dearer than life itself." Sooner than surrender it, Caesar appealed to arms. A constitutional pretext was provided by the violence of his adversaries: Caesar stood in defence of the rights of the tribunes and the liberties of the Roman People. But that was not the plea which Caesar himself valued most— it was his personal honour.

His enemies appeared to have triumphed. They had driven a wedge between the two dynasts, winning over to their side the power and prestige of Pompeius. They would be able to deal with Pompeius later. It might not come to open war; and Pompeius was still in their control so long as he was not at the head of an army in the field. Upon Caesar they had thrust the choice between civil war and political extinction. . . .

Caesar was constrained to appeal to his army for protection. At last the enemies of Caesar had succeeded in ensnaring Pompeius and in working the constitution against the craftiest politican of the day: he was declared a public enemy if he did not lay down his command before a certain day. By invoking constitutional sanctions against Caesar, a small faction misrepresented the true wishes of a vast majority in the Senate, in Rome, and in Italy. They pretended that the issue lay between a rebellious proconsul and legitimate authority. Such venturesome expedients are commonly the work of hot blood and muddled heads. The error was double and damning. Disillusion followed swiftly. Even Cato was dismayed. It had confidently been expected that the solid and respectable classes in the towns of Italy would rally in defence of the authority of the Senate and the liberties of the Roman People, that all the land would rise as one man against the invader. Nothing of the kind happened. Italy was apathetic to the war-cry of the Republic in danger, sceptical about its champions. . . .

Caesar, it is true, had only a legion to hand: the bulk of his army was still far away. But he swept down the eastern coast of Italy, gathering troops, momentum and confidence as he went. Within two months of the crossing of the Rubicon he was master of Italy. Pompeius made his escape across the Adriatic carrying with him several legions and a large number of senators, a grievous burden of revenge and recrimination. The enemies of Caesar had counted upon capitulation or a short and easy war.

They had lost the first round. Then a second blow, quite beyond calculation: before the summer was out the generals of Pompeius in Spain were outmanoeuvred and overcome. Yet even so, until the legions joined battle on the plain of Pharsalus, the odds lay heavily against Caesar. Fortune, the devotion of his veteran legionaries and the divided counsels of his adversaries secured the crowning victory.

But three years more of fighting were needed to stamp out the last and bitter resistance of the Pompeian cause in Africa and in Spain.

"They would have it thus," said Caesar as he gazed upon the Roman dead at Pharsalus, half in patriot grief for the havoc of civil war, half in impatience and resentment. They had cheated Caesar of the true glory of a Roman aristocrat—to contend with his peers for primacy, not to destroy them. His enemies had the laugh of him in death. Even Pharsalus was not the end. His former ally, the great Pompeius, glorious from victories in all quarters of the world, lay unburied on an Egyptian beach, slain by a renegade Roman, the hireling of a foreign king. Dead, too, and killed by Romans, were Caesar's rivals and enemies, many illustrious consulars. Ahenobarbus fought and fell at Pharsalus, and Q. Metellus Scipio ended worthy of his ancestors; while Cato chose to fall by his own hand rather than witness the domination of Caesar and the destruction of the Free State.

That was the nemesis of ambition and glory, to be thwarted in the end. After such wreckage, the task of rebuilding confronted him, stern and thankless. Without the sincere and patriotic co-operation of the governing class, the attempt would be all in vain, the mere creation of arbitrary power, doomed to perish in violence. . . .

Under these unfavourable auspices, a Sulla but for *clementia*, a Gracchus but lacking a revolutionary programme, Caesar established his Dictatorship. His rule began as the triumph of a faction in civil war: he made it his task to transcend faction, and in so doing wrought his own destruction. A champion of the People, he had to curb the People's rights, as Sulla had done. To rule, he needed the support of the *nobiles*, yet he had to curtail their privileges and repress their dangerous ambitions.

In name and function Caesar's office was to set the State in order again (*rei publicae constituendae*). Despite odious memories of Sulla, the choice of the Dictatorship was recommended by its comprehensive powers and freedom from the tribunician veto. Caesar knew that secret enemies would soon direct that deadly weapon against one who had used it with such dexterity in the past and who more recently claimed to be asserting the rights of the tribunes, the liberty of the Roman People. He was not mistaken. Yet he required special powers: after a civil war the need was patent. The Dictator's task might well demand several years. In 46 B.C. his powers were prolonged to a tenure of ten years, an ominous sign. A gleam of hope that the emergency period would be quite short flickered up for a moment, to wane at once and perish utterly. In January 44 B.C. Caesar was voted the Dictatorship for life. About the same time decrees of the Senate ordained that an oath of allegiance should be taken in his name. Was this the measure of his ordering of the Roman State? Was this a *res publica constituta*?

It was disquieting. Little had been done to repair the ravages of civil war and promote social regeneration. For that there was sore need, as both his adherents and his former adversaries pointed out. From Pompeius, from Cato and from the oligarchy, no hope of reform. But Caesar seemed different: he had consistently advocated the cause of the oppressed, whether Roman, Italian or provincial. He had shown that he was not afraid of vested interests. But Caesar was not a revolutionary. . . .

[He] postponed decision about the permanent ordering of the State. It was too difficult. Instead, he would set out for the wars again, to Macedonia and to the eastern frontier of the Empire. At Rome he was hampered: abroad he might enjoy his conscious mastery of men and events, as before in Gaul. Easy victories—but not the urgent needs of the Roman People.

About Caesar's ultimate designs there can be opinion, but no certainty. The acts and projects of his Dictatorship do not reveal them. For the rest, the evidence is partisan—or posthumous. No statement of unrealized intentions is a safe guide to history, for it is unverifiable and therefore the most attractive form of misrepresentation. The enemies of Caesar spread rumours to discredit the living Dictator: Caesar dead became a god and a myth, passing from the realm of history into literature and legend, declamation and propaganda. . . .

Yet speculation cannot be debarred from playing round the high and momentous theme of the last designs of Caesar the Dictator. It has been supposed and contended that Caesar either desired to establish or had actually inaugurated an institution unheard of in Rome and unimagined there—monarchic rule, despotic and absolute, based upon worship of the ruler, after the pattern of the monarchies of the Hellenistic East. Thus may Caesar be represented as the heir in all things of Alexander the Macedonian and as the anticipator of Caracalla, a king and a god incarnate, levelling class and nation, ruling a subject, united and uniform world by right divine.

This extreme simplification of long and diverse ages of history seems to suggest that Caesar alone of contemporary Roman statesmen possessed either a wide vision of the future or a singular and elementary blindness to the present. But this is only a Caesar of myth or rational construction. . . .

If Caesar must be judged, it is by facts and not by alleged intentions. As his acts and his writings reveal him, Caesar stands out as a realist and an opportunist. In the short time at his disposal he can hardly have made plans for a long future or laid the foundation of a consistent government. Whatever it might be, it would owe more to the needs of the moment than to alien or theoretical models. More important the business in hand; it was expedited in swift and arbitrary fashion. Caesar made plans and decisions in the company of his intimates and secretaries: the Senate voted but did not deliberate. As the Dictator was on the point of departing in the spring of 44 B.C. for several years of campaigning in the Balkans and the East, he tied up magistracies and provincial commands in advance by placing them, according to the traditional Roman way, in the hands of loyal partisans, or of reconciled Pompeians whose good sense should guarantee peace. For that period, at least, a salutary pause from political activity: with the lapse of time the situation might become clearer in one way or another. . . .

At the moment it was intolerable: the autocrat became impatient, annoyed by covert opposition, petty criticism and laudations of dead Cato. That he was unpopular he well knew. "For all his genius, Caesar could not see a way out," as one of his friends was subsequently to remark. And there was no going back. To Caesar's clear mind and love of rapid decision, this brought a tragic sense of impotence and frustration—he had been all things and it was no good. He had surpassed the good fortune of Sulla Felix and the glory of Pompeius Magnus. In vain—reckless ambition had ruined the Roman State and baffled itself in the end. Of the melancholy that descended upon Caesar there stands the best of testimony—"my life has been long enough, whether reckoned in years or in renown." The words were remembered. The most eloquent of his contemporaries did not disdain to plagiarize them.

The question of ultimate intentions becomes irrelevant. Caesar was slain for what he was, not for what he might become. . . .

It is not necessary to believe that Caesar planned to establish at Rome a "Hellenistic Monarchy," whatever meaning may attach to that phrase. The Dictatorship was enough. The rule of the *nobiles*, he could see, was an anachronism in a world-empire; and so was the power of the Roman plebs when all Italy enjoyed the franchise. Caesar in truth was more conservative and Roman than many have fancied; and no Roman conceived of government save through an oligarchy. But Caesar was being forced into an autocratic position. It meant the lasting domination of one man instead of the rule of the law, the constitution and the Senate; it announced the triumph soon or late of new forces and new ideas, the elevation of the army and the provinces, the depression of the traditional governing class. Caesar's autocracy appeared to be much more than a temporary expedient to liquidate the heritage of the Civil War and reinvigorate the organs of the Roman State. It was going to last—and the Roman aristocracy was not to be permitted to govern and exploit the Empire in its own fashion. The tragedies of history do not arise from the conflict of conventional right and wrong. They are more august and more complex. Caesar and Brutus each had right on his side. . . .

144 Makers of World History

Without a party a statesman is nothing. He sometimes forgets that awkward fact. If the leader or principal agent of a faction goes beyond the wishes of his allies and emancipates himself from control, he may have to be dropped or suppressed. . . .

When Caesar took the Dictatorship for life and the sworn allegiance of senators, it seemed clear that he had escaped from the shackles of party to supreme and personal rule. For this reason, certain of the most prominent of his adherents combined with Republicans and Pompeians to remove their leader. The Caesarian party thus split by the assassination of the Dictator none the less survived, joined for a few months with Republicans in a new and precarious front of security and vested interests led by the Dictator's political deputy until a new leader, emerging unexpected, at first tore it in pieces again, but ultimately, after conquering the last of his rivals, converted the old Caesarian party into a national government in a transformed State. The composition and vicissitudes of that party, though less dramatic in unity of theme than the careers and exploits of the successive leaders, will yet help to recall the ineffable complexities of authentic history.

Review and Study Questions

1. Compare Caesar with Alexander the Great.
2. Why was Caesar assassinated?
3. How did Caesar interpret the nature of his rule over the Roman Empire?
4. Caesar has been viewed as the assassin of the Republic. Do you agree? Why?

Suggestions for Further Reading

As in the case of Alexander, the ancient sources for the life of Julius Caesar are among the liveliest and most entertaining accounts of him. Students are encouraged to read the rest of Suetonius's sketch beyond what is excerpted in this chapter. They are also encouraged to read Plutarch's Life of Caesar, which, as we have noted, he wrote to be compared with his Life of Alexander. Plutarch and Suetonius between them give us most of the anecdotal matter commonly associated with Caesar. We have in addition, as also noted above, the considerable volume of Caesar's own writings in several attractive modern editions, *The Gallic War*, tr. and ed. Moses Hadas (New York: Modern Library, 1957), tr. J. Warrington (New York: Heritage, 1955), and tr. S.

A. Handford (Baltimore: Penguin, 1965); and *The Civil War,* ed. and tr. Jane F. Mitchell (Baltimore: Penguin, 1967). We also have references to Caesar scattered throughout the works of such contemporaries as Cicero and Sallust.

Caesar has always been a fascinating figure, and there are an impossibly large number of biographies of him. Two can be especially recommended to students. Probably the best brief biography is J. P. V. D. Balsdon, *Julius Caesar and Rome* (London: The English Universities Press, 1967), an authoritative work by an established authority, another in the excellent "Teach Yourself History Library" series. Students may prefer the somewhat larger and more lavish Michael Grant, *Caesar* (London: Weidenfeld and Nicolson, 1974), in the "Great Lives" series; it is interesting and readable as well as authoritative, another book by one of the best modern popularizers of ancient history. Zwi Yavetz, *Julius Caesar and his Public Image* (Ithaca, N.Y.: Cornell University Press, 1983) attempts to assess the various answers to the question of why Caesar was assassinated. Students will find the last chapter, "Public Opinion and the Ides of March," particularly useful as a summary and review of the problem.

There are also many books dealing with Caesar's era and the late Roman republic. One of the best of these, and one that combines the account of the man and the era, is Matthias Gelzer, *Caesar: Politician and Statesman,* tr. Peter Needham (Cambridge, Mass.: Harvard University Press, 1968). Despite its relentlessly prosaic quality, it is an important interpretive work by a great German scholar, stressing Caesar as a political figure of genius and paralleling the views of Sir Ronald Syme, which are represented in this chapter. A somewhat broader account, still considered a standard work by many authorities, is that of F. E. Adcock in chs. 15–17 in vol. 9 of the *Cambridge Ancient History* (Cambridge, England: Cambridge University Press, 1932). Also recommended are R. E. Smith, *The Failure of the Roman Republic* (Cambridge, England: Cambridge University Press, 1955); the somewhat more detailed Erich S. Gruen, *The Last Generation of the Roman Republic* (Berkeley: University of California Press, 1974); and the now famous small study by Lily Ross Taylor, *Party Politics in the Age of Caesar* (Berkeley: University of California Press, 1975 [1949]).

Finally, two special studies are recommended, the attractive small book by F. E. Adcock, *Caesar as Man of Letters* (Cambridge, England: Cambridge University Press, 1956), and Gen. John F. C. Fuller, *Julius Caesar: Man, Soldier, and Tyrant* (New Brunswick, N.J.: Rutgers University Press, 1965), a lively, opinionated, and somewhat debunking book by a great military historian about Caesar as a less-than-brilliant general.

MUHAMMAD: THE MESSENGER OF GOD

c. 570   Born
c. 595   Married Khadijah
c. 610   Beginning of his revelations
   622   The "Hegira" flight to Medina
   624   Battle of Badr
   630   Conquest of Mecca
   632   Died

Muhammad, who was to found one of the world's most widespread religions, was born in the Arabian town of Mecca in about 570. Mecca was one of a number of merchant communities that had sprung up along the Arabian shore of the Red Sea, on the main caravan route leading from the Persian Gulf and Yemen to Syria and the Mediterranean. Muhammad was the son of a respectable Meccan family, which most likely engaged in commerce but was not of the "inner" merchant aristocracy dominating the town. Little is known of Muhammad's early life except that he was orphaned; he was probably raised first by his grandfather and then by an uncle. It is probable that Muhammad engaged in commerce.

As in the case of every great religious leader, the figure of Muhammad has been obscured by a mass of pious tradition. We know that he married a rich widow, Khadijah, who was some years older than himself. Says the Koran, "Did not He [God] find thee needy, and suffice thee?" (93:6–8). Having been thus "sufficed," Muhammad assumed the management of a considerable estate and probably lived much like any other Meccan merchant.

When he was about forty, Muhammad received the earliest of a series of divine revelations upon which he based his religious teachings. There is no record of whether this revelation came as a result of an arduous spiritual search or as an unbidden insight. At first Muham-

147

mad confined his teaching to his family; then he extended it to friends. Eventually he began to preach more widely and openly, seeking converts whom he called Muslims, "submissive to God." In contrast to the polytheism then prevalent in Arabia, Muhammad recognized only one God, Allah, and spoke of himself as God's messenger or prophet. And, like the ancient Hebrew prophets, he condemned polytheism and idolatry.

His success was modest, but it was sufficient to alarm the merchant aristocracy of Mecca. In a society in which religion and politics were inseparable, the revolutionary nature of Muhammad's religious teachings implied the possibility of political unrest. And political unrest is a threat to commerce. Moreover, Mecca was not only an economic but also a religious center for the various gods of the desert people who came to trade there. In a shrine called the Kaaba were housed the sacred stones representing the primitive gods of the Arabic tribes, and this along with other shrines attracted pilgrims, and hence, business to Mecca. It is not surprising then that public opinion mobilized against this dangerous radical who, by his attack on idolatry and other beliefs, threatened both the prosperity and the religious status of his city. He had also begun to criticize the merchant leaders for their rapacity and lack of charity.

By 621 Muhammad and his followers were in dire circumstances. They were being bitterly persecuted. The chief of the Hashimite clan, to which Muhammad himself belonged and who had protected him, died, as did Muhammad's devoted wife Khadijah. He had even sent some eighty of his disciples to Abyssinia for their own protection. Then, suddenly, a change occurred. Two of the tribes of Yathrib, a city some three hundred miles to the north of Mecca, sent for Muhammad. Some of their members had heard him speak, and they now sought him as a "wise man" and mediator to bring peace among their warring clans and factions. His followers preceded him in small groups. Then Muhammad himself fled to his new home city, which he named Medinat un Nabi, "the City of the Prophet," soon shortened to Medina. This was the "Hegira," the flight, of the year 622. It was later considered to mark the beginning of Islam—appropriately enough, for it was in Medina that Islam first became a state and a culture. Ultimately it was to become a world empire and a world religion.

The Founding of Islam

IBN ISHAQ'S *SIRAT RASUL ALLAH*

Muhammad wrote nothing himself, and none of his early disciples or immediate successors left any written record of the prophet. He declared his revelations to his followers, many of whom knew them by heart. Some of the revelations were dictated or written down later, but at his death there was no one complete and authoritative text. It was only in the following generation that Muhammad's successors commanded that the revelations be collected "from palm branches and tablets of stone and the hearts of men." This was done by the chief secretary of the prophet, and by the year 651 the collection was completed. This was the Koran, "The Reading," the one sacred book of Islam.

While devout Muslims believe that every word of the Koran is the word of God, Muhammad was the prophet through whom God's word was revealed, and there are occasional references to him in it. But such scattered references do not constitute even the outline of a biography. The enormous collections of traditions (Hadith), or stories about Muhammad that began to be assembled even before his death, are almost useless as a source of reliable biographical detail. It is only in the eighth and ninth centuries, when formal biographies begin to appear, that we have sources on which to base a true biographical account. There are several of these, but the most comprehensive and reliable is the Sirat Rasul Allah *of Ibn Ishaq*—The Book of Campaigns and (the Prophet's) Biography.

Ibn Ishaq was born in Medina about 707 and died in Baghdad in 773. His account of Muhammad is based on interviews with eyewitnesses and other near contemporaries, and on other largely oral records and traditions. He subjected his sources to considerable skeptical scrutiny, often saying that his informant "alleged" something to be true or that God only knows whether a particular statement is true or not. He was regarded by his Arabic contemporaries as the "best informed man" about his subject: "Knowledge will remain in Medina as long as Ibn Ishaq lives." The eminent modern western authority Alfred Guillaume agrees: "He has given us the only systematic straightforward account of the life of Muhammad which, apart from legends and stories of miracles, deserves to be accepted as history in the full sense of the word."[1] His book was edited and preserved by another scholar, Abdul-Malik ibn Hisham, about a century later.

---

[1]A. Guillaume, "The Biography of the Prophet in Recent Research," *Islamic Quarterly* 1 (1954), 8.

We pick up his account with the events leading up to Muhammad's flight from Mecca to Medina.

When Quraysh[2] became insolent towards God and rejected His gracious purpose, accused His prophet of lying, and ill treated and exiled those who served Him and proclaimed His unity, believed in His prophet, and held fast to His religion, He gave permission to His apostle to fight and to protect himself against those who wronged them and treated them badly. . . .

When God had given permission to fight and this clan of the Anṣār[3] had pledged their support to him in Islam and to help him and his followers, and the Muslims who had taken refuge with them, the apostle commanded his companions, the emigrants of his people and those Muslims who were with him in Mecca, to emigrate to Medina and to link up with their brethren the Anṣār. 'God will make for you brethren and houses in which you may be safe.' So they went out in companies, and the apostle stayed in Mecca waiting for his Lord's permission to leave Mecca and migrate to Medina. . . . After his companions had left, the apostle stayed in Mecca waiting for permission to migrate. Except for Abū Bakr and 'Alī, none of his supporters were left but those under restraint and those who had been forced to apostatize. The former kept asking the apostle for permission to emigrate and he would answer, 'Don't be in a hurry; it may be that God will give you a companion.' Abū Bakr hoped that it would be Muhammad himself. . . .

Among the verses of the Quran which God sent down about that day . . . are: 'And when the unbelievers plot to shut thee up or to kill thee or to drive thee out they plot, but God plots also, and God is the best of plotters,' and 'Or they say he is a poet for whom we may expect the misfortune of fate. Say: Go on expecting for I am with you among the expectant.'

It was then that God gave permission to his prophet to migrate. Now Abū Bakr was a man of means, and at the time that he asked the apostle's permission to migrate and he replied 'Do not hurry; perhaps God will give you a companion,' hoping that the apostle meant himself he bought two camels and kept them tied up in his house supplying them with fodder in preparation for departure. . . .

---

[2]Quraysh (or Koreish), the name of the leading tribe in Mecca, is used to refer to the whole city's population.—Ed.

[3]This term means "helpers" and refers to those citizens of Medina who joined his cause.—Ed.

According to what I have been told none knew when the apostle left except 'Alī and Abū Bakr and the latter's family. I have heard that the apostle told 'Alī about his departure and ordered him to stay behind in Mecca in order to return goods which men had deposited with the apostle; for anyone in Mecca who had property which he was anxious about left it with him because of his notorious honesty and trustworthiness.

When the apostle decided to go he came to Abū Bakr and the two of them left by a window in the back of the latter's house and made for a cave on Thaur, a mountain below Mecca. . . .

The apostle ordered that a mosque should be built, and he stayed with Abū Ayyūb until the mosque and his houses were completed. The apostle joined in the work to encourage the Muslims to work and the *muhājirīn*[4] and the *anṣār* laboured hard. . . .

The apostle lived in Abū Ayyūb's house until his mosque and dwelling-houses were built; then he removed to his own quarters. . . .

The apostle stayed in Medina from the month of Rabī'u'l-awwal to Ṣafar of the following year until his mosque and his quarters were built. This tribe of the Anṣār all accepted Islam and every house of the Anṣār accepted Islam except Khaṭma, Wāqif, Wā'il, and Umayya who were the Aus Allah, a clan of Aus who clung to their heathenism.

The apostle wrote a document[5] concerning the emigrants and the helpers in which he made a friendly agreement with the Jews and established them in their religion and their property, and stated the reciprocal obligations, as follows: In the name of God the Compassionate, the Merciful. This is a document from Muhammad the prophet [governing the relations] between the believers and Muslims of Quraysh and Yathrib, and those who followed them and joined them and laboured with them. They are one community (*umma*) to the exclusion of all men. The Quraysh emigrants according to their present custom shall pay the bloodwit within their number and shall redeem their prisoners with the kindness and justice common among believers. . . .

A believer shall not take as an ally the freedman of another Muslim against him. The God-fearing believers shall be against the rebellious or him who seeks to spread injustice, or sin or enmity,

---

[4]This is another term for his followers from Mecca.—ED.

[5]This is the document known as the Constitution of Medina. It is reproduced and analyzed in W. Montgomery Watt, *Muhammad at Medina* (Oxford: The Clarendon Press, 1956), pp. 221 ff.—ED.

or corruption between believers; the hand of every man shall be against him even if he be a son of one of them. A believer shall not slay a believer for the sake of an unbeliever, nor shall he aid an unbeliever against a believer. God's protection is one, the least of them may give protection to a stranger on their behalf. Believers are friends one to the other to the exclusion of outsiders. To the Jew who follows us belong help and equality. He shall not be wronged nor shall his enemies be aided. The peace of the believers is indivisible. No separate peace shall be made when believers are fighting in the way of God. Conditions must be fair and equitable to all. In every foray a rider must take another behind him. The believers must avenge the blood of one another shed in the way of God. The God-fearing believers enjoy the best and most upright guidance. No polytheist shall take the property or person of Quraysh under his protection nor shall he intervene against a believer. Whosoever is convicted of killing a believer without good reason shall be subject to retaliation unless the next of kin is satisfied (with blood-money), and the believers shall be against him as one man, and they are bound to take action against him.

It shall not be lawful to a believer who holds by what is in this document and believes in God and the last day to help an evil-doer or to shelter him. The curse of God and His anger on the day of resurrection will be upon him if he does, and neither repentance nor ransom will be received from him. Whenever you differ about a matter it must be referred to God and to Muhammad.

The Jews shall contribute to the cost of war so long as they are fighting alongside the believers. The Jews of the B. 'Auf are one community with the believers (the Jews have their religion and the Muslims have theirs), their freedmen and their persons except those who behave unjustly and sinfully, for they hurt but themselves and their families. The same applies to the Jews of the B. al-Najjār, B. al-Ḥārith, B. Sā'ida, B. Jusham, B. al-Aus, B. Tha'laba, and the Jafna, a clan of the Tha'laba and the B. al-Shuṭayba. Loyalty is a protection against treachery. The freedmen of Tha'laba are as themselves. The close friends of the Jews are as themselves. None of them shall go out to war save with the permission of Muhammad, but he shall not be prevented from taking revenge for a wound. He who slays a man without warning slays himself and his household, unless it be one who has wronged him, for God will accept that. The Jews must bear their expenses and the Muslims their expenses. Each must help the other against anyone who attacks the people of this document. They must seek mutual advice and consultation, and loyalty is a protection against treachery. A man is not liable for his ally's misdeeds. The wronged must be helped. The Jews must pay with the believers so long as war lasts. Yathrib shall be a sanctuary for the people of this document. A stranger under protection shall be as his host doing no harm and committing no crime. A woman shall only be given protection with the consent of her family. If any dispute or controversy likely to cause trouble should arise it must be referred to God and to Muhammad the apostle of God. God accepts what is nearest to piety and goodness in this document. Quraysh and their helpers shall not be given protection. The contracting parties are bound to help one another against any attack on Yathrib. If they are called to make peace and maintain it they must do so; and if they make a similar demand on the Muslims it must be carried out except in the case of a holy war. Every one shall have his portion from the side to which he belongs, the Jews of al-Aus, their freedmen and themselves have the same standing with the people of this document in pure loyalty from the people of this document.

Loyalty is a protection against treachery: He who acquires aught acquires it for himself. God approves of this document. This deed will not protect the unjust and the sinner. The man who goes forth to fight and the man who stays at home in the city is safe unless he has been unjust and sinned. God is the protector of the good and God-fearing man and Muhammad is the apostle of God. . . .

The apostle instituted brotherhood between his fellow emigrants and the helpers, and he said according to what I have heard—and I appeal to God lest I should attribute to him words that he did not say—'Let each of you take a brother in God.' He himself took 'Alī by the hand and said, 'This is my brother.' So God's apostle, the lord of the sent ones and leader of the God-fearing, apostle of the Lord of the worlds, the peerless and unequalled, and 'Alī b. Abū Ṭālib became brothers. . . .

When the apostle was firmly settled in Medina and his brethren the emigrants were gathered to him and the affairs of the helpers were arranged Islam became firmly established. Prayer was instituted, the alms tax and fasting were prescribed, legal punishments fixed, the forbidden and the permitted prescribed, and Islam took up its abode with them. It was this clan of the helpers who 'have taken up their abode (in the city of the prophet) and in the faith.' When the apostle first came, the people gathered to him for prayer at the appointed times without being summoned. At first the apostle thought of using a trumpet like that of the Jews who used it to summon to prayer. Afterwards he disliked the idea and ordered a clapper to be made, so it was duly fashioned to be beaten when the Muslims should pray.

The Prophet and the True Believer

SAYED AMEER ALI

*From the time of Ibn Ishaq to the present, Muslim biographers have contin-
ued to write about Muhammad's life, and their accounts have tended to be
uncritical and adulatory of the prophet—as do all such apologetic works.
Nevertheless, these biographies form one of the strands making up the tradition of Islam. One of the most widely accepted of them is Sayed Ameer Ali,*
The Spirit of Islam: A History of the Evolution and Ideals of Islam, with a Life of the Prophet, *rev. ed. (London: Chatto and Windus,
1978 [1891].* Sayed Ameer Ali *was an English-trained Indian lawyer and
judge in Bengal, and a devout Muslim. He was a prolific writer; some of
his books dealt with his profession—he was an authority on the law of
evidence—but most of them dealt with Islam. In 1873 he published* Critical Examination of the Life and Teachings of Mohammed, *in 1880*
Personal Law of the Mohammedans, *in 1893* The Ethics of Islam,
and in 1899 A Short History of the Saracens. *But his best-known book
was* The Spirit of Islam, *from which the following passage is excerpted.*

*The passage deals with Muhammad's consolidation of his position in Me-
dina, his work as a political leader and administrator, and his actions as
the head of his new religion. It also deals with the increasing hostility between Muhammad and the important Jewish community of Medina. The
reader should note, in the account, the pervasive tone of harshness toward
the Jews, their actions, and their motives; the unfailing clemency of Muhammad; and even the intervention of angelic forces on the side of Islam at the
Battle of Badr.*

At this time there were three distinct parties in Medîna. The
Muhâjirîn (the Exiles) and the Ansâr (the Helpers) formed the kernel
of Islâm. Their devotion to the Prophet was unbounded. . . .

But the Jews, who may be said to have formed the third party,
constituted the most serious element of danger. They had close business relations with the Koreish, and their ramifications extended into
various parts hostile to the Faith. At first they were inclined to look
with some favour on the preachings of Mohammed. He could not, of
course, be their promised Messiah, but perhaps a weak dreamer, a
humble preacher, dependent upon the hospitality of their old enemies, now their patrons, the Aus and the Khazraj, might become their

avenger, help them in conquering the Arabs, and found for them a new kingdom of Judah. With this aim in view, they had joined with the Medinites in a half-hearted welcome to the Prophet. And for a time they maintained a pacific attitude. But it was only for a time; for barely a month had gone by before the old spirit of rebellion, which had led them to crucify their prophets, found vent in open seditions and secret treachery. One of the first acts of Mohammed after his arrival in Medîna was to weld together the heterogeneous and conflicting elements of which the city and its suburbs were composed, into an orderly confederation. With this object he had granted a charter to the people, by which the rights and obligations of the Moslems *inter se,* and of the Moslems and Jews, were clearly defined. And the Jews, borne down for the moment by the irresistible character of the movement, had gladly accepted the Pact. . . .

No kindness or generosity, however, on the part of the Prophet would satisfy the Jews; nothing could conciliate the bitter feelings with which they were animated. Enraged that they could not use him as their instrument for the conversion of Arabia to Judaism, and that his belief was so much simpler than their Talmudic legends, they soon broke off, and ranged themselves on the side of the enemies of the new Faith. And when asked which they preferred, idolatry or Islâm, they, like many Christian controversialists, declared they preferred idolatry, with all its attendant evils, to the creed of Mohammed. . . .

And now came the moment of severest trial to Islâm. Barely had the Prophet time to put the city in a state of defence and organise the Believers, before the blow descended upon him. Medîna itself was honeycombed by sedition and treachery. And it became the duty of Mohammed to take serious measures to guard against that dreaded catastrophe which a rising within, or a sudden attack from without, would have entailed upon his followers. He was not simply a preacher of Islâm; he was also the guardian of the lives and liberties of his people. As a Prophet, he could afford to ignore the revilings and the gibes of his enemies; but as the head of the State, "the general in a time of almost continual warfare," when Medîna was kept in a state of military defence and under a sort of military discipline, he could not overlook treachery. He was bound by his duty to his subjects to suppress a party that might have led, and almost did lead to the sack of the city by investing armies. The safety of the State required the proscription of the traitors, who were either sowing the seeds of sedition within Medîna or carrying information to the common enemy. Some half a dozen were placed under the ban, outlawed, and executed. We are, however, anticipating the course of events in referring to these executions.

The Koreish army was afield before Mohammed received God's command to do battle to His enemies.

He who never in his life had wielded a weapon, to whom the sight of human suffering caused intense pain and pity, and who, against all the canons of Arab manliness, wept bitterly at the loss of his children or disciples, whose character ever remained so tender and so pathetic as to cause his enemies to call him womanish,—this man was now compelled, from the necessities of the situation, and against his own inclination, to repel the attacks of the enemy by force of arms, to organise his followers for purposes of self-defence, and often to send out expeditions to anticipate treacherous and sudden onslaughts. Hitherto, Arab warfare consisted of sudden and murderous forays, often made in the night or in the early morn; isolated combats or a general melée, when the attacked were aware of the designs of the attacking party. Mohammed, with a thorough knowledge of the habits of his people, had frequently to guard against these sudden onslaughts by sending forth reconnoitring parties.

The Meccans and their allies commenced raiding up to the very vicinity of Medîna, destroying the fruit-trees of the Moslems, and carrying away their flocks. A force, consisting of a thousand well-equipped men, marched under the noted Abû Jahl, "the Father of Ignorance," towards Medîna to destroy the Moslems, and to protect one of their caravans bringing munitions of war. The Moslems received timely notice of the movement, and a body of three hundred disciples proceeded at once to forestall the heathens by occupying the valley of Badr, upon which Abû Jahl was moving. When Mohammed saw the infidel army arrogantly advancing into the valley, raising his hands towards heaven, like the prophets of Israel, he prayed that the little band of the Faithful might not be destroyed: "O Lord, forget not Thy promise of assistance. O Lord, if this little band were to perish, there will be none to offer unto Thee pure worship."

Three of the Koreish advanced into the open space which divided the Moslems from the idolaters, and, according to Arab usage, challenged three champions from the Moslem ranks to single combat. Hamza, Ali, and Obaidah accepted the challenge, and came out conquerors. The engagement then became general. At one time the fortunes of the field wavered, but Mohammed's appeal to his people decided the fate of the battle. "It was a stormy winter day. A piercing blast swept across the valley." It seemed as if the angels of heaven were warring for the Moslems. Indeed, to the earnest minds of Mohammed and his followers, who, like the early Christians, saw God's providence "in all the gifts of nature, in every relation of life, at each turn of their affairs, individual or public,"—to them those blasts of wind and sand, the elements warring against the enemies of God, at that critical moment appeared veritable succour sent from heaven; as angels riding on the wings of the wind, and driving the faithless idolaters before them in confusion. The Meccans were driven back with great loss; many of their chiefs were slain; and Abû Jahl fell a victim to his unruly pride. . . .

The remarkable circumstances which led to the victory of Badr, and the results which followed from it, made a deep impression on the minds of the Moslems. They firmly believed that the angels of heaven had battled on their side against the unbelieving host. . . .

The defeat of the idolaters at Badr was felt as keenly by the Jews as by the Meccans. Immediately after this battle a distinguished member of their race, called Ka'b, the son of Ashraf, belonging to the tribe of Nazîr, publicly deploring the ill-success of the idolaters, proceeded towards Mecca. Finding the people there plunged in grief, he spared no exertion to revive their courage. . . . His acts were openly directed against the commonwealth of which he was a member. He belonged to a tribe which had entered into the Compact with the Moslems, and pledged itself for the internal as well as the external safety of the State. Another Jew of the Nazîr, Abû Râf'e Sallâm, son of Abu'l Hukaik, was equally wild and bitter against the Musulmans. He inhabited, with a fraction of his tribe, the territories of Khaibar, four or five days' journey to the north-west of Medîna. Detesting Mohammed and the Musulmans, he made use of every endeavour to excite the neighbouring Arab tribes, such as the Sulaim and the Ghatafân, against them. It was impossible for the Musulman Commonwealth to tolerate this open treachery on the part of those to whom every consideration had been shown, with the object of securing their neutrality, if not their support. The very existence of the Moslem community was at stake; and every principle of safety required that these traitorous designs should be quietly frustrated. The sentence of outlawry was executed upon them by the Medinites themselves—in one case by a member of the tribe of Aus, in the other by a Khazrajite. . . . The Jews had openly and knowingly infringed the terms of their compact. It was necessary to put a stop to this with a firm hand, or farewell to all hope of peace and security. Consequently Mohammed proceeded at once to the quarter of the Banî-Kainukâ', and required them to enter definitely into the Moslem Commonwealth by embracing Islâm, or to vacate Medîna. The reply of the Jews was couched in the most offensive terms. "O, Mohammed, do not be elated with the victory over thy people (the Koreish). Thou hast had an affair with men ignorant of the art of war. If thou art desirous of having any dealings with us, we shall show thee that we are men." They then shut themselves up in their fortress, and set Mohammed's authority at defiance. But their reduction was an absolute duty, and siege was accordingly laid to their stronghold without loss of time. After fifteen days they surrendered. At first it was intended to inflict some severe punishment on them, but the clemency of Mohammed's nature overcame the dictates of justice, and the Banî-Kainukâ' were simply banished.

A Western Assessment of Muhammad

WILLIAM MONTGOMERY WATT

In Medina, Muhammad made himself the head of a growing politico-religious movement. In 630 he was able to conquer Mecca and to make the city of his birth the permanent center of Islam. Two years later Muhammad died. He had formed the scattered polyglot of Arab tribes into an Arab nation and armed it with a powerful new religion.

In the course of the next generation Islam exploded out of the Near East to become a world political force. Arab armies defeated the Byzantines in Syria and Asia Minor. They swept away the weak structures of Byzantine authority in North Africa and, within a century, they had established themselves facing the western Christians in Spain and along the shores of the Mediterranean. It was in the ensuing long period of confrontation that the traditional suspicion and hostility between Islam and the West developed.

If the Muslim biographical tradition of Muhammad has been adulatory and uncritical, the western tradition has been equally unrestrained in its hostility toward him, beginning with the accounts of the twelfth century that picture him as Mahound "the great enemy," "the prince of darkness." Although it moderated somewhat over time, the fundamental hostility of this western view persisted well into the nineteenth century. Indeed, it has only been in the last generation that western scholars have seriously turned to the task of creating a reliable and sympathetic picture of the prophet of Islam.

One of the leading figures in this revisionist revolution has been William Montgomery Watt, from whose most important book, Muhammad at Medina, *the following passage is taken. Watt is Professor of Arabic and Islamic Studies at the University of Edinburgh and past chairman of the Association of British Orientalists. It has been his life's work "to reach an objective view of Muhammad's character," as a precondition for meaningful understanding between the Muslim world and our own.*

Several accounts have been preserved of the appearance of Muḥammad, and, as they largely agree, they are perhaps near the truth, though there is a tendency in some of them to paint a picture of the ideal man. According to these accounts Muḥammad was of average height or a little above the average. His chest and shoulders were broad, and altogether he was of a sturdy build. His arms, or perhaps rather forearms, were long, and his hands and feet rough. His forehead was large and prominent, and he had a hooked nose and large black eyes with a touch of brown. The hair of his head was long and thick, straight or slightly curled. His beard also was thick, and he had a thin line of fine hair on his neck and chest. His cheeks were spare, his mouth large, and he had a pleasant smile. In complexion he was fair. He always walked as if he were rushing downhill, and others had difficulty in keeping up with him. When he turned in any direction, he did so with his whole body.

He was given to sadness, and there were long periods of silence when he was deep in thought; yet he never rested but was always busy with something. He never spoke unnecessarily. What he said was always to the point and sufficient to make his meaning clear, but there was no padding. From first to last he spoke rapidly. Over his feelings he had a firm control. When he was annoyed he would turn aside; when he was pleased, he lowered his eyes. His time was carefully apportioned according to the various demands on him. In his dealings with people he was above all tactful. He could be severe at times, but in the main he was not rough but gentle. His laugh was mostly a smile.

There are many stories illustrating his gentleness and tenderness of feeling. Even if some of them are not true, the probability is that the general picture is sound. There seems to be no reason, for instance, for doubting the truth of the story of how he broke the news of the death of Ja'far b. Abī Ṭālib to his widow Asmā' bint 'Umays; the story is said to have been told by Asmā' herself to her grand-daughter. She had been busy one morning with her household duties, which had included tanning forty hides and kneading dough, when Muḥammad called. She collected her children—she had three sons by Ja'far—washed their faces and anointed them. When Muḥammad entered, he asked for the sons of Ja'far. She brought them, and Muḥammad put his arms round them and smelt them (as a mother would a baby). Then his eyes filled with tears and he burst out weeping. 'Have you heard something about Ja'far?', she asked, and he told her that he had been killed. Later he instructed some of his people to prepare food for Ja'far's household, 'for they are too busy today to think about themselves'. About the same time the little daughter of Zayd b. Ḥārithah (who had been killed along with Ja'far) came to him in tears to be comforted, and he wept along with her; afterwards, when questioned about this, he said it was because of the great love between Zayd and himself. The memory of his first wife Khadījah could also soften his heart. After Badr the husband of his daughter Zaynab was among the prisoners taken by the Muslims, and Zaynab sent a necklace of Khadījah's to Muḥammad for a ransom, but he was so moved at the sight of it that he set the man free without payment.

Muḥammad seems to have felt especial tenderness towards children, and to have got on well with them. Perhaps it was an expression of the yearning of a man who had seen all his sons die in infancy. Much of his paternal affection went to his adopted son Zayd, who has just been mentioned. . . .

He was able to enter into the spirit of childish games and had many friends among children. 'Ā'ishah was still a child when he married her, and she continued to play with her toys. He would ask her what they were. 'Solomon's horses', she replied, and Muḥammad smiled. . . . His kindness extended even to animals, and this is something remarkable for Muḥammad's century and part of the world. As his men marched towards Mecca just before the conquest they passed a bitch with puppies, and Muḥammad not merely gave orders that they were not to be disturbed, but posted a man to see that the orders were carried out. . . .

These are interesting sidelights on the personality of Muḥammad, and fill out the picture of him we form from his conduct of public affairs. He gained men's respect and confidence by the religious basis of his activity and by such qualities as courage, resoluteness, impartiality, firmness inclining to severity but tempered by generosity. In addition to these, however, he had a charm of manner which won their affection and secured their devotion.

Of all the world's great men none has been so much maligned as Muḥammad. It is easy to see how this has come about. For centuries Islam was the great enemy of Christendom, for Christendom was in direct contact with no other organized states comparable in power to the Muslims. . . . The aim of the present discussion is to work towards a more objective attitude with regard to the moral criticisms inherited from medieval times. The main points are three. Muḥammad has been alleged to be insincere, to be sensual, and to be treacherous.

The allegation of insincerity or imposture was vigorously attacked by Thomas Carlyle over a hundred years ago, has been increasingly opposed by scholarly opinion since then, and yet is still sometimes made. The extreme form of the view was that Muḥammad did not believe in his revelations and did not in any sense receive them from 'outside himself', but deliberately composed them, and then published them in such a way as to deceive people into following him, so gaining power to satisfy his ambition and his lust. Such a view is incredible. Above all it gives no satisfying explanation of Muḥammad's readiness to endure hardship in his Meccan days, of the respect in which he was held by men of high intelligence and upright character, and of his success in founding a world religion which has produced men of undoubted saintliness. These matters can only be satisfactorily explained and understood on the assumption that Muḥammad was sincere, that is, that he genuinely believed that what we now know as the Qur'ān was not the product of his own mind, but came to him from God and was true. . . .

When we come to the other two allegations, however, namely, that Muḥammad was morally defective in that he was treacherous and sensual, the discussion has to embrace not merely factual points, but also the question of the standard by which the acts have to be judged. . . .

The allegation of treachery may be taken to cover a number of criticisms made by European writers. It applies most clearly to such acts as the breaking of his agreements with the Jews and his one-sided denunciation of the treaty of al-Ḥudaybiyah with the Meccans. It may also, however, be taken to include the infringement either of the sacred month or of the sacred territory on the expedition to Nakhlah when the first Meccan blood was shed, the mass execution of the Jewish clan of Qurayẓah, and the orders or encouragement given to his followers to remove dangerous opponents by assassination. . . .

Now the Islamic community or *ummah* was thought of as a tribe. Towards tribes with which it had agreements, it had duties and obligations, and these were scrupulously observed according to the standards of the day; Muḥammad even paid blood-money to a man who was really but not technically responsible for the death of several Muslims. Where a tribe was at war with the Muslims, however, or had no agreement, they had no obligations towards it even of what we would call common decency. If contemporaries showed some surprise at the execution of all the males of Qurayẓah, it was because Muḥammad was not afraid of any consequences of such an act; the behaviour of Qurayẓah during the siege of Medina was regarded as having cancelled their agreement with Muḥammad. Similarly, the terms of the treaty of al-Ḥudaybiyah had been broken by the Meccans before Muḥammad denounced it, and the individuals who were assassinated had forfeited any claim to friendly treatment by Muḥammad through their propaganda against him. So far were the Muslims who killed them from feeling any qualms that one of them, describing the return from the deed, wrote that they returned with the head of their victim 'five honourable men, steady and true, and God was the sixth with us'. This is so much in keeping with the spirit of pre-Islamic times that it is almost certainly authentic; but, even if not, it shows the attitude of the early Muslims. . . .

Again, the common European and Christian criticism that Muḥammad was a sensualist or, in the blunter language of the seventeenth century, an 'old lecher', fades away when examined in the light of the standards of Muḥammad's time. There was a strain in early Muslim thought which tended to magnify the common—or perhaps we should say 'superhuman'—humanity of their prophet. There is even a tradition to the effect that his virility was such that he was able to satisfy all his wives in a single night. This looks like an invention, for the usual account is that he gave his wives a night each in turn, but it shows the outlook of some at least of his followers.[6] The early Muslims looked askance at celibacy and checked any movements towards it, and even rigorous ascetics in Islam have commonly been married. . . .

In general, then, there was nothing in Muḥammad's marital relationships which his contemporaries regarded as incompatible with his prophethood. They did not consider him a voluptuary any more than they considered him a scoundrel. The sources record criticisms of him, but these are based on no moral criterion, but on a conservatism which was akin to superstition. Though later Muslims might produce colourful stories of Muḥammad's susceptibility to feminine charm, and though there is no reason to suppose that he disregarded the factor of physical attraction, it is practically certain that he had his feelings towards the fair sex well under control, and that he did not enter into marriages except when they were politically and socially desirable.

It is possible, too, to go further and, while restricting oneself to the standpoint of Muḥammad's time, to turn the alleged instances of treachery and sensuality into matter for praise. In his day and generation Muḥammad was a social reformer, indeed a reformer even in the sphere of morals. He created a new system of social security and a new family structure, both of which were a vast improvement on what went before. In this way he adapted for settled communities all that was best in the morality of the nomad, and established a religious and social framework for the life of a sixth of the human race today. That is not the work of a traitor or a lecher. . . .

Circumstances of place and time favoured Muḥammad. Various forces combined to set the stage for his life-work and for the subsequent expansion of Islam. . . . There was nothing inevitable or automatic about the spread of the Arabs and the growth of the Islamic community. But for a remarkable combination of qualities in Muḥammad it is improbable that the expansion would have taken place, and these vast forces might easily have spent themselves in raids on Syria and 'Irāq without any lasting consequences. In particular we may

---

[6]Muhammad had eleven wives in all.—ED.

distinguish three great gifts Muḥammad had, each of which was indispensable to the total achievement.

First there is what may be called his gift as a seer. Through him—or, on the orthodox Muslim view, through the revelations made to him—the Arab world was given an ideological framework within which the resolution of its social tensions became possible. The provision of such a framework involved both insight into the fundamental causes of the social malaise of the time, and the genius to express this insight in a form which would stir the hearer to the depths of his being. The European reader may be 'put off' by the Qur'ān, but it was admirably suited to the needs and conditions of the day.

Secondly, there is Muḥammad's wisdom as a statesman. The conceptual structure found in the Qur'ān was merely a framework. The framework had to support a building of concrete policies and concrete institutions. . . . His wisdom in these matters is shown by the rapid expansion of his small state to a world-empire and by the adaptation of his social institutions to many different environments and their continuance for thirteen centuries.

Thirdly, there is his skill and tact as an administrator and his wisdom in the choice of men to whom to delegate administrative details. Sound institutions and a sound policy will not go far if the execution of affairs is faulty and fumbling. When Muḥammad died, the state he had founded was a 'going concern', able to withstand the shock of his removal and, once it had recovered from this shock, to expand at prodigious speed.

Review and Study Questions

1. What sort of man was Muhammad? Compare him with (a) the Buddha, (b) Confucius, (c) Jesus Christ.

2. What was the role of the Jews of Medina in the early history of Islam?

3. What was the nature of the community Muhammad established?

Suggestions for Further Reading

The contemporary and near-contemporary sources for the life of Muhammad present all the difficulties already referred to and more. While limited as a biographic source, the *Koran* ought to be sampled by interested students. Of the several available English translations, the best and the one that comes closest to conveying the impression made on Muslims by the original is *The Koran Interpreted,* a translation by Arthur J. Arberry (New York: Macmillan, 1955), although the standard edition is probably still *The Koran,* tr. J. M. Rodwell (London and New York: J. M. Dent and E. P. Dutton, Everyman's Library, 1909). Another alternative edition is *The Qur'an,* tr. Richard Bell (Edinburgh: T. and T. Clark, 1937–39). A useful work is W. Montgomery Watt, *Companion to the Qur'an* (London: Allen and Unwin, 1967).

Alfred Guillaume, *The Traditions of Islam* (New York: Books for Libraries—Arno Press, 1980) is devoted to the Hadith, the traditional sayings and anecdotes about Muhammad, and includes a substantial selection from them. Of the early biographies of Muhammad, students may read further from Ibn Ishaq's *Sirat Rasul Allah* in *The Life of Muhammad, A Translation of Ishaq's Sirat Rasul Allah,* intro. A. Guillaume (Lahore, Karachi, Dacca: Oxford University Press Pakistan Branch, 1970 [1955]), excerpted for this chapter. Another early work is al-Waqidi's *Maghazi,* ed. J. M. B. Jones, dealing extensively with Muhammad's military campaigns and his relations with the people of Medina and the surrounding tribes. A good critique of the early historical sources is A. Guillaume, "The Biography of the Prophet in Recent Research," *Islamic Quarterly,* 1 (1954), 5–11.

Of the traditional Muslim biographies of Muhammad, in addition to Sayed Ameer Ali, *The Spirit of Islam: A History of the Evolution and Ideals of Islam, with a Life of the Prophet,* rev. ed. (London: Chatto and Windus, 1978 [1891]), a simple and straightforward example is Muhammad Zafrulla Khan, *Muhammad: Seal of the Prophets* (London: Routledge and Kegan Paul, 1980), whose aim is to help "a seeker after truth to determine whether he was truly the divine instrument chosen for the regeneration of mankind through the ages." A somewhat more sophisticated example is Muhammad Husayn Haykal, *The Life of Mohammed,* best sampled in the extensive excerpts in a critical work, Antonie Wessels, *A Modern Arabic Biography of Muhammad, A Critical Study of Muhammad Husayn Haykal's Hayat Muhammad* (Leiden: Brill, 1972).

Among the best modern western critical biographies of Muhammad is W. Montgomery Watt, *Muhammad at Medina* (Oxford: The Clarendon Press, 1956), excerpted for this chapter. It needs to be read, however, along with his earlier companion volume, *Muhammad at Mecca* (Oxford: The Clarendon Press, 1953). The material in both these books is condensed in a smaller volume by Watt, *Muhammad Prophet and Statesman* (Oxford: Oxford University Press, 1961). Maxime Rodinson, *Mohammed,* tr. Anne Carter (New York: Pantheon, 1971) is an excellent work by an able French scholar who, however, is more interested in the ideology of Islam than in its prophet. Two interesting works, both by British military men who spent their lives in the Near East and both popular laymen's biographies, are R. V. C. Bodley, *The Messenger: The Life of Mohammed* (New York: Greenwood Press, 1946) and John Bagot Glubb, *The Life and Times of Muhammad* (New York: Stein and Day, 1970).

Among the many general works on the history and culture of the Islamic world, two in particular are recommended: Philip K. Hitti, *History of the Arabs, From the Earliest Times to the Present*, 5th ed. rev. (London: Macmillan, 1953) and Bernard Lewis, *The Arabs in History*, 3rd ed. (London: Hutchinson, 1964). Recommended also is *The Cambridge History of Islam*, 4 vols. (Cambridge: Cambridge University Press, 1979), especially vols. I and IA.

MURASAKI SHIKIBU: THE LADY OF THE SHINING PRINCE

c. 973	Born
c. 998	Married
1001	Widowed
1005–6	Entered the service of the Empress Shoshi
c. 1010	Completed most of *The Tale of Genji*
c. 1026	Died

The greatest work of Japanese prose literature, the earliest novel in any language, and one of the great novels of world literature, *The Tale of Genji,* was written by a woman, the Lady Murasaki Shikibu, in the early eleventh century. Even more remarkably, the culture of the Heian Age, to which she belonged—one of the most important periods of Japanese history—was almost totally dominated by women like Murasaki. This situation, nearly unique in the course of Japanese history, resulted from a peculiar constellation of events.

Early Japan was shaped by the older, richer culture of China. In late prehistoric times, elements of Chinese culture, including the fabrication of iron and bronze and the wet cultivation of rice, began to spread to Korea and Japan. By the fifth century A.D. Japan was ruled by a hereditary imperial dynasty, the Yamato. In the following century two important influences were introduced into Japan, both from China. One was the structural notion of central government, with its hierarchies of court ranks; the other was Buddhism. In the early eighth century the Japanese—again on the model of China—built their first capital city, at Nara. Within less than a century the capital was moved to Kyoto, where it remained for more than a thousand years. It was called Heian-kyo, "the capital of peace and tranquility," and it became a brilliant center of art and culture.

The emperor was the cultural leader of the emerging Japanese society, the focal point of its empire and its religion, and the central figure of its elaborate court pageantry; but the real political authority of the nation was in the hands of a powerful family, the Fujiwara clan. The Fujiwara ruled not as emperors but as regents, and their influence was exercised through the women of their clan, whom they strategically placed as consorts of the emperor and wives of members of the imperial family. The Fujiwara regents actively encouraged the further development of the rich, patterned society of the court, in which the emperor spent his life performing elaborate rituals and acting as the central figure in the equally elaborate religious festivals designed to assure the continued welfare of the state.

This highly artificial court society reached its zenith in the so-called Heian Age, from the tenth to the twelfth century. The daughters of the Fujiwara, as consorts of successive emperors and wives of other imperial figures, took a leading role. They surrounded themselves with other talented women who vied with one another in learning and religious observance, in poetic composition, and in fine writing.

Earlier Japanese writing had been completely dominated by Chinese influence, and all the serious literature and records of Japan—histories, chronicles, works of geography and law, and official documents—were written in a cumbersome, adapted Chinese script. Further, they were written exclusively by male scholars; women were not considered sufficiently intelligent to learn the Chinese script. Instead, the native Japanese language was relegated to the use of women, in a script called *Kana* that had been developed in the ninth century. It was even called "women's writing." Ironically, while the laborious and tedious works of their male contemporaries have virtually disappeared, the works of "women's writing" survive to depict for us their society and the activities of their lives in letters, diaries, poems, stories, and in *The Tale of Genji,* the masterpiece of the Heian court lady Murasaki Shikibu.

The Tale of Genji

MURASAKI SHIKIBU

In spite of the fame of The Tale of Genji, *which was honored in its own time and has been ever since, its author remains stubbornly obscure. In part this is surely because of Murasaki's own reticence. It was simply not seemly for a lady of the court to flaunt the details of her personal life. For example, we have no portrait of her and no literary description. There was in Heian Japan a tradition of vigorous and realistic portraiture of men, especially of important men, but not of women. Even if women had been depicted, the depictions would not have been realistic. Women were typically swathed in so many layers of clothing that they often literally could not move. Their faces were painted with a dead-white face powder, presumably to conceal their features; their teeth were blackened at the dictate of high fashion. We do not even know Murasaki's real name. Murasaki is the name of one of the leading characters in her novel and probably was used to refer to the author indirectly.* Shikibu *was a title held by her father, who was Senior Secretary in the imperial Bureau of Ceremonial. Her father, though a member of the great Fujiwara clan, belonged to a lesser branch of the family and never rose to high office. He was a scholar, a poet, and a minor administrative functionary.*

Murasaki was probably born in 973 in the provincial capital where her father was posted. We know almost nothing about her youth. In 998 she married Fujiwara no Nobutaka, an associate and distant relative of her father and an older man who already had three wives. In spite of this, Murasaki's marriage was apparently happy enough, and she had a daughter in 999. Her husband died of an epidemic in 1001.

To fill the emptiness of her widowhood, Murasaki is thought to have begun writing The Tale of Genji *at some time during the next four or five years. In 1005 or 1006 she entered the service of the court. She may have been selected by the Fujiwara regent Michinaga as tutor and lady-in-waiting to his daughter, the young Empress Shoshi. Murasaki led a rather retiring life at court and seems never to have enjoyed a great court title. But her familiarity with the court and with its people and their manners is reflected in* The Tale of Genji, *which she substantially completed by 1010. She may have departed the court as early as the following year, when the Empress Shoshi retired to a private residence. We know that Murasaki was, by this time, deeply interested in Buddhism, and had contemplated becoming a Buddhist nun. The date of her death is unknown—it may have been as early as 1014 or as late as 1026, more likely the latter.*

In contrast to the sketchy details of Murasaki's biography we have the teeming tapestry of her novel, with its endless details about the life of the court. One critic has called it "a great and sophisticated work of fictional history." The Tale of Genji *is a rambling, episodic work spanning more than fifty years. Its central theme is the amorous adventures of Genji, "The Shining Prince." He is of noble birth, the son of the emperor. Genji is rich, wise, and witty, but his wit and wisdom are almost entirely expended on planning or concealing seductions and dwelling upon the liaisons of love. Yet this is not an erotic book. Murasaki is a woman of "discriminating and delicate taste, and a deep understanding of the emotions of the human heart. She is interested not in the details of her hero's conquests, but in the subtlest refinements of human intercourse; not in the lovers' embraces, but in their longings and their regrets."[1] And she is interested in the context in which the love affairs take place—the charming entertainments, the solemn ceremonies at shrines and monasteries, the archery and equestrian contests, the contests of poetry, painting, and perfume blending. She tells us of the delicacy of sentiment of the ladies and gentlemen of the court, the nuances of gesture and innuendo, the refinements of costume, rich beyond belief, with each color and fabric and pattern steeped in symbolism.*

The modern reader is most affected by the incredible artificiality of this society and the equally incredible triviality of its concerns. There are almost no real intellectual interests. Even the Buddhism that played so prominent a part in the court society tended to be mainly a matter of external forms subscribed to with a bland disregard for the incompatibility of Buddhism with either the imported Confucianism or the native Japanese Shinto cult. Instead of meaningful spiritual or intellectual questions, the courtiers, nobles, and officials of the court were preoccupied with manners, taste, and empty formalism. However, one gains the distinct impression that Murasaki herself is dissatisfied with the emptiness of the court life that she describes so faithfully.

The Tale of Genji *is in no sense an autobiographical novel. Yet, in an occasional passage, there is a shadowy reflection of the author and of her concerns. The following excerpt is one such passage. In it Genji makes fun of the romances that the court ladies love to read. But he is drawn up short by one of the ladies, Tamakazura, "the most avid reader of all," who insists that the romances are really a vehicle for the expression of truth. After a moment's half-ironic reflection, Genji agrees, and suggests that "the two of us set down our story and give them a really interesting one." It is a*

---

[1]George Sansom, *A History of Japan to 1334* (Stanford: Stanford University Press, 1958), p. 179.

suggestion too ridiculous and amusing for Tamakazura even to imagine:
"She hid her face in her sleeves."
    The excerpt begins with one of those interminable entertainments that
filled the life of the court, this one an equestrian archery contest.

Genji went out to the stands toward midafternoon. All the princes
were there, as he had predicted. The equestrian archery was freer
and more varied than at the palace. The officers of the guard joined
in, and everyone sat entranced through the afternoon. The women
may not have understood all the finer points, but the uniforms of
even the common guardsmen were magnificent and the horsemanship was complicated and exciting. The grounds were very wide,
fronting also on Murasaki's southeast quarter, where young women
were watching. There was music and dancing, Chinese polo music
and the Korean dragon dance. As night came on, the triumphal
music rang out high and wild. The guardsmen were richly rewarded
according to their several ranks. It was very late when the assembly
dispersed.

    Genji spent the night with the lady of the orange blossoms. . . .
They were good friends, he and she, and no more, and they went to
separate beds. Genji wondered when they had begun to drift apart. . . .
She had let him have her bed and spread quilts for herself outside the
curtains. She had in the course of time come to accept such arrangements as proper, and he did not suggest changing them.

    The rains of early summer continued without a break, even gloom-
ier than in most years. The ladies at Rokujō amused themselves with
illustrated romances. . . . Tamakazura was the most avid reader of all.
She quite lost herself in pictures and stories and would spend whole
days with them. Several of her young women were well informed in
literary matters. She came upon all sorts of interesting and shocking
incidents (she could not be sure whether they were true or not), but
she found little that resembled her own unfortunate career. . . .

    Genji could not help noticing the clutter of pictures and manu-
scripts. "What a nuisance this all is," he said one day. "Women seem to
have been born to be cheerfully deceived. They know perfectly well
that in all these old stories there is scarcely a shred of truth, and yet
they are captured and made sport of by the whole range of trivialities
and go on scribbling them down, quite unaware that in these warm
rains their hair is all dank and knotted."

    He smiled. "What would we do if there were not these old romances
to relieve our boredom? But amid all the fabrication I must admit that
I do find real emotions and plausible chains of events. We can be
quite aware of the frivolity and the idleness and still be moved. We

have to feel a little sorry for a charming princess in the depths of gloom. Sometimes a series of absurd and grotesque incidents which we know to be quite improbable holds our interest, and afterwards we must blush that it was so. Yet even then we can see what it was that held us. Sometimes I stand and listen to the stories they read to my daughter, and I think to myself that there certainly are good talkers in the world. I think that these yarns must come from people much practiced in lying. But perhaps that is not the whole of the story?"

She pushed away her inkstone. "I can see that that would be the view of someone much given to lying himself. For my part, I am convinced of their truthfulness."

He laughed. "I have been rude and unfair to your romances, haven't I. They have set down and preserved happenings from the age of the gods to our own. *The Chronicles of Japan* and the rest are a mere fragment of the whole truth. It is your romances that fill in the details.

"We are not told of things that happened to specific people exactly as they happened; but the beginning is when there are good things and bad things, things that happen in this life which one never tires of seeing and hearing about, things which one cannot bear not to tell of and must pass on for all generations. If the storyteller wishes to speak well, then he chooses the good things; and if he wishes to hold the reader's attention he chooses bad things, extraordinarily bad things. Good things and bad things alike, they are things of this world and no other.

"Writers in other countries approach the matter differently. Old stories in our own are different from new. There are differences in the degree of seriousness. But to dismiss them as lies is itself to depart from the truth. Even in the writ which the Buddha drew from his noble heart are parables, devices for pointing obliquely at the truth. To the ignorant they may seem to operate at cross purposes. The Greater Vehicle is full of them, but the general burden is always the same. The difference between enlightenment and confusion is of about the same order as the difference between the good and the bad in a romance. If one takes the generous view, then nothing is empty and useless."

He now seemed bent on establishing the uses of fiction.

"But tell me: is there in any of your old stories a proper, upright fool like myself?" He came closer. "I doubt that even among the most unworldly of your heroines there is one who manages to be as distant and unnoticing as you are. Suppose the two of us set down our story and give the world a really interesting one."

"I think it very likely that the world will take notice of our curious story even if we do not go to the trouble." She hid her face in her sleeves.

The Diary

MURASAKI SHIKIBU

With Murasaki's Diary *we are on somewhat more solid ground concerning the details of her life than in* The Tale of Genji. *On the other hand, the* Diary *covers only some two years of her life, 1008–10. She had been a member of the empress's household for several years, and the excerpted passage comes near the end of her period of court service. Still, she dwells not so much on the facts of her life as on the reactions of others to her. She conveys very clearly her own increasing melancholy, the spitefulness of many of her female companions, her criticisms of their deportment, and, at the end, her own increasing attraction to Buddhism. We gain a powerful impression of a talented, learned woman who is both bound by the traditions of the court and disillusioned with them.*

63. For instance, whenever the Master of Her Majesty's Household Tadanobu arrives with a message for Her Majesty, the senior women are so helpless and childish that they hardly ever come out to greet him, and, when they do, they seem unable to say anything in the least appropriate. It's not that they are at a loss for words, and it's not that they are lacking in intelligence; it's just that they feel so self-conscious and embarrassed that they are afraid of saying something silly, so they refuse to say anything at all and try to make themselves as invisible as possible. Women in other households cannot possibly act in such a manner! Once one has entered this sort of world even the highest born of ladies falls into line, but our women still seem to act as though they were little girls at home. If a woman of a lower rank comes out to greet him, Major Counselor Tadanobu takes it in very bad grace, so there are even times when he leaves without seeing anyone, either because the right woman has gone home or because those women who are in their rooms refuse to come out. Other nobles, the kind who often visit Her Majesty with messages, seem to have secret understandings with particular women of their choice and retire somewhat crestfallen if they happen to be absent. It is hardly surprising that

they take every opportunity they can to complain that the place is moribund.

The women in the High Priestess' household[2] must obviously look down on us for this. But, even so, it makes little sense to ridicule others by saying: "We are the only ones of note. Everyone else is as good as blind and deaf when it comes to taste." It is very easy to criticize people, but a far more difficult task to keep oneself in check, and it is while one forgets this truth, lauds oneself to the skies, treats everyone else as worthless and generally despises others, that one's true character is often clearly revealed. . . .

I criticize other women like this, but here is one who has managed to survive this far without having achieved anything of note and has nothing to rely on in the future that might afford her the slightest consolation. Yet, perhaps because I still retain the conviction that I am not the kind of person to abandon herself completely to despair, on autumn evenings, when nostalgia is at its most poignant, I go out and sit on the veranda to gaze in reverie. "Is this the moon that used to praise my beauty?" I say to myself, as I conjure up memories of the past. Then, realizing that I am making precisely that mistake which must be avoided, I become uneasy and move inside a little, while still, of course, continuing to fret and worry.

67. I remember how in the cool of the evening I used to play the koto to myself, rather badly; I was always worried lest someone were to hear me and realize that I was just "adding to the sadness of it all." How silly of me, and yet how sad! So now my two kotos, one of thirteen strings and the other of six, stand in a miserable little closet blackened with soot, ready tuned but idle. Through neglect—I forgot, for example, to ask that the bridges be removed on rainy days— they have accumulated the dust and lean there now against a cupboard, their necks jammed between that and a pillar, with a biwa standing on either side.[3]

There is also a pair of large cupboards crammed full to bursting point. One is full of old poems and tales that have become the home for countless silverfish that scatter in such an unpleasant manner that no one cares to look at them any more; the other is full of Chinese books which have lain unattended ever since he who carefully collected them passed away. Whenever my loneliness threatens to overwhelm me, I take out one or two of them to look at. But my women gather together behind my back. "It's because she goes on like this

---

[2]Referring to the ladies of another, rival court, that of the High Priestess of the Kamo Shrines.—ED.

[3]The *biwa* was a flutelike instrument also popular with the court nobility.—ED.

that she is so miserable. What kind of lady is it who reads Chinese books?" they whisper. "In the past it was not even the done thing to read sutras!"[4] "Yes," I feel like replying, "but I've never seen anyone who lived longer just because they obeyed a prohibition!" But that would be inconsiderate of me, for what they say is not unreasonable.

68. Everyone reacts differently. Some are cheerful, open-hearted, and forthcoming; others are born pessimists, amused by nothing, the kind who search through old letters, carry out penances, intone sutras without end, and clack their beads, all of which I find most unseemly. So aware am I of my women's prying eyes that I hesitate to do even those things a woman in my position should allow herself to do. How much more so at court, where I do have many things I wish to say but always think better of it. There would be no point, I tell myself, in explaining to people who would never understand, and as it would only be causing trouble with women who think of nothing but themselves and are always carping, I just keep my thoughts to myself. It is very rare that one finds people of true understanding; for the most part they judge everything by their own standards and ignore everyone else's opinion.

69. So I seem to be misunderstood, and they think that I am shy. There have been times when I have been forced to sit in their company, and on such occasions I have tried to avoid their petty criticisms, not because I am particularly shy but because I consider it all so distasteful; as a result, I am now known as somewhat of a dullard.

"Well, we never expected this!" they all say. "No one liked her. They all said she was pretentious, awkward, difficult to approach, prickly, too fond of her tales, haughty, prone to versifying, disdainful, cantankerous, and scornful. But when you meet her, she is strangely meek, a completely different person altogether!"

How embarrassing! Do they really look upon me as such a dull thing, I wonder? But I am what I am and so act accordingly. Her Majesty too has often remarked that she had thought I was not the kind of person with whom she could ever relax, but that now I have become closer to her than any of the others. I am so perversely standoffish; if only I can avoid putting off those for whom I have genuine respect. . . .

71. There is a woman called Saemon no Naishi, who, for some strange reason, took a dislike to me, I cannot think why. I heard all sorts of malicious rumors about myself.

His Majesty was listening to someone reading the *Tale of Genji* aloud. "She must have read the Chronicles of Japan!" he said. "She

---

[4]Sutras were Buddhist scriptures.—ED.

seems very learned." Saemon no Naishi heard this and apparently jumped to conclusions, spreading it abroad among the senior courtiers that I was flaunting my learning. She gave me the nickname Our Lady of the Chronicles. How utterly ridiculous! Would I, who hesitate to reveal my learning in front of my women at home, ever think of doing so at court?

When my brother, Secretary at the Ministry of Ceremonial, was a young boy learning the Chinese classics, I was in the habit of listening to him and I became unusually proficient at understanding those passages which he found too difficult to grasp. Father, a most learned man, was always regretting the fact: "Just my luck!" he would say. "What a pity she was not born a man!" But then gradually I realized that people were saying, "It's bad enough when a man flaunts his learning; she will come to no good," and ever since then I have avoided writing even the simplest character. My handwriting is appalling. And as for those classics, or whatever they are called, that I used to read, I gave them up entirely. Still I kept on hearing these malicious remarks. Worried what people would think if they heard such rumors, I pretended to be unable to read even the inscriptions on the screens. Then Her Majesty asked me to read to her here and there from the Collected Works of Po Chü-i,[5] and, because she evinced a desire to know more about such things, we carefully chose a time when other women would not be present and, amateur that I was, I read with her the two books of Po Chü-i's New Ballads in secret; we started the summer before last. I hid this fact from the others, as did Her Majesty, but somehow His Excellency and the Emperor got wind of it and they had some beautiful copies made of various Chinese books, which His Excellency then presented to Her Majesty. That gossip Saemon no Naishi could never have found out that Her Majesty had actually asked me to study with her, for, if she had, I would never have heard the last of it. Ah what a prattling, tiresome world it is!

72. Now I shall be absolutely frank. I care little for what others say. I have decided to put my trust in Amitābha[6] and immerse myself in reading sutras. You might expect me to have no compunction in becoming a nun, for I have lost what little attachment I retained for the trials and pains that life has to offer, and yet still I hesitate; even if I were to commit myself to turning my back on the world, there might still be moments of irresolution before he came for me, trailing clouds

---

[5]Po Chü-i (772–846) was a Chinese poet of the T'ang dynasty whose works were very popular in Heian Japan.—Ed.

[6]Amitābha (or Amida) was a Buddhist deity.—Ed.

of glory. The time too is ripe. If I get much older my eyesight will surely weaken to the point that I shall be unable to read the sutras, and my spirits will fail. It may seem that I am merely going through the motions of being a true believer, but I assure you that I can think of little else at the present moment. But then someone with as much to atone for as myself may not qualify for salvation; there are so many things that serve to remind one of the transgressions of a former existence. Ah the wretchedness of it all!

A Historical Appraisal

IVAN MORRIS

Given the scanty facts we have about Murasaki's life, how can we put together even a biographical sketch? The answer is to take those few facts we do have and extrapolate from them and from passages in her two most important books, the Diary *and* The Tale of Genji—*in short, to find the author in her work.*

This is a nearly irresistible temptation when dealing with the author of one of the world's greatest literary works, and many scholars have done it. One of the most successful was Ivan Morris, from whose The World of the Shining Prince: Court Life in Ancient Japan *the following passage is taken.*

'Pretty yet shy, shrinking from sight, unsociable, fond of old tales, conceited, so wrapped up in poetry that other people hardly exist, spitefully looking down on the whole world—such is the unpleasant opinion that people have of me. Yet when they come to know me they say that I am strangely gentle, quite unlike what they had been led to believe. I know that people look down on me like some old outcast, but I have become accustomed to all this, and tell myself, "My nature is as it is." '

This is one of the few parts of her diary in which Murasaki turns her acute power of description towards herself. It is a revealing passage. She was what would nowadays be labelled as an introvert and, typically, she was convinced that people misunderstood her. The diary suggests that Murasaki got little pleasure from the casual social relations, the gossip, and the badinage that occupied most of the other ladies at court. She had the reputation of being virtuous (an unusual one in her circle), and we have reason to believe that she was something of a prude. . . .

To what extent does Murasaki's life provide a clue to her character? Our fund of facts about Japan's first and greatest novelist is soon exhausted. She was born in the seventies of the tenth century into a minor, though very literary, branch of the Fujiwara family. From her earliest youth she lived in a cultured atmosphere among people well versed in the classics, whose pastime it was to compose elegant, if not very original, verses in Chinese. Her father, Tametoki, was an ambitious and fairly successful official, who started his career as a student of literature preparing for what roughly corresponds to a D.Lit. degree. He had slowly worked his way up the government hierarchy, largely thanks to the influence of his kinsman, the all-powerful Michinaga, to whom he regularly sent appeals in the form of stereotyped Chinese poetry. Tametoki's grandfather was a poet of some note and he in turn was the great-grandson of Fuyutsugu, an illustrious statesman and *littérateur,* who had greatly contributed to establishing the fortunes of the Fujiwara family in the early part of the preceding century. In short, Murasaki had the advantage of belonging to a family with a long tradition of scholarly and artistic interests.

Tametoki had great ambitions for his eldest son and made sure that he had all the benefits of a classical education. A knowledge of Chinese history and literature was essential for any worth-while political career, and in Murasaki's diary father and son are described poring over Ssu-ma Ch'ien's *Historical Records.* For women this type of study was far from being an asset. Many of the court ladies had a smattering of classical knowledge, but anything more serious might label a woman as being unconventional and, worse still, a blue-stocking. This prejudice did not deter Murasaki, and we find her profiting from her brother's studies to learn what she could herself. Tametoki does not appear to have prevented his daughter from indulging in these odd pursuits, but it is doubtful whether he encouraged her. On one unfortunate occasion (mentioned in the diary) he observed his two children at their lessons and realized that Murasaki was more adept at memorizing Chinese characters than her brother. This inspired the well-known lament, 'If only you were a boy, how happy I should be!' Nobunori, the brother in question, entered government service with a post in the Ministry of Ceremonial (where his father had also served); later he was attached to his father's staff in the province of Echigo, where he died in about 1013 at an early age. Like most well-bred young men of his time he wrote conventional poetry.

We know little about Murasaki's youth. It seems likely that a good deal of her time was devoted to reading and study; for she became familiar with the standard Chinese and Buddhist classics and was also widely read in the literature of her own country. This may well have deterred potential suitors. In any case she was not betrothed until about twenty, an advanced age for girls of her time. It was of course a *mariage de convenance:* her husband was a kinsman and appears to have been considerably older.

It did not last long. In 1001 (the first fairly definite date in Murasaki's life) her husband died, probably in an epidemic. . . .

For five years after her husband's death Murasaki lived at home in retirement, and it was almost certainly during this period that she began work on her novel. In 1004 her father's poems finally produced the desired effect and he was appointed governor of the province of Echizen, some eighty miles from the capital. Shortly thereafter he arranged for his daughter to enter court as maid-of-honour to Michinaga's daughter, the nineteen-year-old consort of the young Emperor Ichijō. Murasaki began her diary in 1008 and kept it for about two years. It gives a vivid picture of her life at court, but does not help us to fix any accurate chronology; for the Heian diary was an impressionistic literary form rather than a systematic record of events.

Ichijō died in 1011 at the age of thirty-one and was succeeded by his first cousin. The Empress, accompanied by her suite (in which Murasaki was presumably included), moved to one of the 'detached palaces' and embarked on her sixty-year period of staid retirement. In the same year Murasaki's father was made governor of the large northern province of Echigo. His son joined him there, but died after a couple of years. . . .

During all this time we know absolutely nothing about the life of Murasaki Shikibu. There is little factual basis for the traditional view that she became a nun in 1015 and died in 1031. On the other hand, there is some evidence that she continued in the service of the Empress Dowager; for *Tales of Glory,* in an entry dated the eighth month of 1025, speaks of 'Echigo no Ben, daughter of Murasaki Shikibu, a lady-in-waiting at court'. Six years later, however, Murasaki's name is conspicuously absent from a list of ladies who are mentioned as having travelled in the Empress Dowager's suite on a flower-viewing expedition. It is probable, then, though by no means certain, that Murasaki either died or retired into the seclusion of a convent at some time between 1025 and 1031 at the age of about fifty.

While we have few facts about Murasaki's life, the diary and *The Tale of Genji* do provide ample evidence about her knowledge and her experience of the world. Even the most cursory reading of the novel will suggest how intimately she was acquainted with the aristocratic life of her time, not only at court, but in town mansions and in remoter houses beyond the limits of the capital. Murasaki had keenly observed how different kinds of men and women spoke and behaved, and she had tried to enter into their feelings and to know why they acted as they did. She was sensitive to the natural surroundings in which these people lived and to the subtle effects that these surroundings had on them. Possibly she deserved her reputation for being virtuous (though Michinaga, for one, doubted it); but this did not prevent her from being keenly interested in love between men and women and in all the conflicting emotions and other complexities that it involved. Indeed many people have regarded her novel as primarily a study of the varied manifestations of sexual and romantic love. . . .

We know from the diary that Murasaki's interest in Chinese literature was no youthful whim. Her husband was a specialist in the subject and at his death he appears to have left a substantial Chinese library. Murasaki mentions that she would occasionally read some of the volumes to while away the long days when she was on leave from court and living at her father's house. Since Chinese studies were socially taboo for her sex, Murasaki's maids expressed dismay, mingled with dire forebodings, when they observed their mistress at this unorthodox pastime: 'My women gather round me and say, "Madam, if you go on like this, there won't be much happiness in store for you. Why should you read books in Chinese characters? In the old days they wouldn't even let women read the sutras." '

At court Murasaki was at great pains to hide her knowledge of the foreign classics; and fear that the other ladies would find out about her interests (as of course they did) seems to have become a sort of complex. The young empress was also eager to explore these illicit realms, and Murasaki mentions that for some years she has clandestinely been teaching her mistress parts of Po Chü-i's collected works when no one else was present.

If Murasaki had a fair knowledge of Chinese literature—or rather, of that somewhat scattered selection of Chinese literature that circulated in Heian Kyō—she was well versed in the writing of her own country, and we can assume that she was familiar with the principal Japanese works until her time. The diary tells us that when *The Tale of Genji* was read to Emperor Ichijō he commented, 'The person who wrote this must have been reading *The Chronicles of Japan* and is surely very learned'. The Emperor's remark was no doubt well intentioned, but it was responsible for Murasaki's acquiring the nickname of 'the lady of the Chronicles' (*Nihongi no tsubone*), which she so greatly resented.

Apart from historical works and official court annals, Murasaki was well acquainted with the wealth of Japanese poetry beginning with the vast *Manyō Shū* anthology (*The Collection of Ten Thousand Leaves*) compiled in the eighth century. She was widely read in the vernacular *kanabun* literature, which had developed so brilliantly during the first two centuries of the Heian period—the diaries, the travel records, and the miscellaneous jottings, of which only a small portion has survived to the present day. Above all, she must have used her long leisure hours at home to steep herself in those voluminous tales or romances known as *monogatari,* the form in which she was to establish her own name.

Murasaki's diary throws considerable light on her knowledge of Buddhism and on her attitude to religion. Her writing shows that she knew a great deal about the intricate Buddhist ceremonial, its hierarchy, and its monastic orders; and we have evidence that she was familiar, not only with the official writings of Tendai (the sect with which she was mainly associated), but with the names, and to some extent the contents, of the other principal scriptures that were known in Japan. Above all, she shows herself to have been imbued with the underlying spirit of Buddhism common to all the sects—the sense of universal impermanence. This is reflected in the thoughts and words of her principal characters; and in the diary itself we find a direct and moving affirmation of faith:

'All the things of this world are sad and tiresome. But from now on I shall fear nothing. Whatever others may do or say, I shall recite my prayers tirelessly to Amida Buddha. And when in my mind the things of this world have come to assume no more importance or stability than the vanishing dew, then I shall exert all my efforts to become a wise and holy person.' . . .

Finally, what were the circumstances under which Murasaki wrote her novel? . . .

We know from references in the diary that at least part of the book was being circulated at court in 1008. In describing a party given to celebrate the birth of the Empress' first child, Murasaki mentions this incident: ' "Well, now," said the Captain of the Outer Palace Guards, "I expect that little Murasaki must be about here somewhere." "There's no one here like Genji," thought I to myself, "so what should Murasaki be doing in this place?" ' . . .

Some of the events in the novel seem to have been taken from things that actually happened at court in 1013 and 1017, but this cannot be accepted as positive evidence. The only other reliable date occurs in the *Sarashina Diary.*[7] I quote the passage at some length, since it gives a good idea of the impression that Murasaki's book made on one young girl at the time, and also of how hard it was to come by a copy:

---

[7]This was another contemporary diary, that of a thirteen-year-old girl, also preserved, like Murasaki's.—ED.

'I read *Waka Murasaki* and a few of the other [early] books in *The Tale of Genji,* and I longed to see the later parts. . . . But we were still new to the capital and it was not easy to find copies. I was burning with impatience and curiosity, and in my prayers I used to say, "Let me see the whole!" When my parents went to the Kōryū Temple for a retreat, this was the only thing I asked for. Yet all my hopes were in vain.

'I was feeling most dejected about it when one day I called on an aunt of mine who had come up from the country. She received me very affectionately and showed the greatest interest in me. "What a pretty girl you've grown up to be!" said she. Then, as I was leaving, she asked, "What would you like as a present? I am sure you don't want anything too practical. I'd like to give you something that you will really enjoy."

'And so it was that she presented me with fifty-odd volumes of *The Tale of Genji* in a special case, together with [numerous other *monogatari*]. Oh, how happy I was when I came home with all these books in a bag! In the past I had only been able to have an occasional flurried look at parts of *The Tale of Genji.* Now I had it all in front of me and I could lie undisturbed behind my screen, taking the books out one by one and enjoying them to my heart's content. I wouldn't have changed places with the Empress herself.'

Since *The Tale of Genji* consists of fifty-four books, this would seem to be fairly good evidence that most of the novel, if not all, was completed and in circulation by 1022, the date to which this passage refers. It seems plausible that Murasaki started writing shortly after her husband's death when she was living at home, say in about 1002, and that she continued with occasional interruptions during her long period of service at court until about 1020, when she had completed some fifty books.

Review and Study Questions

1. How does Murasaki's writing reflect her society? How does it reflect her own private life?
2. What was the status of women in Heian Japan?
3. How did Murasaki's devout Buddhism affect her outlook on life?

Suggestions for Further Reading

The standard English translation of *The Tale of Genji* was done by Arthur Waley in 1935. See *The Tale of Genji: A Novel in Six Parts* by Lady Murasaki, tr. Arthur Waley (New York: Modern Library, 1960). It was the first English translation of the work and had come to be regarded as a classic of English literature. But it is limited in several serious ways. Waley was arbitrary and often followed his personal views rather than the text. He sometimes mistranslated passages or simply ignored sections of the text that he did not agree with. A better translation is Murasaki Shikibu, *The Tale of Genji*, tr. Edward G. Seidensticker (New York: Knopf, 1976), excerpted for this chapter. This stays much closer to the text and picks up its fundamental ironic undertones. Marian Ury, reviewing the book in *Harvard Journal of Asiatic Studies*, 37 (1977), 201, insists that this is the first true representation of the Genji in English. The best edition of the *Diary* is that excerpted for this chapter, Richard Bowring, *Murasaki Shikibu: Her Diary and Poetic Memoirs, A Translation and Study* (Princeton: Princeton University Press, 1982). There is an older edition of the *Diary*, among other works in *Diaries of Court Ladies of Old Japan*, tr. Annie Shepley Omori and Kochi Doi, intro. Amy Lowell (Tokyo: Kenkusha, 1935). This work, however, is somewhat inferior to Bowring's and has much less substantial editorial apparatus and notes.

The best interpretive work on Murasaki and her works is Ivan Morris, *The World of the Shining Prince: Court Life in Ancient Japan* (New York: Knopf, 1964), excerpted for this chapter. There are also several specialized studies that are useful for various aspects of her life and work. Two are in *Medieval Japan: Essays in Institutional History*, ed. John W. Hall and Jeffrey P. Mass (New Haven and London: Yale University Press, 1974): G. Cameron Hurst III, "The Structure of the Heian Court: Some Thoughts on the Nature of 'Familial Authority' in Heian Japan," and John W. Hall, "Kyoto as Historical Background." Another useful study is William H. McCullough, "Japanese Marriage Institutions in the Heian Period," *Harvard Journal of Asiatic Studies*, 27 (1967), 103–67. Another is *Ukifune: Love in The Tale of Genji*, ed. Andrew Pekarik (New York: Columbia University Press, 1982).

Among the historical studies of Murasaki's period, one of the best is George Sansom, *A History of Japan to 1334* (Stanford: Stanford University Press, 1958). Another is Robert Karl Reischauer, *Early Japanese History (c. 40 B.C.–A.D. 1167), Part A* (Princeton and Oxford: Princeton University Press and Oxford University Press, 1937). Especially recommended is the brief and readable Jonathan Norton Leonard, *Early Japan* (New York: Time–Life Books, 1968), a volume in the "Great Ages of Man" series. A respected general history that can be recommended is by Edwin O. Reischauer, *Japan: The Story of a Nation*, rev. ed. (New York: Knopf, 1974), the great American interpreter of things Japanese.

There are no full-scale biographies of Murasaki in English or in any other western language and only two in Japanese, both of them roundly criticized by western scholars.

ELEANOR OF AQUITAINE AND THE WRATH OF GOD

c. 1122	Born
1137	Married the future Louis VII of France
1147–1149	Second crusade
1152	Divorced from Louis VII and married to the future Henry II of England
1192–1194	Regent during captivity of Richard I
1204	Died

Eleanor of Aquitaine was one of the most remarkable and important figures in medieval history. In her own right, she was duchess of the vast domain of Aquitaine and countess of Poitou, the wife first of Louis VII of France and then of Henry II of England, the mother of "good King Richard" and "bad King John," patroness of poets and minstrels. Tradition remembers her as beautiful and passionate, headstrong and willful. But beyond that intriguing traditional reputation, she is a figure only imperfectly seen and, ironically enough, seen at all largely through the accounts of her enemies.

The sources of medieval history are scanty at best and tend, moreover, to record men's doings in a preponderantly man's world. Even the greatest of medieval women appear in the records of their time as conveyors of properties and channels for noble blood lines, and we know of them only that they were "good and faithful wives"—or that they were not. So it is with Eleanor. We do not even have a contemporary description of her. Troubadour poets sang rapturously of her "crystal cheeks," her "locks like threads of gold," her eyes "like Orient pearls." One even proclaims:

> Were the world all mine,
> From the sea to the Rhine,

185

> I'd give it all
> If so be the Queen of England
> Lay in my arms.

In sober fact, we do not know what color her eyes were, nor her hair, whether it was indeed "like threads of gold" or raven black. Even the few pictorial representations we have of her—including her tomb effigy at the Abbey of Fontevrault—are purely conventional.

But Eleanor's part in the great events of her time was real enough. It began with her marriage, at the age of fifteen, to Louis the young king, son of Louis VI (Louis the Fat) of France. Her father, the turbulent Duke William X of Aquitaine, had died suddenly and unexpectedly on pilgrimage to Spain, leaving Eleanor his heir. And, in feudal law, the disposition of both Eleanor and her fiefs was a matter to be decided by her father's overlord, Louis VI of France. Duke William had been Louis's most intractable vassal, and his death was a priceless opportunity not only to put an end to the contumaciousness of Aquitaine but to tie that large and wealthy duchy to the French realm. Louis decided that the interests of his house were best served by the marriage of Eleanor to his son. And so, it was done. There is no record of how either the young bride or the young groom responded, only an account of the brilliant assemblage that gathered to witness the ceremony in Bordeaux and to accompany the couple back by weary stages to Paris. In the course of this journey, the aged King Louis died. His son was now Louis VII, the Duchess Eleanor now queen of France. The year was 1137.

We must not imagine that Eleanor was a very happy bride in those first years of her marriage. Paris was a cold and gloomy northern city, very different from sunny Provence, and the Capetian castles in which she lived were dark and uncomfortable. The king—her husband— had an inexhaustible thirst for devotion and piety and surrounded himself with ecclesiastical advisers, confessors, theologians, and barren, quibbling scholars, so unlike the more robust and charming practitioners of the *gai savoir* (merry learning) with whom Eleanor had grown up at her father's court. Nor was Louis very happy, for he and his young wife had two daughters, Marie and Alix, but no son, no member of what was then considered "the better sex" to be groomed for the Capetian throne.

Then word reached Paris of the fall of Edessa in the distant Latin Kingdom of Jerusalem, one of those fortress principalities to secure the Holy Land dating from the first crusade almost half a century before. The resurgence of Moslem power was clearly seen to threaten the Holy Land, and the call for a second crusade went out. The pious King Louis took the cross—to the consternation of his more realistic advisers. And Eleanor insisted upon accompanying him. Whatever Louis and his fellow crusaders may have thought about this matter, Eleanor's position as a great vassal who could summon a substantial host of warriors from her own lands made her support crucial: and her support was contingent upon her going in person. There is a persistent legend that the queen and her ladies decked themselves out as Amazons in anticipation of their role in the coming military adventure.

But the military adventure itself turned into a military disaster. The second crusade was a dismal failure. The French forces of Louis VII were seriously defeated by the Turks, and the German contingent led by the Emperor Conrad III was almost wiped out. Both the French and the Germans accused the Byzantine Greeks of treachery. There were disagreements among the Western knights, and many of them simply abandoned the crusade and returned home. There were divided counsels among those who remained and mistrust between them and the Christian lords of the Eastern principalities. And there were continued military blunders and defeats. Tempers were short, old quarrels flared, new ones commenced.

In this atmosphere, what had apparently been a growing estrangement between King Louis and Queen Eleanor became an open break. Their troubles were aggravated by what was then considered the boldness and outspokenness of the queen and in particular by her attentions to her handsome uncle, only eight years older than she, Raymond of Poitiers, Prince of Antioch. It may have been no more than an innocent flirtation. But Louis thought otherwise. He brooded not only on his queen's conduct but on what he perceived as her failure to produce a son for him, and his mind turned to divorce, the grounds for which were to be found in consanguinity, a marriage within the prohibited degree of blood relationship, which was the usual legal pretext for the dissolution of feudal marriages no longer bearable or profitable.

Eleanor and the Chroniclers

WILLIAM OF TYRE
AND JOHN OF SALISBURY

Eleanor's role in the second crusade is scarcely mentioned by the chroniclers who recorded the deeds of its other leading figures. Odo of Deuil, a monk of the French royal monastery of St. Denis and the chaplain of Louis VII, wrote the most detailed account of Louis's part in the crusade—De profectione Ludovici VII in orientem—*but he makes only four passing references to the queen in the entire narrative. Odo clearly had reason to favor the cause of the king, his master. And, for one reason or another, so did the few other chroniclers who give any account at all of the estrangement between Louis and Eleanor. The most detailed is that of William, Archbishop of Tyre. William is generally regarded as the best of all the chroniclers of the crusades, but he was not present at the time of this crisis and we do not know what source he used. In any event, he regarded the behavior of the queen and the resulting breach with her husband as part of a cynical attempt by Raymond of Antioch to turn the crusade to his own advantage. Here is the account of William of Tyre.*

For many days Raymond, prince of Antioch, had eagerly awaited the arrival of the king of the Franks. When he learned that the king had landed in his domains, he summoned all the nobles of the land and the chief leaders of the people and went out to meet him with a chosen escort. He greeted the king with much reverence and conducted him with great pomp into the city of Antioch, where he was met by the clergy and the people. Long before this time—in fact, as soon as he heard that Louis was coming—Raymond had conceived the idea that by his aid he might be able to enlarge the principality of Antioch. With this in mind, therefore, even before the king started on the pilgrimage, the prince had sent to him in France a large store of noble gifts and treasures of great price in the hope of winning his favor. He also counted greatly on the interest of the queen with the lord king, for she had been his inseparable companion on his pilgrimage. She was Raymond's niece, and eldest daughter of Count William of Poitou, his brother.

As we have said, therefore, Raymond showed the king every attention on his arrival. He likewise displayed a similar care for the nobles and chief men in the royal retinue and gave them many proofs of his great liberality. In short, he outdid all in showing honor to each one according to his rank and handled everything with the greatest magnificence. He felt a lively hope that with the assistance of the king and his troops he would be able to subjugate the neighboring cities, namely, Aleppo, Shayzar, and several others. Nor would this hope have been futile, could he have induced the king and his chief men to undertake the work. For the arrival of King Louis had brought such fear to our enemies that now they not only distrusted their own strength but even despaired of life itself.

Raymond had already more than once approached the king privately in regard to the plans which he had in mind. Now he came before the members of the king's suite and his own nobles and explained with due formality how his request could be accomplished without difficulty and at the same time be of advantage and renown to themselves. The king, however, ardently desired to go to Jerusalem to fulfil his vows, and his determination was irrevocable. When Raymond found that he could not induce the king to join him, his attitude changed. Frustrated in his ambitious designs, he began to hate the king's ways; he openly plotted against him and took means to do him injury. He resolved also to deprive him of his wife, either by force or by secret intrigue. The queen readily assented to this design, for she was a foolish woman. Her conduct before and after this time showed her to be, as we have said, far from circumspect. Contrary to her royal dignity, she disregarded her marriage vows and was unfaithful to her husband.

As soon as the king discovered these plots, he took means to provide for his life and safety by anticipating the designs of the prince. By the advice of his chief nobles, he hastened his departure and secretly left Antioch with his people. Thus the splendid aspect of his affairs was completely changed, and the end was quite unlike the beginning. His coming had been attended with pomp and glory; but fortune is fickle, and his departure was ignominious.

The only other substantial account of the events leading to the divorce of Louis and Eleanor is that of the great twelfth-century ecclesiastic and intellectual, John of Salisbury, in his Historia Pontificalis. *In one respect, John was even further removed from the events than was William of Tyre. He had no direct knowledge of the East at all and was, at this time, in Rome on a mission from the see of Canterbury and attached to the papal court. We do not know what source he used for the events in Antioch. It is likely that he is simply repeating the story as he heard it from members of Louis's retinue, for the hostility against Eleanor that already animated Louis's close supporters is clearly present in John's ac-*

*count. It is also possible that the hostility of the account and its strong
pro-French bias is related to the later time at which John's work was actually written, about 1163. At this time, John was involved in the growing
bitterness between Thomas Becket, whom he supported, and Henry II of
England, who had just sent John into exile for his support of Becket. John
found refuge in France.*

But in any event, the account in the Historia Pontificalis *is strongly
favorable to Louis, even to the extent of ascribing to Eleanor the initiative
in the proposal for the divorce.*

In the year of grace 1149 the most Christian king of the Franks reached
Antioch, after the destruction of his armies in the east, and was nobly
entertained there by Prince Raymond, brother of the late William,
count of Poitiers. He was as it happened the queen's uncle, and owed
the king loyalty, affection and respect for many reasons. But whilst they
remained there to console, heal and revive the survivors from the
wreck of the army, the attentions paid by the prince to the queen, and
his constant, indeed almost continuous, conversation with her, aroused
the king's suspicions. These were greatly strengthened when the
queen wished to remain behind, although the king was preparing to
leave, and the prince made every effort to keep her, if the king would
give his consent. And when the king made haste to tear her away, she
mentioned their kinship, saying it was not lawful for them to remain
together as man and wife, since they were related in the fourth and
fifth degrees. Even before their departure a rumour to that effect had
been heard in France, where the late Bartholomew bishop of Laon had
calculated the degrees of kinship; but it was not certain whether the
reckoning was true or false. At this the king was deeply moved; and
although he loved the queen almost beyond reason he consented to
divorce her if his counsellors and the French nobility would allow it.
There was one knight amongst the king's secretaries, called Terricus
Gualerancius, a eunuch whom the queen had always hated and
mocked, but who was faithful and had the king's ear like his father's
before him. He boldly persuaded the king not to suffer her to dally
longer at Antioch, both because "guilt under kinship's guise could lie
concealed," and because it would be a lasting shame to the kingdom of
the Franks if in addition to all the other disasters it was reported that
the king had been deserted by his wife, or robbed of her. So he argued,
either because he hated the queen or because he really believed it,
moved perchance by widespread rumour. In consequence, she was
torn away and forced to leave for Jerusalem with the king; and, their
mutual anger growing greater, the wound remained, hide it as best
they might.

In the next passage, John is on more familiar ground since he was in Rome, a familiar of the curia and of Pope Eugenius III, and perhaps even a witness to some of the events he describes.

In the year of grace eleven hundred and fifty the king of the Franks returned home. But the galleys of the Emperor of Constantinople lay in wait for him on his return, capturing the queen and all who were journeying in her ship. The king was appealed to to return to his Byzantine brother and friend, and force was being brought to bear on him when the galleys of the king of Sicily came to the rescue. Freeing the queen and releasing the king, they escorted them back to Sicily rejoicing, with honour and triumph. This was done by order of the king of Sicily, who feared the wiles of the Greeks and desired an opportunity of showing his devotion to the king and queen of the Franks. Now therefore he hastened to meet him with an ample retinue, and escorted him most honourably to Palermo, heaping gifts both on him and on all his followers; thereafter he travelled with him right across his territory to Ceprano, supplying all his needs on the way. This is the last point on the frontier between the principality of Capua and Campania, which is papal territory.

At Ceprano the cardinals and officials of the church met the king and, providing him with all that he desired, escorted him to Tusculum to the lord pope, who received him with such tenderness and reverence that one would have said he was welcoming an angel of the Lord rather than a mortal man. He reconciled the king and queen, after hearing severally the accounts each gave of the estrangement begun at Antioch, and forbade any future mention of their consanguinity: confirming their marriage, both orally and in writing, he commanded under pain of anathema that no word should be spoken against it and that it should not be dissolved under any pretext whatever. This ruling plainly delighted the king, for he loved the queen passionately, in an almost childish way. The pope made them sleep in the same bed, which he had had decked with priceless hangings of his own; and daily during their brief visit he strove by friendly converse to restore love between them. He heaped gifts upon them; and when the moment for departure came, though he was a stern man, he could not hold back his tears, but sent them on their way blessing them and the kingdom of the Franks, which was higher in his esteem than all the kingdoms of the world.

Eleanor, the Queen of Hearts

AMY KELLY

Despite "the lord pope's" good offices, his tears and his blessing, even his threat of anathema, the estrangement between Louis and Eleanor continued. Louis was adamant, and finally, in the spring of 1152 at a solemn synod in Beaugency on the Loire, Louis's representatives argued the case of the consanguinity of their lord and his queen, and the Archbishop of Sens proclaimed their marriage invalid. The Archbishop of Bordeaux, the queen's surrogate, sought only the assurance that her lands be restored. But this had already been arranged, as had all the other details of this elaborate royal charade. Eleanor was not even present. She had already returned to Poitou.

But Eleanor was not destined to reign as a dowager duchess in her own domains. Within two months, she married Henry, Duke of Normandy. He was not only the Norman duke but also the heir to the fiefs of his father, Geoffrey Plantagenet, Count of Maine and Anjou. These already substantial lands, when joined to those of his new bride, made Henry lord of a nearly solid block of territories that stretched from the English Channel to the Mediterranean and from Bordeaux to the Vexin, hardly a day's ride from Paris. At one stroke, Henry of Anjou had become the greatest feudatory of France, with lands and resources many times the size of those held by his nominal overlord, King Louis VII. Two years later, another piece of Henry's inheritance came into his hands. His mother, Matilda, was the daughter of the English King Henry I and had never ceased to press the claim of her son to the English throne. The reign of King Stephen was coming to an end, and he had no surviving heirs. At his death in 1154, Henry of Anjou claimed his crown, and there was none to deny him. Eleanor was a queen once more.

But this time, she had a very different king. Henry II was as godless as Louis had been pious, as flamboyant as Louis had been humble. Where Louis was stubborn and persistent, Henry was furiously energetic and decisive. The setting was at hand for one of the classic confrontations of medieval history that was to stretch into the following generation of the kings of both France and England.

As for Eleanor, the sources are once more almost silent. We do know that she and Henry produced a large family. The eldest son, William, born before the succession to England, died in childhood. But in 1155 came Henry; in 1156, their first daughter, Matilda; in 1157 came Richard, to be called the Lion Hearted; in 1158 came Geoffrey; in 1161, Eleanor; in 1165, Johanna; and in 1166, John. We know that through the early years of her marriage to Henry, Eleanor was often with him at court and sometimes presided in his absence, a fact attested by writs and seals. But her marriage was by no means serene. There were long periods of separation during which the king was known to be unfaithful. The incidents of his infidelity had grown more flagrant with the passing years. At about the time of prince John's birth in 1166, Henry was involved with a paramour of spectacular beauty, Rosamond Clifford. Their affair was the object of such celebration by poets, balladeers, and wags alike that Eleanor may have decided that her bed and her dignity could no longer endure such an affront. But there may have been other matters at issue. The queen may have become alarmed at her husband's efforts to substitute his rule for hers in her dower lands.

In any case, about 1170 she returned to Poitou with her favorite son, Richard, whom she installed as her heir for the lands of Poitou and Aquitaine. For the next three or four years she lived in her old capital of Poitiers, separated from her husband. In these years of self-imposed exile, Eleanor not only reasserted her rights to her own lands, but created a center in Poitiers for the practice of the troubadour culture and l'amour courtois that had long been associated with her family.

The following passage, from Amy Kelly's Eleanor of Aquitaine and the Four Kings—*the book that has come to be regarded as the standard work on Eleanor—is a brilliant reconstruction of this period of Eleanor's life.*

When the countess of Poitou settled down to rule her own heritage, she took her residence in Poitiers, which offered a wide eye-sweep on the world of still operative kings. In the recent Plantagenet building program her ancestral city, the seat and necropolis of her forebears, had been magnificently enlarged and rebuilt, and it stood at her coming thoroughly renewed, a gleaming exemplar of urban elegance. The site rose superbly amidst encircling rivers. Its narrow Merovingian area had lately been extended to include with new and ampler walls parishes that had previously straggled over its outer slopes; ancient quarters had been cleared of immemorial decay; new churches and collegials had sprung up; the cathedral of Saint Pierre was enriched; markets and shops of tradesmen and artisans bore witness to renewed life among the *bourgeoisie;* bridges fanned out to suburbs and monastic establishments lying beyond the streams that moated the city. Brimming with sunshine, the valleys ebbed far away below—hamlet and croft, mill and vineyard—to a haze as blue as the vintage. . . .

When Eleanor came in about 1170 to take full possession of her newly restored city of Poitiers and to install her favorite son there as ruling count and duke in her own patrimony, she was no mere game piece as were most feudal women, to be moved like a queen in chess. She had learned her role as *domina* in Paris, Byzantium, Antioch, London, and Rouen, and knew her value in the feudal world. She was prepared of her own unguided wisdom to reject the imperfect destinies to which she had been, as it were, assigned. In this, her third important role in history, she was the pawn of neither prince nor prelate, the victim of no dynastic scheme. She came as her own mistress, the most sophisticated of women, equipped with plans to establish her own assize, to inaugurate a regime dedicated neither to Mars nor to the Pope, nor to any king, but to Minerva, Venus, and the Virgin. She was resolved to escape from secondary roles, to assert her independent sovereignty in her own citadel, to dispense her own justice, her own patronage, and when at leisure, to survey, like the Empress of Byzantium, a vast decorum in her precincts. . . .

The heirs of Poitou and Aquitaine who came to the queen's high place for their vassals' homage, their squires' training, and their courtiers' service, were truculent youths, boisterous young men from the baronial strongholds of the south without the Norman or Frankish sense of nationality, bred on feuds and violence, some of them with rich fiefs and proud lineage, but with little solidarity and no business but local warfare and daredevil escapade. The custom of lateral rather than vertical inheritance of fiefs in vogue in some parts of Poitou and Aquitaine—the system by which lands passed through a whole generation before descending to the next generation—produced a vast number of landless but expectant younger men, foot-loose, unemployed, ambitious, yet dependent upon the reluctant bounty of uncles and brothers, or their own violent exploits. These wild young men were a deep anxiety not only to the heads of their houses, but to the Kings of France and England and to the Pope in Rome. They were the stuff of which rebellion and schism are made. For two generations the church had done what it could with the problem of their unemployment, marching hordes out of Europe on crusade and rounding other hordes into the cloister.

It was with this spirited world of princes and princesses, of apprentice knights and chatelaines, at once the school and the court of young Richard, that the duchess, busy as she was with the multifarious business of a feudal suzerain, had to deal in her palace in Poitiers. . . .

Eleanor found a willing and helpful deputy to assist her in the person of Marie, Countess of Champagne, her daughter by Louis of France. Marie, now entrusted to Eleanor's tutelage, was a well-educated young woman and apparently well disposed to her mother's plans.

. . . The character of the milieu which Marie appears to have set up in Poitiers suggests a genuine sympathy between the queen and her daughter who had so long been sundered by the bleak fortuities of life. Old relationships were knit up. Something native blossomed in the countess, who shone with a special luster in her mother's court. The young Count of Poitou learned to love particularly his half sister Marie and forever to regard the Poitiers of her dispensation as the world's citadel of valor, the seat of courtesy, and the fountainhead of poetic inspiration. Long after, in his darkest hours, it was to her good graces he appealed. The countess, having carte blanche to proceed with the very necessary business of getting control of her academy, must have striven first for order. Since the miscellaneous and high-spirited young persons in her charge had not learned order from the liturgy nor yet from hagiography, the countess bethought her, like many an astute pedagogue, to deduce her principles from something more germane to their interests. She did not precisely invent her regime; rather she appropriated it from the abundant resources at her hand.

The liberal court of Eleanor had again drawn a company of those gifted persons who thrive by talent or by art. Poets, *conteurs* purveying romance, ecclesiastics with Latin literature at their tongues' end and mere clerks with smatterings of Ovid learned from quotation books, chroniclers engaged upon the sober epic of the Plantagenets, came to their haven in Poitiers. The queen and the countess, with their native poetic tradition, were the natural patrons of the troubadours. It will be seen that the Countess Marie's resources were rich and abundant, but not so formalized as to afford the disciplines for a royal academy nor give substance to a social ritual. The great hall was ready for her grand assize; the expectant court already thronged to gape at its suggestive splendors. . . .

At least one other important source Marie employed. She levied upon the social traditions of her Poitevin forebears. Nostredame relates that in Provence chatelaines were accustomed to entertain their seasonal assemblies with so-called "courts of love," in which, just as feudal vassals brought their grievances to the assizes of their overlords for regulation, litigants in love's thrall brought their problems for the judgment of the ladies. André in his famous work[1] makes

---

[1]André, simply known as the Chaplain, a scholar of this court whose work *Tractatus de Amore* is referred to here, one of the basic works on medieval chivalry and the courts of love.—ED.

reference to antecedent decisions in questions of an amatory nature by "les dames de Gascogne," and the poetry of the troubadours presupposes a milieu in which their doctrines of homage and deference could be exploited. Thus we have in Andre's *Tractatus* the framework of Ovid with the central emphasis reversed, the Arthurian code of manners, the southern ritual of the "courts of love," all burnished with a golden wash of troubadour poetry learned by the queen's forebears and their vassals in the deep Midi, probably beyond the barrier of the Pyrenees. Marie made these familiar materials the vehicle for her woman's doctrine of civility, and in so doing, she transformed the gross and cynical pagan doctrines of Ovid into something more ideal, the woman's canon, the chivalric code of manners. Manners, she plainly saw, were after all the fine residuum of philosophies, the very flower of ethics. . . .

With this anatomy of the whole corpus of love in hand, Marie organized the rabble of soldiers, fighting cocks, jousters, springers, riding masters, troubadours, Poitevin nobles and debutantes, young chatelaines, adolescent princes, and infant princesses in the great hall of Poitiers. Of this pandemonium the countess fashioned a seemly and elegant society, the fame of which spread to the world. Here was a woman's assize to draw men from the excitements of the tilt and the hunt, from dice and games to feminine society, an assize to outlaw boorishness and compel the tribute of adulation to female majesty. . . .

While the ladies, well-accoutered, sit above upon the dais, the sterner portion of society purged, according to the code, from the odors of the kennels and the highway and free for a time from spurs and falcons, range themselves about the stone benches that line the walls, stirring the fragrant rushes with neatly pointed shoe. There are doubtless preludes of music luring the last reluctant knight from the gaming table, *tensons* or *pastourelles*, the plucking of rotes, the "voicing of a fair song and sweet," perhaps even some of the more complicated musical harmonies so ill-received by the clerical critics in London; a Breton *lai* adding an episode to Arthurian romance, or a chapter in the tale of "sad-man" Tristram, bringing a gush of tears from the tender audience clustered about the queen and the Countess of Champagne.

After the romance of the evening in the queen's court, the jury comes to attention upon petition of a young knight in the hall. He bespeaks the judgment of the queen and her ladies upon a point of conduct, through an advocate, of course, so he may remain anonymous. A certain knight, the advocate deposes, has sworn to his lady, as the hard condition of obtaining her love, that he will upon no provocation boast of her merits in company. But one day he overhears detractors heaping his mistress with calumnies. Forgetting his vow in the heat of his passion, he warms to eloquence in defense of his lady. This coming to her ears, she repudiates her champion. Does the lover, who admits he has broken his pledge to his mistress, deserve in this instance to be driven from her presence?

The Countess of Champagne, subduing suggestions from the floor and the buzz of conference upon the dais, renders the judgment of the areopagus. The lady in the case, anonymous of course, is at fault, declares the Countess Marie. She has laid upon her lover a vow too impossibly difficult. The lover has been remiss, no doubt, in breaking his vow to his mistress, no matter what cruel hardship it involves; but he deserves leniency for the merit of his ardor and his constancy. The jury recommends that the stern lady reinstate the plaintiff. The court takes down the judgment. It constitutes a precedent. Does anyone guess the identity of the young pair whose estrangement is thus delicately knit up by the countess? As a bit of suspense it is delicious. As a theme for talk, how loosening to the tongue!

A disappointed petitioner brings forward a case, through an advocate, involving the question whether love survives marriage. The countess, applying her mind to the code, which says that marriage is no proper obstacle to lovers (*Causa coniugii ab amore non est excusatio recta*), and after grave deliberation with her ladies, creates a sensation in the court by expressing doubt whether love in the ideal sense can exist between spouses. This is so arresting a proposition that the observations of the countess are referred to the queen for corroboration, and all wait upon the opinion of this deeply experienced judge. The queen with dignity affirms that she cannot gainsay the Countess of Champagne, though she finds it admirable that a wife should find love and marriage consonant. Eleanor, Queen of France and then of England, had learned at fifty-two that, as another medieval lady put it, "Mortal love is but the licking of honey from thorns."

Eleanor the Regent

MARION MEADE

During the years of Eleanor's dalliance at Poitiers, her husband's larger world had been turned upside down by his quarrel with Thomas Becket. It had not ended even with the martyrdom of that troublesome prelate at the altar of Canterbury in 1170. The question of whether Henry ordered

*Becket's murder or not—and he probably did not—is quite immaterial. For
he bore its consequences. And its principal consequence was to give to the
French king a priceless justification to move against Henry and his fiefs.
What is more, Henry's own sons were as often as not in league with the
French king. With some of them, Henry had been too hard, with others too
soft. And when he favored one, the others feared and plotted against the
favorite of the moment. Even Henry's proposed disposition of his estates and
titles served only to further their quarrels with each other and with him.
These quarrels reached their first climax in the great rebellion of 1173, in
which Henry the young king, Richard, and Geoffrey were in open alliance
with Louis of France against their father. To the alliance flocked rebellious
barons from Scotland to Aquitaine. Henry charged Eleanor with sedition
and with embittering their sons against him. As the rebellion faltered and
then was quelled, Henry was reconciled, however fitfully, with his sons but
not their mother. With Eleanor, Henry was unyielding. She was impris-
oned, first at Salisbury Castle, later at Winchester and other places, for the
next sixteen years. One must imagine that the captivity was genteel, but it
was nonetheless real. From time to time, she was released for a holiday visit
to court or to participate in some stormy family council.
    In the last years of Eleanor's imprisonment, two of her sons, Henry and
Geoffrey, died, but the surviving sons, Richard and John, could still intrigue against their father. They did so in league with a new and more
dangerous Capetian enemy, Philip II Augustus, the able and energetic son
of Louis VII, who had followed him to the throne in 1180. Henry II's final
years were filled with his sons' rebellion, and he died in 1189 shamed by
defeat at their hands. It was only after Henry's death and the succession of
Richard that Eleanor was released from her captivity.
    With none of her ardor dimmed, the queen, now almost seventy, set about
to serve her favored son, now king at last. While Richard was still on the
Continent, Eleanor assumed the regency and on her own authority
convoked a court at Westminster to demand the oaths of loyalty from the
English feudality to their new king. She then traveled to other centers to
take similar obeisances and to set the affairs of the kingdom in order. Her
son arrived for an undisputed coronation in the summer of 1189.
    But Richard's thoughts in that triumphal summer season were not upon
the affairs of England or any of his other lands. He had already taken the
cross almost two years before, and the third crusade was about to begin. The
Lion Hearted was to be its greatest hero.
    The third crusade, despite Richard's heroics, was as unsuccessful as the
second. And, after three years, during which most of his fellow crusaders
had declared their vows discharged and returned to their own lands—
including his Capetian rival, Philip Augustus—Richard started for home.
    We pick up the story of his return—with its delays and betrayals—and of
Eleanor's role in it from her recent biography, by Marion Meade,* **Eleanor**

of Aquitaine: A Biography. *Meade's book is broadly revisionist, and the basis of her revisionism is her feminism. Meade observes that "the historical record, written to accommodate men" has judged Eleanor ". . . a bitch, harlot, adultress, and monster" and that this is not surprising "for she was one of those rare women who altogether refused to be bound by the rules of proper behavior for her sex; she did as she pleased, although not without agonizing personal struggle" (p. ix). In Meade's account, as in any other account of Eleanor, there is much latitude for interpretation, given the pervasive silence of contemporary chronicles. Meade further argues that even these are "riddled with lies since monks and historians—in the twelfth century one and the same—have always abhorred emancipated women" (p. xi). Meade intends to redress the balance. And she does so, in no part of her account more forcefully than in the following passage.*

In England, Eleanor was expecting her son home for Christmas. All through November and early December companies of Crusaders had begun arriving in the kingdom; in the ports and marketplaces there were firsthand reports of the king's deeds in Palestine and plans for celebrations once he arrived. But the days passed without news, and newly arrived contingents of soldiers expressed astonishment that they had beaten the king home although they had left Acre after Richard. Along the coast, lookouts peered into the foggy Channel in hope of sighting the royal vessel, and messengers waited to race over the frozen roads toward London with the news of the king's landing. Eleanor learned that Berengaria and Joanna[2] had safely reached Rome, but of her son, weeks overdue, there was an alarming lack of information. She held a cheerless Christmas court at Westminster, her apprehension mounting with each day, her silent fears being expressed openly in the ale houses along the Thames: The king had encountered some calamity, a storm along the Adriatic coast no doubt, and now he would never return.

Three days after Christmas, the whereabouts of the tardy Richard Plantagenet became known, not at Westminster but at the Cité Palace in Paris. On December 28, Philip Augustus received an astounding letter from his good friend Henry Hohenstaufen, the Holy Roman emperor:[3]

---

[2]Berengaria was Richard's wife—a Spanish princess he had married, at Eleanor's urging, on his way to the crusade. Joanna was Richard's sister, the widowed Queen of Sicily, whom he had taken under his protection to Palestine.—ED.

[3]The Plantagenet kings were related by marriage to the great German feudal family, the Welfs, who were the most dangerous rivals to the imperial house of Hohenstaufen. The Angevins, including Richard, had frequently supported the Welfs, hence the emperor's hostility.—ED.

We have thought it proper to inform your nobleness that while the enemy of our empire and the disturber of your kingdom, Richard, King of England, was crossing the sea to his dominions, it chanced that the winds caused him to be shipwrecked in the region of Istria, at a place which lies between Aquila and Venice. . . . The roads being duly watched and the entire area well-guarded, our dearly beloved cousin Leopold, Duke of Austria, captured the king in a humble house in a village near Vienna. Inasmuch as he is now in our power, and has always done his utmost for your annoyance and disturbance, we have thought it proper to relay this information to your nobleness.

Shortly after the first of the new year, 1193, the archbishop of Rouen was able to send Eleanor a copy of the letter, accompanied by a covering note in which he cited whatever comforting quotations he could recall from Scripture to cover an outrage of this magnitude.

Eleanor's most imperative problem—finding the location where Richard was being held prisoner—she tackled with her usual energy and resourcefulness. From all points, emissaries were dispatched to find the king: Eleanor herself sent the abbots of Boxley and Pontrobert to roam the villages of Bavaria and Swabia, following every lead and rumor; Hubert Walter, bishop of Salisbury, stopping in Italy on his way home from the Crusade, changed course and hastened to Germany; even William Longchamp, the exiled chancellor, set out at once from Paris to trace his master. It was not until March, however, that Richard's chaplain, Anselm, who had shared many of the king's misadventures, arrived in England, and Eleanor was able to obtain authentic details [including the fact that Richard was being held in a remote castle of Durrenstein in Austria].

Treachery was rife not only in Germany but in Paris and Rouen; it even percolated rapidly in the queen's own family. Before Eleanor could take steps to secure Coeur de Lion's release, she was faced with more immediate catastrophes in the form of Philip Augustus and his newest ally, her son John. These two proceeded on the assumption that Richard, king of England, was dead. Or as good as dead. But before Eleanor could take her youngest son in hand, he fled to Normandy, where he declared himself the king's heir, an announcement the Norman barons greeted with disdain. John did not wait to convince them, proceeding instead to Paris, where he did homage to Philip for the Plantagenet Continental domains and furthermore agreeing to confirm Philip's right to the Vexin.[4] . . . In the meantime, Eleanor, "who then ruled England," had taken the precaution of

---

[4]The Vexin was an area at the juncture of Normandy, Anjou, and the Île de France, long disputed by the English and French kings.—ED.

closing the Channel ports and ordering the defense of the eastern coast against a possible invasion, her hastily mustered home guard being instructed to wield any weapon that came to hand, including their plowing tools.

At this point, Eleanor's dilemma in regard to her sons would have taxed the most patient of mothers. John, returning to England, swaggered about the countryside proclaiming himself the next king of England—perhaps he sincerely believed that Richard would never be released alive—and, never known for his sensitivity, constantly regaled Eleanor with the latest rumors concerning the fate of her favorite son. Her actions during this period indicate clearly that she failed to take John seriously. Although he was twenty-seven, she thought of him as the baby of the family, always a child showing off and trying to attract attention. Her attitude was probably close to that of Richard's when, a few months later, he was informed of John's machinations: "My brother John is not the man to subjugate a country if there is a person able to make the slightest resistance to his attempts." With one hand, Eleanor deftly managed to anticipate John's plots and render him harmless; with the other, she worked for Richard's release. After Easter, the king had been removed from Durrenstein Castle and the hands of Duke Leopold and, after some haggling, had been taken into custody by Leopold's suzerain, the Holy Roman emperor. As the emperor's prisoner, Richard found himself the object of high-level decisions. His death, it was decided, would achieve no useful purpose; rather the arrogant Plantagenets, or what remained of them, should be made to redeem their kin, but at a price that would bring their provinces to their knees: 100,000 silver marks with two hundred hostages as surety for payment. The hostages, it was specified, were to be chosen from among the leading barons of England and Normandy or from their children.

Relieved as Eleanor must have felt to learn that her son could be purchased, she could only have been appalled at the size of the ransom. The prospect of collecting such an enormous sum, thirty-five tons of pure silver, seemed impossible after Henry's Saladin tithe[5] and Richard's great sale before the Crusade.[6] Where was the money to be found? Where were two hundred noble hostages to be located? At a council convened at Saint Albans on June 1, 1193, she appointed five officers to assist with the dreaded task. During the summer and fall,

---

[5]A tax that Henry had levied for a crusade, hence called after the great Moslem leader Saladin.—ED.

[6]A sale not only of movable property of the crown but that of such protected folk as foreign and Jewish merchants, and what could be extracted from the nobility.—ED.

England became a marketplace to raise the greatest tax in its history. The kingdom was stripped of its wealth: "No subject, lay or clerk, rich or poor, was overlooked. No one could say, 'Behold I am only So-and-So or Such-and-Such, pray let me be excused.' " Barons were taxed one-quarter of a year's income. Churches and abbeys were relieved of their movable wealth, including the crosses on their altars. The Cistercians, who possessed no riches, sheared their flocks and donated a year's crop of wool. Before long, the bars of silver and gold began slowly to pile up in the crypt of Saint Paul's Cathedral under Eleanor's watchful eyes. But not quickly enough to comfort her. Even more painful was the job of recruiting hostages from the great families, their lamentations and pleadings rising like a sulphurous mist all over the kingdom and providing constant agony for the queen.

From Haguenau, where Richard was incarcerated, came a flood of letters to his subjects and most especially to his "much loved mother." He had been received with honor by the emperor and his court, he is well, he hopes to be home soon. He realizes that the ransom will be difficult to raise but he feels sure that his subjects will not shirk their duty; all sums collected should be entrusted to the queen. . . .

It is said that in her anguish she addressed three letters to Pope Celestine III imploring his assistance in securing Richard's release and in her salutation addressed the pontiff as "Eleanor, by the wrath of God, Queen of England." . . . Why, she demands, does the sword of Saint Peter slumber in its scabbard when her son a "most delicate youth," the anointed of the Lord, lies in chains? Why does the pope, a "negligent," "cruel" prevaricator and sluggard, do nothing?

These letters, supposedly written for her by Peter of Blois, are so improbable that it is surprising that many modern historians have accepted them as authentic. While preserved among the letters of Peter of Blois, who is undoubtedly their author—they are characteristic of his style and use his favorite expressions—there is no evidence that they were written for Eleanor or that they were ever sent. Most likely they were rhetorical exercises. No contemporary of Eleanor's mentioned that she wrote to the pope, and not until the seventeenth century were the letters attributed to her. From a diplomatic point of view, they are too fanciful to be genuine; Eleanor, clearheaded and statesmanlike, was never a querulous old woman complaining of age, infirmities, and weariness of life. On the contrary, her contemporaries unanimously credit her with the utmost courage, industry, and political skill. A second point to notice is that the details of the letters misrepresent the facts of Richard's imprisonment. He was never "detained in bonds," and as both she and the pope knew, Celestine had instantly, upon receiving news of Richard's capture, excommunicated Duke Leopold for laying violent hands on a brother Crusader; he had threatened Philip Augustus with an interdict if he trespassed upon Plantagenet territories; and he had menaced the English with interdict should they fail to collect the ransom. Under the circumstances, Celestine had done all he could. In the last analysis, the letters must be viewed as Peter of Blois's perception of Eleanor's feelings, a view that may or may not be accurate.

In December 1193, Eleanor set sail with an imposing retinue of clerks, chaplains, earls, bishops, hostages, and chests containing the ransom. By January 17, 1194, the day scheduled for Richard's release, she had presented herself and the money at Speyer, but no sooner had they arrived than, to her amazement, Henry Hohenstaufen announced a further delay. He had received letters that placed an entirely new light on the matter of the king's liberation. As the gist of the problem emerged, it seemed Philip Augustus and John Plantagenet had offered the emperor an equivalent amount of silver if he could hold Coeur de Lion in custody another nine months, or deliver him up to them. These disclosures, and Henry's serious consideration of the counteroffer, provoked horror from the emperor's own vassals, and after two days of argument, Henry relented. He would liberate Richard as promised if the king of England would do homage to him for all his possessions, including the kingdom of England. This request, a calculated humiliation, would have made Richard a vassal of the Holy Roman emperor, a degradation that the Plantagenets were hard put to accept. Quick to realize the meaninglessness, as well as the illegality, of the required act, Eleanor made an on-the-spot decision. According to Roger of Hovedon, Richard, "by advice of his mother Eleanor, abdicated the throne of the kingdom of England and delivered it to the emperor as the lord of all." On February 4, the king was released "into the hands of his mother" after a captivity of one year six weeks and three days.

Seven weeks later, on March 12, the king's party landed at Sandwich and proceeded directly to Canterbury, where they gave thanks at the tomb of Saint Thomas. By the time they reached London, the city had been decorated, the bells were clanging furiously, and the Londoners ready to give a rapturous welcome to their hero and champion. Her eldest son "hailed with joy upon the Strand," Eleanor looked in vain for the remaining male member of her family, but the youngest Plantagenet was nowhere to be found. Once Richard's release had been confirmed, he had fled to Paris upon Philip Augustus's warning that "beware, the devil is loose." . . .

According to the chronicles, "the king and John became reconciled through the mediation of Queen Eleanor, their mother." In the circumstances, it seemed the safest course as well as the wisest. There was no doubt in Eleanor's mind that the boy, now twenty-eight, could not be held responsible for his actions, that he was, as Richard of Devizes termed him, "light-minded." But at that moment, he was the last of the Plantagenets. With luck, Richard might reign another twenty-five years or more. Who was to say that he would not produce an heir of his own? Thus the queen must have reasoned in the spring of 1194 when her son, after so many adversities, had come home to her.

Review and Study Questions

1. What were Eleanor's motives in her indiscreet flirtation with Raymond of Antioch?
2. What role did Eleanor play in the evolution of medieval chivalric culture?
3. What role did Eleanor play in European political affairs?
4. To what extent should Eleanor be considered a feminist heroine?

Suggestions for Further Reading

As we have seen, despite her importance and inherent interest, there are virtually no contemporary source materials for Eleanor. Thus, whether hostile or sympathetic, the treatments of Eleanor have had to be not so much biographies as life-and-times books. This is true even of the best modern works. Two of them, Amy Kelly, *Eleanor of Aquitaine and the Four Kings* (Cambridge, Mass.: Harvard University Press, 1950), and Marion Meade, *Eleanor of Aquitaine: A Biography* (New York: Hawthorn, 1977), are excerpted in this chapter, and students are encouraged to read further in them. Two additional works are also recommended: Curtis H. Walker, *Eleanor of Aquitaine* (Chapel Hill: University of North Carolina Press, 1950), and Regine Pernoud, *Eleanor of Aquitaine,* tr. P. Wiles (New York: Coward-McCann, 1967), both well written, lively, and fast moving. *Eleanor of Aquitaine: Patron and Politician,* ed. Wm. W. Kibler (Austin: University of Texas Press, 1976), is a series of specialized papers on aspects of Eleanor's life and reign.

Of Eleanor's contemporaries, the best, most comprehensive, and up-to-date work on Henry II is W. L. Warren, *Henry II* (London: Eyre Methuen, 1973). Somewhat less intimidating are the smaller but entirely competent Richard Barber, *Henry Plantagenet* (Totowa, N.J.: Rowman and Littlefield, 1964), and John Schlight, *Henry II Plantagenet,* "Rulers and Statesmen of the World" (New York: Twayne, 1973). Probably the best biography of Richard I is Philip Henderson, *Richard Coeur de Lion: A Biography* (New York: Norton, 1959), but students are also encouraged to read James A. Brundage, *Richard Lion Heart* (New York: Scribners, 1974), largely a study of Richard as soldier and crusader, and a tough, realistic work. The standard work on John is Sidney Painter, *The Reign of King John* (Baltimore: Johns Hopkins University Press, 1949). W. L. Warren, *King John* (Berkeley: University of California Press, 1978), is a somewhat revisionist treatment of John showing him as a hard-working monarch and more the victim than the causer of his troubles—but he still is a far from attractive figure. For Eleanor's French royal contemporaries, see R. Fawtier, *The Capetian Kings of France,* tr. Lionel Butler and R. J. Adam (London: Macmillan, 1960). There are a handful of studies of important nonroyal figures whose lives intertwined with Eleanor's: Sidney Painter, *William Marshall: Knight Errant, Baron, and Regent of England* (Baltimore: Johns Hopkins University Press, 1933); Charles R. Young, *Hubert Walter: Lord of Canterbury and Lord of England* (Durham, N.C.: Duke University Press, 1968); and a number of books on the durable subject of Henry and Becket—the best are Richard Winston, *Thomas Becket* (New York: Knopf, 1967), a tough, skeptical, but solidly source-based work; Dom David Knowles, *Thomas Becket* (London: A. and C. Black, 1970), a scrupulously objective account by a great ecclesiastical historian, but, naturally, most occupied with the arguments of Thomas and the church; and finally, Alfred L. Duggan, *My Life for My Sheep* (New York: Coward-McCann, 1955), a lively novelized account by an experienced historical novelist.

Two special topics relate to Eleanor throughout her life—chivalry and courtly love and the crusades. Both have been much studied and written about. On chivalry and courtly love, see two excellent and well-written background works—John C. Moore, *Love in Twelfth-Century France* (Philadelphia: University of Pennsylvania Press, 1972), and Jack Lindsay, *The Troubadours and Their World of the Twelfth and Thirteenth Centuries* (London: Frederick Muller, 1976), and two equally interesting ones dealing with the actual operation of knightly chivalry as well as its romanticized literary aspects—Sidney Painter, *French Chivalry: Chivalric Ideas and Practices in Medieval France* (Baltimore: Johns Hopkins University Press, 1940), and the more comprehensive Richard Barber, *The Knight and Chivalry* (New York: Scribners, 1970). But the definitive work on chivalry in all its aspects is Maurice Keen, *Chivalry* (New Haven: Yale University Press, 1984). The standard work on the crusades is now *The History of the Crusades* (Philadelphia: University of Pennsylvania, 1955–1962), a great multiauthored work under the general editorship of Kenneth M. Setton: vol. 1, *The First Hundred Years,* ed. M. W. Baldwin, and vol. 2, *The Later Crusades, 1189–1311,* ed. R. L. Wolff. Steven Runciman, *A History of the Crusades,* 3 vols. (Cambridge, England: Cambridge University Press, 1951–1954), may, however, still be the best account. Students may prefer Zoé Oldenbourg, *The Crusades,* tr. Anne Carter (New York: Pantheon, 1966), somewhat less successful than her famous historical novels but still excellent and exciting. For the warfare of the period, students should look at the recent and comprehensive Philippe Contamine, *War in the Middle Ages,* tr. Michael Jones (Oxford: Blackwell, 1984), especially the sections on the Feudal Age and Medieval Society at its prime.

LEONARDO DA VINCI: UNIVERSAL MAN OF THE RENAISSANCE

1452	Born
1472	Admitted to Florentine painters' guild
1482–1499	In service of Ludovico Sforza of Milan
1516	Entered service of Francis I of France
1519	Died

More than any other figure, Leonardo da Vinci is commonly regarded as the exemplar of that uniquely Renaissance ideal *uomo universale,* the universal man.

Leonardo, the spoiled, loved, and pampered illegitimate son of a well-to-do Florentine notary, was born in 1452 at the very midpoint of Florence's magnificent Renaissance century, the Quattrocento. The boy grew up at his father's country home in the village of Vinci. His precocious genius and his talent for drawing led his father to apprentice Leonardo to the artist Verrocchio in Florence. While Verrocchio is best remembered as a sculptor, it should be noted that he was, like most Florentine artists of his time, a versatile master of other artistic crafts, and that his *bottega*—like Ghiberti's earlier or Michelangelo's later—was not only a lively school of craftsmanship and technique but a place where people gathered to gossip and talk over a wide range of subjects. Here the young Leonardo's multiple talents bloomed.

At the age of twenty Leonardo was admitted to the painters' guild and soon after set up his own shop and household. He was well enough received and commissions came his way. But, for reasons that are not entirely clear, he seems not to have been marked for the lavish patronage of the Medici family—as were so many of his fellow artists—or of any other great Florentine houses. The fashion of the moment preferred those artists like Alberti and Botticelli who mingled learned humanism with their art and could converse in Latin with the humanists, poets, and philosophers who dominated the intellectual scene in Florence. But Leonardo knew no Latin. His education consisted only of apprenticeship training and beyond that a hodge-podge of self-instruction directed to his own wide-ranging interests, in some areas profound and original, in others hopelessly limited and naive. It is also possible that Leonardo may simply have set himself apart from the circle of his fellow artists and their patrons. There are hints of alienation and jealousy and even a vaguely worded reference to a homosexual charge against him that was brought before a magistrate and then dropped. But it is most likely that Leonardo's own restless curiosity was already carrying him beyond the practice of his art.

In 1482 Leonardo left Florence for Milan and the court of its lord, Ludovico Sforza, one of the most powerful princes of Italy. In the letter Leonardo wrote commending himself to Ludovico, which has been preserved, he described himself as a military architect, siege and hydraulic engineer, ordnance and demolition expert, architect, sculptor, and painter; he ended the letter, "And if any one of the above-named things seems to anyone to be impossible or not feasible, I am most ready to make the experiment in your park, or in whatever place may please your Excellency, to whom I commend myself with the utmost humility."[1] Humility indeed! The universal man had declared himself.

Leonardo spent the next seventeen years—the most vigorous and productive of his life—at the court of Milan. He painted *The Last Supper* for the Dominican Convent of Santa Maria delle Grazie. He conceived and created the model for what might well have been the world's greatest equestrian statue; but the statue, memorializing Ludovico Sforza's father, the old soldier-duke Francesco, was never cast, and the model was destroyed. In addition, Leonardo created gimcrackery for court balls and fetes—costumes, jewelry, scenery, engines, floats, spectacles. But increasingly he was occupied with studies of a bewildering variety of subjects. The notebooks he kept reveal drawings and notes on the flight of birds and the possibility of human flight; military engineering, tanks, submarines, exploding shells, rapid-firing artillery pieces, and fortifications; bold schemes for city planning and hydraulic engineering; plans for machinery of every sort, pulleys, gears, self-propelled vehicles, a mechanical clock, and a

---

[1]Quoted in E. G. Holt (ed.), *A Documentary History of Art* (New York: Doubleday, 1957), vol. I, pp. 273–275.

file cutter; detailed studies of plant, animal, and human anatomy that go well beyond the needs of an artist; a complete treatise on painting and another on the comparison of the arts. Despite the fact that much of this body of work—including a treatise on perspective that was reputed to be far in advance of other such works—was scattered and lost, some seven thousand pages have survived, all written in a code-like, left-handed, mirror script.

Leonardo's handwriting is of particular interest, for it is indicative of a special side of his nature—almost obsessively secretive, aloof, touchy and suspicious of others. These qualities are part of the traditional image of Leonardo that has been passed down to us, beginning with his earliest biography, by his younger contemporary Vasari.

In Praise of Leonardo

GIORGIO VASARI

Giorgio Vasari (1511–1574) was himself something of a universal man. He was an artist of more than middling ability who worked all over Italy. He was also a respected functionary, the familiar of popes, princes, and dignitaries, as well as artists and scholars. But his most important achievement was his book Lives of the Most Eminent Painters, Sculptors & Architects from Cimabue until our own Time, *the first edition published in Florence in 1550. Wallace K. Ferguson has called it "a masterpiece of art history."[2] In fact, the book is more than a masterpiece of art history, for it virtually created the concept of art history itself.*

Vasari introduces "our present age" with his treatment of Leonardo. But this biography, despite its extravagant praise of Leonardo's genius, is seriously limited. Vasari had access to many of Leonardo's notes, even some that we no longer have. But he was most familiar with the art and artists of Tuscany. It is clear that he had not actually seen several of Leonardo's most important works, in Milan and elsewhere. And much of the information he provided on Leonardo's life was nothing more than current rumor or gossip about him. Vasari, furthermore, was himself a pupil and lifelong admirer of Leonardo's great contemporary Michelangelo (1475–1564), and it was Vasari's thesis that the whole tradition of Italian art reached its fulfillment in Michelangelo. It might be recalled also that Michelangelo despised Leonardo; they had at least one nasty quarrel. And Michelangelo was fond of saying that Leonardo was a technically incompetent craftsman, who could not complete the projects he began. Whether by design or not, this charge became the main line of criticism in Vasari's biography of Leonardo, and it has persisted alongside Leonardo's reputation as an enigmatic genius.

We look now at Vasari's account from Lives of the Most Eminent Painters, Sculptors & Architects.

The greatest gifts are often seen, in the course of nature, rained by celestial influences on human creatures; and sometimes, in supernatural fashion, beauty, grace, and talent are united beyond measure in one single person, in a manner that to whatever such an one turns his

---

[2]In *The Renaissance in Historical Thought: Five Centuries of Interpretation* (Boston: Houghton Mifflin, 1948), p. 60.

attention, his every action is so divine, that, surpassing all other men, it makes itself clearly known as a thing bestowed by God (as it is), and not acquired by human art. This was seen by all mankind in Leonardo da Vinci, in whom, besides a beauty of body never sufficiently extolled, there was an infinite grace in all his actions; and so great was his genius, and such its growth, that to whatever difficulties he turned his mind, he solved them with ease. In him was great bodily strength, joined to dexterity, with a spirit and courage ever royal and magnanimous; and the fame of his name so increased, that not only in his lifetime was he held in esteem, but his reputation became even greater among posterity after his death.

Truly marvellous and celestial was Leonardo, the son of Ser Piero da Vinci; and in learning and in the rudiments of letters he would have made great proficience, if he had not been so variable and unstable, for he set himself to learn many things, and then, after having begun them, abandoned them. Thus, in arithmetic, during the few months that he studied it, he made so much progress, that, by continually suggesting doubts and difficulties to the master who was teaching him, he would very often bewilder him. He gave some little attention to music, and quickly resolved to learn to play the lyre, as one who had by nature a spirit most lofty and full of refinement; wherefore he sang divinely to that instrument, improvising upon it. Nevertheless, although he occupied himself with such a variety of things, he never ceased drawing and working in relief, pursuits which suited his fancy more than any other. Ser Piero, having observed this, and having considered the loftiness of his intellect, one day took some of his drawings and carried them to Andrea del Verrocchio, who was much his friend, and besought him straitly to tell him whether Leonardo, by devoting himself to drawing, would make any proficience. Andrea was astonished to see the extraordinary beginnings of Leonardo, and urged Ser Piero that he should make him study it; wherefore he arranged with Leonardo that he should enter the workshop of Andrea, which Leonardo did with the greatest willingness in the world. And he practised not one branch of art only, but all those in which drawing played a part; and having an intellect so divine and marvellous that he was also an excellent geometrician, he not only worked in sculpture, making in his youth, in clay, some heads of women that are smiling, of which plaster casts are still taken, and likewise some heads of boys which appeared to have issued from the hand of a master; but in architecture, also, he made many drawings both of ground-plans and of other designs of buildings; and he was the first, although but a youth, who suggested the plan of reducing the river Arno to a navigable canal from Pisa to Florence. He made designs of flour-mills, fulling-mills, and engines, which might be driven by the force of water: and since he wished that his profession should be painting, he studied much in drawing after nature. . . . He was continually making models and designs to show men how to re-move mountains with ease, and how to bore them in order to pass from one level to another; and by means of levers, windlasses, and screws, he showed the way to raise and draw great weights, together with methods for emptying harbours, and pumps for removing water from low places, things which his brain never ceased from devising; and of these ideas and labours many drawings may be seen, scattered abroad among our craftsmen; and I myself have seen not a few. . . .

He was so pleasing in conversation, that he attracted to himself the hearts of men. And although he possessed, one might say, nothing, and worked little, he always kept servants and horses, in which latter he took much delight, and particularly in all other animals, which he managed with the greatest love and patience; and this he showed when often passing by the places where birds were sold, for, taking them with his own hand out of their cages, and having paid to those who sold them the price that was asked, he let them fly away into the air, restoring to them their lost liberty. For which reason nature was pleased so to favour him, that, wherever he turned his thought, brain, and mind, he displayed such divine power in his works, that, in giving them their perfection, no one was ever his peer in readiness, vivacity, excellence, beauty, and grace.

It is clear that Leonardo, through his comprehension of art, began many things and never finished one of them, since it seemed to him that the hand was not able to attain to the perfection of art in carrying out the things which he imagined; for the reason that he conceived in idea difficulties so subtle and so marvellous, that they could never be expressed by the hands, be they ever so excellent. And so many were his caprices, that, philosophizing of natural things, he set himself to seek out the properties of herbs, going on even to observe the motions of the heavens, the path of the moon, and the courses of the sun. . . .

He began a panel-picture of the Adoration of the Magi, containing many beautiful things, particularly the heads, which was in the house of Amerigo Benci, opposite the Loggia de' Peruzzi; and this, also, remained unfinished, like his other works.

It came to pass that Giovan Galeazzo, Duke of Milan, being dead, and Lodovico Sforza raised to the same rank, in the year 1494,[3] Leonardo was summoned to Milan in great repute to the Duke, who took much delight in the sound of the lyre, to the end that he might play it: and Leonardo took with him that instrument which he had made with his own hands, in great part of silver, in the form of a

---

[3]The date was actually 1482.—ED.

horse's skull—a thing bizarre and new—in order that the harmony might be of greater volume and more sonorous in tone; with which he surpassed all the musicians who had come together there to play. Besides this, he was the best improviser in verse of his day. The Duke, hearing the marvellous discourse of Leonardo, became so enamoured of his genius, that it was something incredible: and he prevailed upon him by entreaties to paint an altar-panel containing a Nativity, which was sent by the Duke to the Emperor.

He also painted in Milan, for the Friars of S. Dominic, at S. Maria delle Grazie, a Last Supper, a most beautiful and marvellous thing; and to the heads of the Apostles he gave such majesty and beauty, that he left the head of Christ unfinished, not believing that he was able to give it that divine air which is essential to the image of Christ.[4] This work, remaining thus all but finished, has ever been held by the Milanese in the greatest veneration, and also by strangers as well; for Leonardo imagined and succeeded in expressing that anxiety which had seized the Apostles in wishing to know who should betray their Master. . . .

While he was engaged on this work, he proposed to the Duke to make a horse in bronze, of a marvellous greatness, in order to place upon it, as a memorial, the image of the Duke.[5] And on so vast a scale did he begin it and continue it, that it could never be completed. And there are those who have been of the opinion (so various and so often malign out of envy are the judgments of men) that he began it with no intention of finishing it, because, being of so great a size, an incredible difficulty was encountered in seeking to cast it in one piece; and it might also be believed that, from the result, many may have formed such a judgment, since many of his works have remained unfinished. But, in truth, one can believe that his vast and most excellent mind was hampered through being too full of desire, and that his wish ever to seek out excellence upon excellence, and perfection upon perfection, was the reason of it. "Tal che l'opera fosse ritardata dal desio,"[6] as our Petrarca has said. And, indeed, those who saw the great model that Leonardo made in clay vow that they have never seen a more beautiful thing, or a more superb; and it was preserved until the French came to Milan with King Louis of France, and broke it all to pieces.[7] Lost, also, is a little model of it in wax, which was held to be perfect, together with a book on the anatomy of the horse made by him by way of study.

---

[4]The head of Christ was finished, along with the rest of the painting. Vasari was repeating gossip and had not seen the work.—ED.

[5]Rather of the Duke's father, Francesco, the founder of the Sforza dynasty.—ED.

[6]"So that the work was retarded by the very desire of it."—ED.

[7]Louis XII of France. The incident of the model's destruction took place during the French occupation of Milan in 1499.—ED.

He then applied himself, but with greater care, to the anatomy of man, assisted by and in turn assisting, in this research, Messer Marc' Antonio della Torre, an excellent philosopher, who was then lecturing at Pavia, and who wrote of this matter; and he was one of the first (as I have heard tell) that began to illustrate the problems of medicine with the doctrine of Galen, and to throw true light on anatomy, which up to that time had been wrapped in the thick and gross darkness of ignorance. And in this he found marvellous aid in the brain, work, and hand of Leonardo, who made a book drawn in red chalk, and annotated with the pen, of the bodies that he dissected with his own hand, and drew with the greatest diligence; wherein he showed all the frame of the bones; and then added to them, in order, all the nerves, and covered them with muscles; the first attached to the bone, the second that hold the body firm, and the third that move it; and beside them, part by part, he wrote in letters of an ill-shaped character, which he made with the left hand, backwards; and whoever is not practised in reading them cannot understand them, since they are not to be read save with a mirror. . . .

With the fall of Ludovico Sforza and the French occupation of Milan in 1499, the artist returned to Florence.

Leonardo undertook to execute, for Francesco del Giocondo, the portrait of Monna Lisa, his wife; and after toiling over it for four years, he left it unfinished; and the work is now in the collection of King Francis of France, at Fontainebleau. In this head, whoever wished to see how closely art could imitate nature, was able to comprehend it with ease; for in it were counterfeited all the minutenesses that with subtlety are able to be painted. . . .

By reason, then, of the excellence of the works of this divine craftsman, his fame had so increased that all persons who took delight in art—nay, the whole city of Florence—desired that he should leave them some memorial, and it was being proposed everywhere that he should be commissioned to execute some great and notable work, whereby the commonwealth might be honoured and adorned by the great genius, grace and judgment that were seen in the works of Leonardo. And it was decided between the Gonfalonier[8] and the chief citizens, the Great Council Chamber having been newly built . . . and having been finished in great haste, it was ordained by public decree that Leonardo should be given some beautiful work to paint; and so the said hall was allotted to him by Piero Soderini, then Gonfalonier of Justice. Whereupon Leonardo, determining to execute this work, be-

---

[8]The title of the chief magistrate of Florence.—ED.

gan a cartoon in the Sala del Papa, an apartment in S. Maria Novella, representing the story of Niccolò Piccinino,[9] Captain of Duke Filippo of Milan; wherein he designed a group of horsemen who were fighting for a standard, a work that was held to be very excellent and of great mastery, by reason of the marvellous ideas that he had in composing that battle. . . . It is said that, in order to draw that cartoon, he made a most ingenious stage, which was raised by contracting it and lowered by expanding. And conceiving the wish to colour on the wall in oils, he made a composition of so gross an admixture, to act as a binder on the wall, that, going on to paint in the said hall, it began to peel off in such a manner that in a short time he abandoned it, seeing it spoiling.[10] . . .

He went to Rome with Duke Giuliano de' Medici, at the election of Pope Leo,[11] who spent much of his time on philosophical studies, and particularly on alchemy; where, forming a paste of a certain kind of wax, as he walked he shaped animals very thin and full of wind, and, by blowing into them, made them fly through the air, but when the wind ceased they fell to the ground. . . .

He made an infinite number of such follies, and gave his attention to mirrors; and he tried the strangest methods in seeking out oils for painting, and varnish for preserving works when painted. . . . It is related that, a work having been allotted to him by the Pope, he straight-way began to distil oils and herbs, in order to make the varnish; at which Pope Leo said: "Alas! this man will never do anything, for he begins by thinking of the end of the work, before the beginning."

There was very great disdain between Michelagnolo Buonarroti and him, on account of which Michelagnolo departed from Florence, with the excuse of Duke Giuliano, having been summoned by the Pope to the competition for the façade of S. Lorenzo. Leonardo, understanding this, departed and went into France, where the King, having had works by his hand, bore him great affection; and he desired that he should colour the cartoon of S. Anne, but Leonardo, according to his custom, put him off for a long time with words.

Finally, having grown old, he remained ill many months, and, feeling himself near to death, asked to have himself diligently informed of the teaching of the Catholic faith. . . . [He] expired in the arms of the King, in the seventy-fifth year of his age.[12]

---

[9]A mercenary commander who had worked for Florence.—ED.

[10]Michelangelo was assigned a companion panel and also abandoned his work on it before it was completed.—ED.

[11]Pope Leo X, the former Giovanni Cardinal dei Medici.—ED.

[12]Vasari is inaccurate. In the year Leonardo died, 1519, he actually was sixty-seven.—ED.

Leonardo the Scientist

JOHN HERMAN RANDALL, JR.

From Vasari's time to the present, there has clung to the image of Leonardo da Vinci a kind of Faustian quality, linking him to the origins of modern science. Throughout his life, and increasingly from middle age on, Leonardo was preoccupied with technical studies and scientific experiments, often to the detriment of his art. But the judgments of modern scholars on "Leonardo the scientist" are much more varied and more circumspect than those upon "Leonardo the artist."

We turn first to the views of a distinguished philosopher and historian of science, especially medieval and Renaissance science, the long-time Columbia University Professor of Philosophy, John Herman Randall, Jr. This selection is from his article "The Place of Leonardo da Vinci in the Emergence of Modern Science."

Leonardo was not himself a scientist. "Science" is not the hundred-odd aphorisms or "pensieri" that have been pulled out of his Codici and collected, by Richter, Solmi, and others. "Science" is not oracular utterances, however well phrased; it is not bright ideas jotted down in a notebook. "Science" is systematic and methodical thought. . . .

"Science" is not just the appeal to experience, though it involves such an appeal, as Leonardo stated in answering those critics who had censured him as a mere empiric: "If I could not indeed like them cite authors and books, it is a much greater and worthier thing to profess to cite experience, the mistress of their masters." "Science" is not the mere rejection of authority, the case for which is well put by Leonardo: "He who argues by citing an authority is not employing intelligence but rather memory." . . .

It is true that during Leonardo's youth—the second half of the Quattrocento—the intellectual influence of the non-scientific humanists had been making for a kind of St. Martin's summer of the "authority" of the ancients, and that his life coincides with this rebirth of an authoritarian attitude toward the past. Leonardo's protests were magnificent, and doubtless pertinent. But they are not enough to constitute "science." "Science" is not merely fresh, first-hand observation, however detailed and accurate.

Above all, "science" is not the intuitions of a single genius, solitary

218

and alone, however suggestive. It is cooperative inquiry, such as had prevailed in the Italian schools from the time of Pietro d'Abano (†1315; his *Conciliator* appeared earlier)—and such as was to continue till the time of Galileo—the cumulative cooperative inquiry which actually played so large a part in the emergence of modern science. . . .

In practice, Leonardo always becomes fascinated by some particular problem—he has no interest in working out any systematic body of knowledge. His artist's interest in the particular and the concrete, which inspires his careful, precise and accurate observation, is carried further by his inordinate curiosity into a detailed analytic study of the factors involved. His thought seems always to be moving from the particularity of the painter's experience to the universality of intellect and science, without ever quite getting there. . . .

No evidence has ever been offered that anybody in the sixteenth century capable of appreciating scientific ideas ever saw the Codici of Leonardo. . . . But since the scientific ideas expressed therein were all well-known in the universities of Leonardo's day, and were accessible in much more elaborated form in the books the scientists were reading, there seems to be no "problem" of tracing any presumed "influence" of Leonardo on the development of sixteenth-century scientific thought in Italy.

The *Trattato de la Pittura*, or *Paragone*, was not printed until 1651, but its existence in manuscript form suggests that it had been read much earlier by the Urbino circle. It was put together from various manuscripts of Leonardo by an editor whose identity is not known, but who seems to have been responsible for its systematic organization—an organization which later editors have uniformly tried to improve upon.

With Leonardo's anatomical studies, the story is somewhat different. There is no evidence that Vesalius[13] ever actually saw his drawings; but in view of the marked similarities between them and his own much more systematically planned and organized series of drawings, it is difficult to think that he did not. . . .

Turning now from the things that Leonardo, despite all the adulations of his genius, was clearly not, let us try to state what seems to have been his real genius in scientific matters. During the Renaissance, as a result of the surprising dissolution of the rigid boundaries which had previously kept different intellectual traditions, as it were, in watertight compartments, the many different currents of thought which had long been preparing and strengthening themselves during the Middle Ages managed to come together, and to strike fire. The

---

[13]The Flemish anatomist at the University of Padua who in 1543 published the first modern, scientific descriptive treatise on human anatomy.—ED.

explanation of this phenomenon can ultimately be only sociological—the breaking down of the fairly rigid boundaries that had hitherto shut off one discipline and one intellectual tradition from another. Whatever its cause, the confluence of many different intellectual traditions in the fertile, all-too-fertile mind of Leonardo renders his views an unusually happy illustration of the way in which very diverse intellectual traditions managed during the Renaissance to unite together to create what we now call "modern science."

There is first the "scientific tradition," the careful, intelligent, cooperative and cumulative criticism of Aristotelian physics, which began with William of Ockham.[14] . . . In his reading Leonardo was in touch with this scientific tradition, as Duhem has shown.

There is secondly Leonardo's enthusiasm for mathematics, which goes far beyond its obvious instrumental use. It is very hard to assay the precise sense in which Leonardo thought of mathematics as the alphabet of nature: in this area much work remains to be done. There seems to be in Leonardo no trace of the popular contemporary Pythagoreanism or Platonism. If we examine Leonardo's conception of mathematics as depicted in his drawings, not as inadequately stated in his prose, we find that it differs markedly from the static and very geometrical notion of Dürer.[15] It is movement, not geometrical relations, that Leonardo is trying to capture. There is much in his drawings that suggests a world envisaged in terms of the calculus—like the world of Leibniz[16]—rather than in terms of the purely geometrical vision of the Greek tradition. In his mathematical vision of the world, Leonardo seems to belong to the realm of "dynamic" and "Faustian" attitudes, rather than to the static geometrical perfection of Greek thought.

There is thirdly the tradition of what Edgar Zilsel has called the "superior craftsman"—the man who is not afraid to take an idea and try it out, to experiment with it. . . . As a pupil of Verrocchio [Leonardo] had no fastidious objections to sullying his hands with "experiment." This habit of Leonardo's of descending from the academic cathedra and actually trying out the ideas of which he read had broad repercussions: it is one of the activities of Leonardo that seems to have become generally known, and to have awakened emulation. The consequences of Leonardo's willingness to experiment are to be found in the "practical geometry" of Tartaglia, the greatest of the sixteenth-century Italian mathematicians. Galileo, of course, was in

---

[14]The important nominalist philosopher of the early fourteenth century.—ED.

[15]The great German artist, a contemporary of Leonardo.—ED.

[16]The great German philosopher and mathematician of the seventeenth century who shares with Newton the discovery of the calculus.—ED.

this tradition of the "practical geometers"; he too was an indefatigable inventor. Indeed, Leonardo can fairly claim to belong not to the line of scientists but to the noble tradition of the inventors. . . .

Many of Leonardo's aphorisms treat the matter of the proper intellectual method. He has much to say on the relation between "reason" and "experience," and what he says used to lead commentators to impute to him the anticipation of Francis Bacon's "inductive method"—God save the mark, as though that had anything to do with the method employed by the pioneering scientists of the seventeenth century!

Neither experience alone nor reason alone will suffice. "Those who are enamored of practice without science are like the pilot who boards his ship without helm or compass, and who is never certain where he is going." On the other hand, pure reasoning is without avail: "Should you say that the sciences which begin and end in the mind have achieved truth, that I will not concede, but rather deny for many reasons; and first, because in such mental discourse there occurs no experience, without which there is no certainty to be found."

But Leonardo does not bother to give any precise definition of what he means by his key terms, "experience," "reason," "certainty," or "truth." Certainty depends on "experience," but "there is no certainty where one of the mathematical sciences cannot apply, or where the subject is not united with mathematics." And—maxim for all inventors!—"Mechanics is the paradise of the mathematical sciences, because in it they come to bear their mathematical fruits." . . .

These aphorisms as to the relation between reason and experience are no doubt rhetorically effective. But we have only to compare such vague utterances with the very detailed analyses of precisely the same methodological relation which were being carried out at this very time in the Aristotelian schools of the Italian universities to realize the difference between an artist's insights and the scientist's analysis.

Leonardo was above all else the anatomist of nature. He could see, and with his draughtsmanship depict clearly, the bony skeleton of the world—the geological strata and their indicated past. He could also see everywhere nature's simple machines in operation—in man and in the non-human world alike. . . .

As a genuine contributor, then, to the descriptive sciences, Leonardo reported with his pencil fundamental aspects of nature the great machine—in anatomy, geology, and hydrostatics. As a writer rather than as a graphic reporter, Leonardo shows himself an extremely intelligent reader. But he was clearly never so much the scientist as when he had his pencil in hand, and was penetrating to the mechanical structure of what he was observing.

Leonardo the Technologist

LADISLAO RETI

A substantial group of modern scholars agrees with Randall. Some, how-
ever, do not. In the following selection, we will sample the views of one of
them, Ladislao Reti, a historian of science and medicine and an authority
on Leonardo's scientific and technical manuscripts. Reti not only attaches
more importance to Leonardo's scientific work than does Randall; he vigor-
ously denies Randall's charges that Leonardo failed to exhibit a sustained,
systematic body of scientific thought; that he stood alone outside the tradition
of science; that he failed to develop a methodological terminology; and that
he failed to influence the evolution of science beyond his own time. But most
of all, Reti disputes Randall's view that science is abstract conception.
Rather, he takes the position that science must be the accumulation of par-
ticular observations and applications. Reti views "Leonardo the scientist" as
"Leonardo the technologist," and he insists that a technologist of such bril-
liance and inventiveness as Leonardo cannot be so readily dismissed. "The
greatest engineer of all times" surely deserves a place in the history of
science.

Varied as Leonardo's interests were, statistical analysis of his writings
points to technology as the main subject. As was acutely pointed out
by Bertrand Gille in a recent book, judging by the surviving original
documents, Leonardo's métier was rather an engineer's than an
artist's.

However we may feel about this opinion, it is disturbing to take an
inventory of Leonardo's paintings, of which no more than half a
dozen are unanimously authenticated by the world's leading experts.

Contrast this evident disinclination to paint with the incredible toil
and patience Leonardo lavished on scientific and technical studies,
particularly in the fields of geometry, mechanics, and engineering.
Here his very indulgence elicited curious reactions from his contemporaries and in the minds of his late biographers. They regretted that
a man endowed with such divine artistic genius should waste the
precious hours of his life in such vain pursuits. And, of course, as the
well-known episodes of his artistic career testify, this exposed him not
only to criticism but also to serious inconveniences.

But were Leonardo's nonartistic activities truly marginal?

Documentary evidence proves that every official appointment refers to him not only as an artist but as an engineer as well.

At the court of Ludovico il Moro he was *Ingeniarius et pinctor.*[17] Cesare Borgia called him his most beloved *Architecto et Engengero Generale.*[18] When he returned to Florence he was immediately consulted as military engineer. . . . Louis XII called him *nostre chier et bien amé Léonard da Vincy, nostre paintre et ingenieur ordinaire.*[19] Even in Rome, despite the pope's famous remark on hearing of Leonardo's experiments with varnishes preparatory to beginning an artistic commission, Leonardo's duties clearly included technical work, as is documented by three rough copies of a letter to his patron Giuliano de' Medici. Nor was his position different when he went to France at the invitation of Francis I. The official burial document calls him *Lionard de Vincy, noble millanois, premier peinctre et ingenieur et architecte du Roy, mescanichien d'Estat, et anchien directeur du peincture du Duc de Milan.*[20]

We can thus see that Leonardo had a lively interest in the mechanical arts and engineering from his earliest youth, as evidenced by the oldest drawing in the Codex Atlanticus, to the end of his industrious life. Thousands of his drawings witness to it, from fleeting sketches (though always executed with the most uncanny bravura) to presentation projects finished in chiaroscuro wash. Often these sketches and drawings are accompanied by a descriptive text, comments, and discussion.

The drawings and writings of Leonardo on technical matters, though scattered throughout the notebooks and especially in the Codex Atlanticus (a true order probably never existed nor did the author attempt to make one), represent an important and unique source for the history of technology. . . .

It is far from my intention and beyond my possibilities to discuss Leonardo's technology as a whole on this occasion. Enough is said when we remember that there is hardly a field of applied mechanics where Leonardo's searching mind has left no trace in the pages of his notebooks. To illustrate Leonardo's methods I shall limit myself to discussing some little-known aspects of how he dealt with the main problem of technology, the harnessing of energy to perform useful work.

---

[17]Engineer and painter.—ED.

[18]Architect and Engineer-General.—ED.

[19]Our dear and well-loved Leonardo da Vinci, our painter and engineer ordinary.—ED.

[20]Leonardo da Vinci, Milanese nobleman, first painter and engineer and architect of the King, state technician, and former director of painting of the Duke of Milan.—ED.

At the time of Leonardo the waterwheel had been improved and in some favored places wind was used to grind corn or pump water. But the main burden of human industry still rested on the muscle power of man or animal. Little thought was given to how this should be used. Animals were attached to carts or traction devices; fortunately collar harness was already in use, multiplying by five the pulling strength of the horse. Men worked tools by hand, turned cranks, or operated treadmills. Of course, power could be gained, sacrificing time, with the help of levers, screws, gears, and pulleys. Little attention was given to the problems of friction, strength of materials, and to the rational development of power transmission. At least this is the picture suggested by studying the few manuscripts that precede Leonardo, devoted to technological matters.

Leonardo's approach was fundamentally different. He firmly believed that technological problems must be dealt with not by blindly following traditional solutions but according to scientific rules deduced from observation and experiment.

When Leonardo searched for the most efficient ways of using the human motor, the force of every limb, of every muscle, was analyzed and measured. Leonardo was the first engineer who tried to find a quantitative equivalent for the forms of energy available.

In MS H (written *ca.* 1494) on folios 43*v* and 44*r* (figs. 1 and 2) there are two beautiful sketches showing the estimation of human muscular effort with the help of a dynamometer. The force is mea-

Figure 1
MS H, fol. 43*v*.

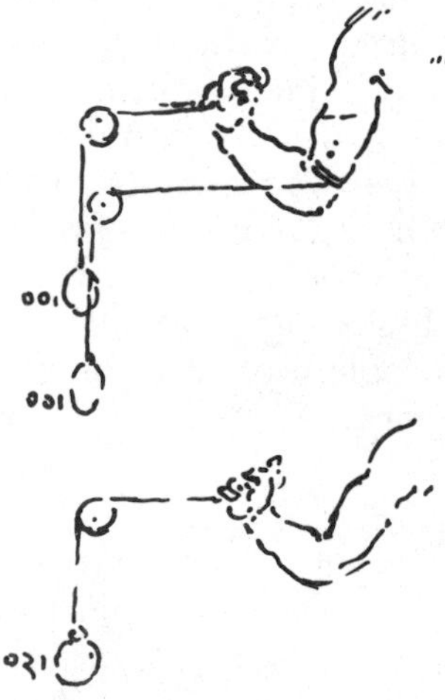

Figure 2
MS H, fol. 44*r*.

sured in pounds which represent the lifting capacity of the group of muscles under scrutiny. In figure 1 no less than six different cases covering the whole body are examined, while in figure 2 Leonardo tries to compare the force of the arm in different positions and points of attachment. Between the last two drawings a diagram shows the arm as a compound lever. In many other instances Leonardo compares the human body with a mechanical system, anticipating Borelli. We shall see one of them on folio 164*r, a* of the Codex Atlanticus. . . .

The interest of Leonardo in the maximum efficiency of muscle power is understandable. It was the only motor he could have used in a flying machine; a project that aroused his ambition as early as the year 1488 and in which he remained interested till the end of his life.

The efficiency of the human motor depends not only on its intrinsic strength but also on the ways the force is applied. Indeed, what is the greatest strength a man can generate, without the help of mechanical devices like levers, gears, or pulleys? In a very interesting passage of MS A, folio 30*v* (fig. 3), Leonardo answers the question:

A man pulling a weight balanced against himself (as in lifting a weight with the help of a single block) cannot pull more than his own weight. And if he has to raise it, he will raise as much more than his weight, as his strength may be more than that of another man. The greatest force a man can apply, with equal velocity and impetus, will be when he sets his feet on one end of the balance and then leans his shoulders against some stable support. This will raise, at the other end of the balance, a weight equal to his own, and added to that, as much weight as he can carry on his shoulders.

Masterly executed marginal sketches illustrate the three different cases. The problem has been already touched on folio 90*v* of MS B, where the following suggestion is made beside a similar sketch: "See at the mill how much is your weight, stepping on the balance and pressing with your shoulders against something."

But Leonardo was always anxious to integrate theory with application. His own advice was: "When you put together the science of the motions of water, remember to include under each proposition its application and use, in order that this science may not be useless" (MS F, fol. 2*v*).

I should like to select, among many, a few cases in which Leonardo demonstrates the usefulness of his rules. One of them is pile driving for foundation work or the regulation of river banks. The simplest pile-driving machine consists of a movable frame, provided with a drop hammer raised by men pulling at a rope provided with hand lines. After being raised, the hammer is released by a trigger. The

Figure 3

MS A, fol. 30*v*.

Figure 4

Belidor, *Architecture Hydraulique*, pt. 2,
p. 128, pl. 8.

operation is repeated until the pile has been sunk to the necessary
depth. In Belidor's classic treatise we may see the figure of this age-
old device (fig. 4).

Leonardo, often engaged in architectural and hydraulic projects,
obviously had a more than theoretical interest in the operation. . . .

As for the practical improvements, I should like to present a group
of notes on this subject, from the Leicester Codex, folio 28*v*, which so
far as I know have never been reproduced, commented upon, or
translated. Marginal drawings (figs. 5 and 6) illustrate the text.

The very best way to drive piles (*ficcare i pali a castello*) is when the man
lifts so much of the weight of the hammer as is his own weight. And
this shall be done in as much time as the man, without burden, is able
to climb a ladder quickly. Now, this man shall put his foot immediately
in the stirrup and he will descend with so much weight as his weight
exceeds that of the hammer. If you want to check it thoroughly, you
can have him carry a stone weighing a pound. He will lift so much

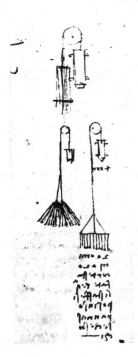

Figure 5
MS Leicester, fol. 28*v*.

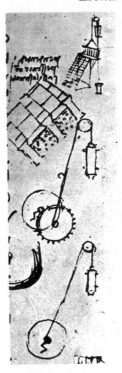

Figure 6
MS Leicester, fol. 28*v*.

weight as is his own on descending from the top of the ladder and the hammer will raise and remain on top, locked by itself, until the man dismounts the stirrup and again climbs the ladder. When you unlock the hammer with a string, it will descend furiously on top of the pile you want to drive in. And with the same speed the stirrup will rise again to the feet of the man. And this shall be done again and again. And if you want to have more men, take several ropes that end in one rope and several ladders to allow the men to reach the top of the ladders at the same time. Now, at a signal from the foreman, they shall put their feet in the stirrups and climb the ladder again. They will rest while descending and there is not much fatigue in climbing the ladders because it is done with feet and hands, and all the weight of the man that is charged on the hands will not burden the feet. But one man shall always give the signal.

Pile driving by raising the hammer by hand is not very useful, because a man cannot raise his own weight if he does not sustain it with his arms. This cannot be done unless the rope he is using is perpendicular to the center of his gravity. And this happens only to one of the men in a crowd who is pulling on the hammer.

We can further observe in the sketches of the Leicester Codex that Belidor's first two improvements had already been considered by Leonardo: the substitution of a large wheel for the block and use of a capstan or a winch. . . .

A last word on the pile driver of Leonardo. He spoke of a hammer that is locked and unlocked by itself. In the pile driver drawn on folio 289r, e of the Codex Atlanticus (fig. 7) we can observe the kind of mechanism Leonardo was hinting at. It is amazing to verify the identity of this device with that of the mentioned, improved pile driver of Belidor (fig. 8). According to the French author, the machine had been invented by Vauloue, a London watchmaker, and used at the construction of the famous Westminster bridge, that is, in 1738–1750. The story is recorded also by Desaguliers. Devices of this type are still used.

Many notes and sketches of Leonardo refer to the construction of canals, a subject that often turns up in the manuscripts. . . .

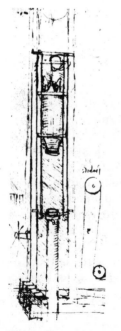

Figure 7
Codex Atlanticus, fol. 289r, e.

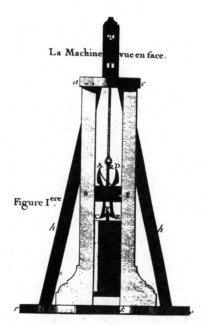

Figure 8
Belidor, *Architecture Hydraulique.*

He began by analyzing the best ways of disposing men to work if this had to be done by hand. For those calculations Leonardo even constructed a kind of chronometer on the nature of which Augusto Marinoni tells us more. He filled many sheets, extremely interesting in themselves, with calculations and sketches (e.g., C.A., fol. 210*r, a*), arriving at the conclusion that the only reasonable solution was to mechanize the whole operation. It was not only a matter of digging. The excavated material had to be cleared and transported a long way. For this purpose wheeled vehicles were considered next and rejected.

Leonardo did not underestimate wheeled vehicles. He notes that "the cart has the first place among all human inventions, particularly when it has the right proportions, although I have never seen such a one." But a cart is useful only on level ground; on steep runs the weight nullifies the effort of the animal. Besides, "to fill the carts requires more time than needed for the transport itself" (C.A., fol. 164*r, a*). . . .

The well-known folio 211*r, a* of the Codex Atlanticus shows the theoretical justification of this statement; less noticed are the beautiful sketches above the main drawing, where the influence of the relative thickness of the axle on the movement is measured by an amazingly modern-looking dynamometer. On folio 340*v, d,* of the same codex, a similar arrangement is suggested for the measurement of the force required in pulling a four-wheeled vehicle. Leonardo was to use the same type of apparatus to gauge the force of a waterfall (C. Fors. III, fol. 47*r*) and to determine the power requirement of a grain mill (*ibid.*, fol. 46*v*), anticipating the classic experiments of Smeaton.

After rejecting wheeled vehicles as unsuitable for excavation work and recognizing that a large and deep canal could not economically be dug by hand, Leonardo examined the possibility of substituting progressive hand shoveling from level to level by excavation machines combined with a system of cranes. Power was again his main concern.

To activate a crane, in addition to a horse-driven capstan, the only transportable motor available at the time would have been a treadmill, a machine that converts muscle power into rotary motion. . . .

Leonardo did not invent the external treadmill; there are older examples as far back as Vitruvius. But he was the first to use the principle rationally and in accordance with sound engineering principles. . . .

However, the increasing size of the complex machines created by the imagination of Leonardo required more power than that which could be supplied by the weight of a few men walking on a treadmill, even admitting the most rational mechanical arrangements. Leonardo was well aware of the situation, and wrote: "There you see the best of all motors, made by the ancient architects, that I cleaned from every fault and reduced to the ultimate perfection, with improvements that were not and could not be in its simple state. But I am still not satisfied and I intend to show a way of quicker motion of more usefulness and brevity" (C.A., fol. 370*v*, *c*). . . .

Still, the ultimate perfection had not yet been achieved. There was too much human work in filling and emptying the buckets and, particularly, in the excavation itself, the breaking up and the shoveling of the soil. Let us see how Leonardo the engineer tackled these problems.

Amazingly modern systems for the emptying of the buckets are described and shown on other pages of the Codex Atlanticus. The box is discharged by hitting the ground as in folio 363*r*, *a* (fig. 9), or by releasing the bottom with a string (C.A., fol. 344*r*, *a*), or it is

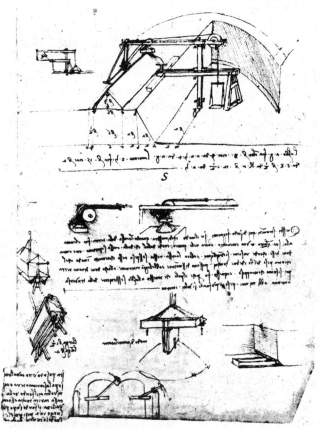

Figure 9
Codex Atlanticus, fol. 363*r*, *a*.

ingeniously overturned with the least possible effort as in folio 294r, *a*. As for the mechanization of the excavation itself, Leonardo offered several solutions that command the admiration of the modern engineer. He devised wheeled scrapers that with the aid of a horse could dig and remove the earth. Their design contains all the main features of modern tools (C.A., fols. 294r, *a*; 389r, *b*; 389v, *c*).

Leonardo's aim, however, was total mechanization. He declared emphatically that in the making of canals "the most useful method would be one by which the soil, removed, would jump by itself quickly on the instrument that will transport it" (C.A., fol. 164r, *a*; C. Ar., fol. 127r–*v*). . . .

A number of reasonable questions advanced by several authors will be echoed at this point. Those marvelously modern-looking projects of Leonardo, do they have reality or are they to be considered as the unfulfilled dreams of an inventor? Are they original or do they come from a long tradition of engineering experience?

These questions can be answered both ways. Leonardo did find ample inspiration in the deeds and writings of his predecessors in the technical arts, and some of his projects were so advanced that they could not have been carried out, for lack of adequate technical support. Others, even if brilliantly conceived, were based on faulty theories and would not work (e.g., the use of syphons more than 30 feet tall).

There can be no doubt, however, that most of Leonardo's technical ideas were grounded in firm and actual experience, even if the corresponding historical records are meager. His canal-building activity in the Romagnas, while in the service of Cesare Borgia, must have been successful in view of his immediate appointment by the Signoria of Florence in a similar capacity after the downfall of his frightful patron. Leonardo's innovations and inventions in the field of mechanical engineering can be traced in the writings of a number of sixteenth- and seventeenth-century authors, especially Cardan, Besson, Ramelli, Zonca, Castelli, Verantius, De Caus, etc. It is useless to speculate about the fact that Leonardo's manuscripts were hardly accessible to those writers: his technological ideas, like those related to the arts, were already incorporated in the common knowledge of the epoch.

But arts and techniques can be easily lost when genius is not understood and assimilated. The technology of the sixteenth and seventeenth centuries was much inferior to the standards set by Leonardo; only at the end of the seventeenth century was there a renewal that led to the beginning of modern engineering. A thorough study of Leonardo's technical activities and ideas, even if presented in the disorderly state of the mutilated and plundered heritage, points to him, as Feldhaus has correctly remarked, as the greatest engineer of all times.

Review and Study Questions

1. How does Vasari both praise and blame Leonardo in his biographical sketch?
2. How do you imagine Leonardo saw himself, as an artist or a scientist? Explain
3. Why do you think Leonardo left so many of his projects uncompleted?
4. Can Leonardo really be considered "the greatest engineer of all times"? Give your reasons.

Suggestions for Further Reading

There are two standard editions of Leonardo's notebooks, Leonardo da Vinci, *Notebooks,* tr. and ed. Edward McCurdy, 2 vols. (London: Cape, 1956), and *The Notebooks of Leonardo da Vinci,* ed. Jean Paul Richter, 2 vols. (New York: Dover, 1970), as well as a small collection of excerpts, Leonardo da Vinci, *Philosophical Diary,* tr. and ed. Wade Baskin (New York: Philosophical Library, 1959). There is also the recent *Leonardo on Painting: An Anthology of Writings by Leonardo da Vinci, with a selection of documents relating to his career as an artist,* ed. Martin Kemp (New Haven: Yale University Press, 1989). Of the many collections of his artistic works, one of the best is *Leonardo da Vinci* (New York: Reynal, 1956), the catalogue of the comprehensive Milan Leonardo Exposition of 1938. Another, relevant to the emphasis of this chapter, is *Leonardo da Vinci: Engineer and Architect* (Montreal: Museum of Fine Arts, 1987), the catalog of a major exhibit in 1987.

Two general works on Leonardo can be recommended—*Leonardo da Vinci: Aspects of the Renaissance Genius,* ed. Morris Philipson (New York: Braziller, 1966), a well-selected set of articles and special studies, and Cecil H. M. Gould, *Leonardo: the Artist and the Non-artist* (Boston: New York Graphic Society, 1975). Both these books recognize the two aspects of Leonardo's life and work that are generally dealt with, the scientific and the artistic. Of the works on Leonardo the artist, the best is Kenneth M. Clark, *Leonardo da Vinci: An Account of His Development as an Artist,* rev. ed. (Baltimore: Penguin, 1958); it may well be the best work on him of any sort. For Leonardo's mechanical engineering interests, the pioneer study is Ivor B. Hart, *The Mechanical Investi-*

gations of Leonardo da Vinci, 2nd ed. (Berkeley: University of California Press, 1963 [1925]), and a later work by Hart updating the research, *The World of Leonardo: Man of Science, Engineer, and Dreamer of Flight* (New York: Viking, 1961). For Leonardo's anatomical studies, see Elmer Belt, *Leonardo the Anatomist* (New York: Greenwood, 1955) and Kenneth D. Keele, *Leonardo da Vinci's "Elements of the Science of Man"* (New York: Academic Press, 1983).

A special interest in Leonardo was stirred by two works of Sigmund Freud, *Leonardo da Vinci: A Study in Psychosexuality,* tr. A. A. Brill (New York: Random House, 1947), and *Leonardo da Vinci and a Memory of His Childhood,* tr. Alan Tyson (New York: Norton, 1964), in which Freud treated Leonardo as the subject of his most extensive attempt at psychohistory. The works are full of errors and not solidly based on research, but they thrust into the forefront of controversy about Leonardo the questions of his homosexuality and the paralyzing duality of his interests in science and art. There are two later important books in this controversy: Kurt R. Sissler, *Leonardo da Vinci: Psychoanalytic Notes on an Enigma* (New York: International Universities Press, 1961), and Raymond S. Stites, *The Sublimation of Leonardo da Vinci, with a Translation of the Codex Trivulzianus* (Washington: Smithsonian, 1970), the latter a large, detailed, and difficult book but an important revisionist study on Freud's tentative conclusions.

Although its assertions and research are now dated, students may still enjoy a famous historical novel, Dmitrii Merezhkovskii, *The Romance of Leonardo da Vinci,* tr. B. G. Guerney (New York: Heritage, 1938).

For the background to Leonardo's biography and the Renaissance, see Wallace K. Ferguson, *Europe in Transition, 1300–1520* (Boston: Houghton Mifflin, 1962), and Ernst Breisach, *Renaissance Europe, 1300–1517* (New York: Macmillan, 1973). And for an attractive and readable book on the Italy that formed Leonardo, see Lauro Martines, *Power and Imagination: City-States in Renaissance Italy* (New York: Knopf, 1979).

MARTIN LUTHER: PROTESTANT SAINT OR "DEVIL IN THE HABIT OF A MONK"?

c. 1483	Born
1505	Entered Augustinian order
1517	The Ninety-five Theses
1521	Diet of Worms and trial of Luther
1525	Married Katherina von Bora
1546	Died

On a summer day in the year 1505, a young German law student was returning to the University of Erfurt after a visit home. He was overtaken by a sudden, violent thunderstorm and struck to the ground by a bolt of lightning. Terrified, he cried out, "St. Anne, help me! I will become a monk." Such vows were usually quickly forgotten, but not this one, for the student was Martin Luther, the man who was to bring about the most profound revolution in the history of the Christian faith. Within a matter of weeks, he disposed of his worldly goods, including his law books, and joined the order of the Augustinian Eremites in Erfurt. His father was furious; his friends were dismayed. And historians and theologians since the sixteenth century have speculated about the motives that compelled him. But this is only one of the questions about Martin Luther that have fascinated scholars and made him the subject of more writing than any other figure in European history.

There was seemingly nothing in his youth or adolescence to account for his decision to become a monk. But once that decision was made, Luther was swept by such a tidal wave of religious intensity that it troubled even his monastic superiors. He prayed for hours on end; he subjected himself to such ascetic rigors that he almost ruined his health; and he confessed his sins over and over again. He was assaulted by what one modern scholar has aptly called "the terror of the holy." God was for him a terrible judge, so perfect and so righteous that sinful man could not even begin to deserve anything at His hands but eternal damnation. Martin Luther was beginning his search for "justification," the sense that somehow, against all odds, he might earn God's grace and escape damnation.

The terror of the holy remained, and the monastic life gave Luther no assurance that God's grace was close at hand. But the very religious disquiet that tormented the young monk also caused his superiors to single him out, for this was the stuff that the great figures of religion were made of—St. Francis, St. Bernard, St. Benedict. Moreover, Brother Martin, for all his inner turmoil, was a bright and capable young man and already well educated, a Master of Arts. Soon he was ordained priest. He was sent on a matter of chapter business to Rome. And his education was continued, but now in theology rather than law.

Then the Elector of Saxony, Frederick the Wise, approached the Erfurt Augustinians in search of faculty members for the newly founded university in his capital town of Wittenberg. Brother Martin was sent. In Wittenberg he taught the arts course, worked at his own studies, and assumed more than a fair share of the parish duties. By 1513 he earned his doctor's degree and began to teach theology. As he prepared a series of lectures on the Psalms, he began to gain new understanding of his texts. And then, while he was working out his lectures on the Epistles of St. Paul, he found meaning in the familiar passage from Romans 1:17 that he had never before perceived. "For therein is the righteousness of God revealed from faith to faith: as it is written, the just shall live by faith." Later Luther said, "This passage of Paul became to me a gate to heaven." Here was the "justification" he had sought so long in vain. People are justified by faith, by the simple act of belief in Christ, in a way that no amount of works, however pious and well intended, no amount of prayers or anguish or penance can insure. Justification by faith was to become the cardinal doctrine of a new religious sect.

But Luther's inward revelation might never have led to a separate sect, much less a Reformation, except for a chain of events external to him. It began with a particularly scandalous sale of indulgences in the neighboring lands of the Archbishop of Mainz. The doctrine of indulgences was the basis of the church's profitable traffic in "pardons," as they were sometimes called, remissions of the temporal penalties for sin. Although the doctrine was an outgrowth of the sacrament of penance, many religious were troubled by it. To Luther, the indulgences that had been bought across the border by some of his parishioners and the outrageous claims for their effectiveness that were being made by the indulgence preacher, the Dominican Johann

Tetzel, seemed a surpassingly bad example of the concept of "works," especially in light of his own increasing conviction that works cannot work salvation in people—only faith "sola fides." In response to this scandalous situation, Luther was led to propose his ninety-five theses against indulgences. The document was dated October 31, 1517, the most famous date in Protestantism. The theses were written in Latin, intended for academic disputation, but somehow they were translated into German and found their way into print. Despite their dry, scholarly prose and formal organization they became a popular, even an inflammatory manifesto. Ecclesiastical authorities, including the offended Archbishop of Mainz, complained to Luther's superiors and eventually to Rome. Luther was pressed to recant, but he refused. Instead, he clung stubbornly not only to his basic position on indulgences but to the ever more revolutionary implications of his belief in justification by faith. Within three years, he had come to reject much of the sacramental theory of the church, nearly all its traditions, and the authority of the pope. In 1520 he defied Pope Leo X's bull of condemnation; in the following year he defied the Emperor Charles V in the famous confrontation at the Diet of Worms. The Lord's good servant had become, in Charles's phrase, "that devil in the habit of a monk." The Catholic Luther had become the Protestant Luther.

The Protestant Luther

MARTIN LUTHER

The image of Luther the Protestant results most directly, of course, from Luther's deeds—his successful act of defiance against established church and established state, his uncanny ability not only to survive but to build around him a new political-religious community vital enough to maintain itself. Luther's Protestant image is also based upon the incredible quantity of his writings—tracts and treatises, sermons, commentaries, translations, disputations, hymns, and letters—nearly a hundred heavy volumes in the standard modern edition. But his image also rests upon an elaborate Protestant tradition that can be traced to Luther himself.

Luther was a voluble and expansive man. Even his formal treatises are rich in anecdotes from his own experience and filled with autobiographical detail. These qualities carried over into his talk, and Luther loved to talk. As the Reformation settled into a political and social reality and Luther married—for he rejected clerical celibacy along with the other doctrines of the old church—his kitchen table became the center of the Protestant world. In addition to his own large family, there were always people visiting— friends and associates, wandering scholars and ecclesiastics, professors and students, and religious refugees. After dinner, when the dishes were cleared and the beer steins passed around, they would talk, Luther usually taking the lead. He had opinions on practically everything—politics, people, theology, education, child raising—and he would reminisce about his own life as well.

Some of the guests took notes on these conversations, and a great many of them have been preserved—six volumes in the German Weimar edition— appropriately called the Tabletalk. *The following selections are from the* Tabletalk. *They are fragments of Luther's own recollections of his experiences of monasticism, his inward struggle to gain a sense of justification, and his defiance of the old church.*

He [Martin Luther] became a monk against the will of his father. When he celebrated his first mass and asked his father why he was angry about the step he took, the father replied reproachfully, "Don't you know that it's written, Honor your father and your mother" [Exod. 20:12]? When he excused himself by saying that he was so frightened by a storm that he was compelled to become a monk, his father answered, "Just so it wasn't a phantom you saw!" . . .

[Luther recalled] "later when I stood there during the mass and began the canon, I was so frightened that I would have fled if I hadn't been admonished by the prior. For when I read the words, 'Thee, therefore, most merciful Father,' etc., and thought I had to speak to God without a Mediator, I felt like fleeing from the world like Judas. Who can bear the majesty of God without Christ as Mediator? In short, as a monk I experienced such horrors; I had to experience them before I could fight them." . . . "I almost fasted myself to death, for again and again I went for three days without taking a drop of water or a morsel of food. I was very serious about it. I really crucified the Lord Christ. I wasn't simply an observer but helped to carry him and pierce [his hands and feet]. God forgive me for it, for I have confessed it openly! This is the truth: the most pious monk is the worst scoundrel. He denies that Christ is the mediator and highpriest and turns him into a judge."

"I chose twenty-one saints and prayed to three every day when I celebrated mass; thus I completed the number every week. I prayed especially to the Blessed Virgin, who with her womanly heart would compassionately appease her Son. . . ."

"When I was a monk I was unwilling to omit any of the prayers, but when I was busy with public lecturing and writing I often accumulated my appointed prayers for a whole week, or even two or three weeks. Then I would take a Saturday off, or shut myself in for as long as three days without food and drink, until I had said the prescribed prayers. This made my head split, and as a consequence I couldn't close my eyes for five nights, lay sick unto death, and went out of my senses. Even after I had quickly recovered and I tried again to read, my head went 'round and 'round. Thus our Lord God drew me, as if by force, from that torment of prayers. To such an extent had I been captive [to human traditions]. . . ."

"I wouldn't take one thousand florins for not having seen Rome because I wouldn't have been able to believe such things if I had been told by somebody without having seen them for myself. We were simply laughed at because we were such pious monks. A Christian was taken to be nothing but a fool. I know priests who said six or seven masses while I said only one. They took money for them and I didn't. In short, there's no disgrace in Italy except to be poor. Murder and theft are still punished a little, for they must do this. Otherwise no sin is too great for them." . . .

[As a young professor in Wittenberg] "the words 'righteous' and 'righteousness of God' struck my conscience like lightning. When I heard them I was exceedingly terrified. If God is righteous [I thought], he must punish. But when by God's grace I pondered, in the tower[1] and heated room of this building, over the words, 'He who through faith is righteous shall live' [Rom. 1:17] and 'the righteousness of God' [Rom. 3:21], I soon came to the conclusion that if we, as righteous men, ought to live from faith and if the righteousness of God should contribute to the salvation of all who believe, then salvation won't be our merit but God's mercy. My spirit was thereby cheered. For it's by the righteousness of God that we're justified and saved through Christ. These words [which had before terrified me] now became more pleasing to me. The Holy Spirit unveiled the Scriptures for me in this tower." . . .

"That works don't merit life, grace, and salvation is clear from this, that works are not spiritual birth but are fruits of this birth. We are not made sons, heirs, righteous, saints, Christians by means of works, but we do good works once we have been made, born, created such. So it's necessary to have life, salvation, and grace before works, just as a tree doesn't deserve to become a tree on account of its fruit but a tree is by nature fitted to bear fruit. Because we're born, created, generated righteous by the Word of grace, we're not fashioned, prepared, or put together as such by means of the law or works. Works merit something else than life, grace, or salvation—namely, praise, glory, favor, and certain extraordinary things—just as a tree deserves to be loved, cultivated, praised, and honored by others on account of its fruit. Urge the birth and substance of the Christian and you will at the same time extinguish the merits of works insofar as grace and salvation from sin, death, and the devil are concerned."

"Infants who have no works are saved by faith alone, and therefore faith alone justifies. If the power of God can do this in one person it can do it in all, because it's not the power of the infant but the power of faith. Nor is it the weakness of the infant that does it, otherwise that weakness would itself be a merit or be equivalent to one. We'd like to defy our Lord God with our works. We'd like to become righteous through them. But he won't allow it. My conscience tells me that I'm not justified by works, but nobody believes it. 'Thou art justified in thy sentence; against thee only have I sinned and done that which is evil in thy sight' [Ps. 51:4]. What is meant by 'forgive us our debts' [Matt. 6:12]? I don't want to be good. What would be easier than for a man to say, 'I am a sinful man' [Luke 5:8]? But thou art a righteous God. That would be bad enough, but we are our own tormentors.

---

[1]The tower was the "privy" of the cloister, and it was there that Luther suddenly saw the significance of justification by faith. Hence Lutheran scholarship refers to his *turmerlebnis,* or "tower experience."—ED.

The Spirit says, 'Righteous art thou' [Ps. 119:137]. The flesh can't say this: 'Thou art justified in thy sentence' [Ps. 51:4].'' . . .

"God led us away from all this in a wonderful way; without my quite being aware of it he took me away from that game more than twenty years ago. How difficult it was at first when we journeyed toward Kemberg[2] after All Saints' Day in the year 1517, when I first made up my mind to write against the crass errors of indulgences! Dr. Jerome Schurff[3] advised against this: 'You wish to write against the pope? What are you trying to do? It won't be tolerated!' I replied, 'And if they have to tolerate it?' Presently Sylvester,[4] master of the sacred palace, entered the arena, fulminating against me with this syllogism: 'Whoever questions what the Roman Church says and does is heretical. Luther questions what the Roman Church says and does, and therefore [he is a heretic].' So it all began." . . .

"At the beginning of the gospel[5] I took steps only very gradually against the impudent Tetzel. Jerome, the bishop of Brandenburg, held me in esteem, and I exhorted him, as the ordinary of the place, to look into the matter and sent him a copy of my *Explanations*[6] before I published them. But nobody was willing to restrain the ranting Tetzel; rather, everybody ventured to defend him. So I proceeded imprudently while the others listened and were worn out under the tyranny. Now that I got into the matter I prayed to God to help me further. One can never pay the pope as he deserves."

The Catholic Luther

HARTMANN GRISAR

The traditional Catholic view of Luther is a hostile one. For Luther's Reformation set the new Protestantism against the old Catholicism with a bitterness and animosity that are apparent even to this day.

---

[2]A nearby monastery where, presumably, they were traveling on some routine parish business.—ED.

[3]A colleague of Luther's in the faculty of law.—ED.

[4]Sylvester Prierias, a papal official and a Dominican, the first dignitary in Rome to attack Luther.—ED.

[5]Luther often used this phrase for the beginning of the Reformation.—ED.

[6]The book Luther wrote explaining and defending his ninety-five theses.—ED.

242 Makers of World History

The following selection is from Martin Luther: His Life and Work, *by the German Jesuit scholar Hartmann Grisar (1845–1932), a shorter and somewhat more pointed work based upon his more famous, six-volume* Luther. *Although Grisar does abandon some of the more outrageous charges of the Catholic polemical tradition and displays an awesome knowledge of the detail of his subject, he is still openly partisan in his account and openly hostile in his interpretation. The passage below focuses on the last years of Luther the Catholic, the years at Wittenberg when Luther, as a young professor of theology, was struggling toward his understanding of justification by faith. Grisar insists that even then Luther was a "bad" Catholic. Instead of the frightened and solitary figure striving against "the terror of the holy," we find a truculent rebel, willfully distorting the rules of his own order and arrogantly preferring his own interpretation of scripture and ecclesiastical tradition to that of the church. Grisar makes Luther seem a selfish and overbearing man, neglectful of his proper religious duties. He finds him misled by his attraction to mysticism and excessive in his ascetic exercises. In short, what Grisar builds is a case for Luther's suffering from "a serious aberration."*

The young professor of Sacred Scripture displayed a pronounced inclination toward mysticism. Mysticism had always been cultivated to a certain extent in the religious orders of the Catholic Church. The reading of Bonaventure had pointed Luther, even as a young monk, to the pious union with God at which Mysticism aims. Toward the close of his lectures on the Psalms, he became acquainted with certain works on Mysticism which he imbibed with great avidity. They were the sermons of Tauler and the tract *"Theologia deutsch."* They dominated his thoughts in 1515. Although these works were not designed to do so, they helped to develop his unecclesiastical ideas. His lively experience of the weakness of the human will induced him to hearken readily to the mystical voices which spoke of the complete relinquishment of man to God, even though he did not understand them perfectly. His opposition to good works opened his mind to a fallacious conception of the doctrines of those books of the mystical life. It appeared to him that, by following such leaders, his internal fears could be dispelled by a calm immersion in the Godhead. . . . In brief, he tried to transform all theology into what he called a theology of the Cross. Misconstruing Tauler's doctrine of perfection he would recognize only the highest motives, namely, reasons of the greatest perfection for himself as well as for others. Fear of divine punishment and hope of divine reward were to be excluded.

These were extravagances that could not aid him, but, on the contrary, involved great dangers to his orthodoxy; in fact, constituted a serious aberration. But he trusted his new lights with the utmost self-confidence. . . .

In the spring of 1515, Luther was elected rural vicar by his fellow Augustinians.

At stated times he visited the monasteries thus entrusted to him. There were eleven of them, including Erfurt and Wittenberg. After the middle of April, 1516, he made a visitation of the congregations of the Order at Dresden, Neustadt on the Orla, Erfurt, Gotha, Langensalza, and Nordhausen. The letters written by him during his term of office as rural vicar, which normally lasted three years, contain practical directions and admonitions concerning monastic discipline and are, in part, quite edifying. Some of his visitations, however, were conducted with such astonishing rapidity that no fruitful results could be expected of them. Thus the visitation of the monastery at Gotha occupied but one hour, that at Langensalza two hours. "In these places," he wrote to Lang, "the Lord will work without us and direct the spiritual and temporal affairs in spite of the devil." At Neustadt he deposed the prior, Michael Dressel, without a hearing, because the brethren could not get along with him. "I did this," he informed Lang in confidence, "because I hoped to rule there myself for the half-year."

In a letter to the same friend he writes as follows about the engagements with which he was overwhelmed at that time: "I really ought to have two secretaries or chancellors. I do hardly anything all day but write letters. . . . I am at the same time preacher to the monastery, have to preach in the refectory, and am even expected to preach daily in the parish church. I am regent of the *studium* [*i.e.*, of the younger monks] and vicar, that is to say prior eleven times over; I have to provide for the delivery of the fish from the Leitzkau pond and to manage the litigation of the Herzberg fellows [monks] at Torgau; I am lecturing on Paul, compiling an exposition on the Psalter, and, as I said before, writing letters most of the time. . . . It is seldom that I have time for the recitation of the Divine Office or to celebrate Mass, and then, too, I have my peculiar temptations from the flesh, the world, and the devil."

The last sentence quoted above contains a remarkable declaration about his spiritual condition and his compliance with his monastic duties at that time. He seldom found time to recite the Divine Office and to say Mass. It was his duty so to arrange his affairs as to be able to comply with these obligations. The canonical hours were strictly prescribed. Saying Mass is the central obligation of every priest, especially if he is a member of a religious order. If Luther did not know how to observe due moderation in his labors; if he was derelict in the principal duties of the spiritual life; it was to be feared that he would gradually drift away from the religious state, particularly in view of the fact that he had adopted a false Mysticism which favored the relaxation of the rule. As rural vicar, it is probable that he did not sustain among the brethren the good old spirit which the zealous Proles had introduced into the society. Of the "temptations of the flesh" which he mentions we learn nothing definite. He was not yet in conflict with his vows. His wrestlings with the devil may signify the fears and terrors to which he was subject. . . . At times, in consequence either of a disordered affection of the heart or of overwork, he was so distressed that he could not eat or drink for a long time. One day he was found seemingly dead in his cell, so completely was he exhausted as a result of agitation and lack of food. . . .

Did Luther subject himself to extraordinary deeds of penance at any period of his monastic life, as he frequently affirmed in his subsequent conflict with the papacy and monasticism, when he was impelled by polemical reasons to describe himself as the type of a holy and mortified monk, one who could not find peace of mind during his whole monastic career? Holding then that peace of mind was simply impossible in the Catholic Church, he arbitrarily misrepresents monasticism, in order to exhibit in a most glaring manner the alleged inherent impossibility of "papistic" ethics to produce the assurance of God's mercy. "I tormented my body by fastings, vigils, and cold. . . . In the observance of these matters I was so precise and superstitious, that I imposed more burdens upon my body than it could bear without danger to health." "If ever a monk got to heaven by monkery, then I should have got there." "I almost died a-fasting, for often I took neither a drop of water nor a morsel of food for three days." . . .

The above picture of singular holiness is produced not by early witnesses, but by assertions which Luther made little by little at a later period of life. The established facts contradict the legend. Perhaps his description is based partly on remembrances of his distracted days in the monastery, or on eccentric efforts to overcome his sombre moods by means of a false piety. His greatest error, and the one which most betrays him, is that he ascribes his fictitious asceticism to all serious-minded members of his monastery, yea, of all monasteries. He would have it that all monks consumed themselves in wailing and grief, wrestling for the peace of God, until he supplied the remedy. It is a rule of the most elementary criticism finally to cut loose from the distorted presentation of the matter which has maintained itself so tenaciously in Protestant biographies of Luther.

It may be admitted that, on the whole, Luther was a dutiful monk for the greatest part of his monastic life. "When I was in the monastery," he stated on one occasion, in 1535, "I was not like the rest of the men, the robbers, the unjust, the adulterous; but I observed chastity, obedience, and poverty."

Yet, after his transfer to Wittenberg, and in consequence of the applause which was accorded to him there, the unpleasant traits of his character, especially his positive insistence on always being in the right, began to manifest themselves more and more disagreeably. . . . His opposition to the so-called doctrine of self-righteousness caused him to form a false conception of righteousness; instead of attacking an heretical error, he combated the true worth of good works and the perfections of the monastic life.

Voluntary poverty, as practiced by the mendicants, was one of the foundations of his Order. The inmates of monastic houses were to live on alms according to the practice introduced by the great Saint Francis of Assisi and for the benefactions received were to devote themselves gratis to the spiritual needs of their fellowmen. Many abuses, it is true, had attached themselves to the mendicant system; self-interest, avarice, and worldly-mindedness infected the itinerant mendicants. But in his explanation of the Psalms Luther attacks the life of poverty *per se:* "O mendicants! O mendicants! O mendicants!" he pathetically exclaims, "who can excuse you? . . . Look to it yourselves," etc. He places the practice of poverty in an unfavorable light. In his criticism of the "self-righteousness" of his irksome enemies, he confronts them with the righteousness of the spirit that cometh from Christ. These people, whom he believed it his duty to expose, were guilty, in his opinion, of a Pharisaical denial of the true righteousness of Christ. His righteousness, and not our good works, effect our salvation; works generate a fleshly sense and boastfulness. These thought processes evince how false mysticism, unclear theological notions, a darkening of the monastic spirit, and passionate obstinacy conspired in Luther's mind. . . .

The germ of Luther's reformatory doctrine is plainly contained in this species of Mysticism. Step by step he had arrived at his new dogma in the above described manner. The system which attacked the basic truths of the Catholic Church, was complete in outline. Before giving a fuller exposition of it, we must consider the individual factors which cooperated in its development in Luther's mind.

Confession and penance were a source of torturing offense to the young monk. Can one obtain peace with God by the performance of penitential works? He discussed this question with Staupitz[7] on an occasion when he sought consolation. Staupitz pointed out to him that all penance must begin and end with love; that all treasures are hidden in Christ, in whom we must trust and whom we must love. . . . Nor was Staupitz the man who could thoroughly free Luther from his doubts about predestination, although Luther says he helped him. His general reference to the wounds of Christ could not permanently set the troubled monk aright. . . . Recalling Staupitz's exhortations, he says, in 1532: We must stop at the wounds of Christ, and may not ponder over the awful ministry. The only remedy consists in dismissing from our minds the possibility of a verdict of damnation. "When I attend to these ideas, I forget what Christ and God are, and sometimes arrive at the conclusion that God is a scoundrel. . . . The idea of predestination causes us to forget God, and the *Laudate* ceases and the *Blasphemate* begins." The part which these struggles had in the origin of his new doctrine, is to be sought in Luther's violent efforts to attain to a certain repose in the fact of his presumptive predestination. . . . In his interpretation of the Epistle of St. Paul to the Romans, given during the years 1515 and 1516, Luther completely unfolded his new doctrine.

Luther between Reform and Reformation

ERWIN ISERLOH

A phenomenon of the last generation or so of Luther scholarship has been the emergence of a new, more balanced, and more charitable Catholic view of him. The polemical tone has almost disappeared, the shortcomings of the old church have been recognized, and Luther himself is interpreted in ways other than simply as a bad Catholic and a worse monk, led by his own overweening hubris *to an inevitable apostasy.*

One of the best of the new Catholic critics is Erwin Iserloh, professor of church history at the University of Münster in Germany. The following

---

[7]Johann Staupitz was a superior of Luther and one of his most trusted friends and confidants. Though Staupitz remained Catholic and in orders, they remained friends for many years.—ED.

selection is taken from his liveliest and most widely read book, The Theses Were Not Posted: Luther Between Reform and Reformation. *It is, quite apart from its point of view, a stunning demonstration of how a thoughtful scholar may use a precise event to reach a general conclusion. The event in this case is the "primal image" of Luther nailing the ninety-five theses to the door of the Castle Church in Wittenberg, thereby defiantly proclaiming the beginning of his rebellion from the church. Iserloh presents evidence that this treasured picture appeared only after Luther's death, that it came not from Luther himself but from his younger associate Philipp Melanchthon, and that Melanchthon had not even witnessed the event. Iserloh goes on to point out that, far from an act of rebellion, Luther's handling of the matter of the theses shows him to have been, at this crucial point, both a good Catholic and a responsible theologian, in Iserloh's phrase, "an obedient rebel." Iserloh argues further that it was not necessary for Luther to have been driven to rebellion; he might well have been kept within the church to its great advantage, as well as his own.*

Our investigation of the sources and the reports concerning October 31, 1517, compels us to conclude that the drama of that day was notably less than what we would suppose from the jubilee celebrations which have been held since 1617 and from the Reformation Day festivals since their inception in 1668. In fact the sources rule out a public posting of the ninety-five theses.

Although October 31, 1517, lacked outward drama it was nevertheless a day of decisive importance. It is the day on which the Reformation began, not because Martin Luther posted his ninety-five theses on the door of the castle church in Wittenberg, but because on this day Luther approached the competent church authorities with his pressing call for reform. On this day he presented them with his theses and the request that they call a halt to the unworthy activities of the indulgence preachers. When the bishops did not respond, or when they sought merely to divert him, Luther circulated his theses privately. The theses spread quickly and were printed in Nürnberg, Leipzig, and Basel. Suddenly they were echoing throughout Germany and beyond its borders in a way that Luther neither foresaw nor intended. The protest that Luther registered before Archbishop Albrecht[8] and the inclusion of the theses with the letter eventually led to the Roman investigation of Luther's works.

Some will surely want to object: Is it not actually of minor importance whether Luther posted his theses in Wittenberg or not? I would

---

[8]The Archbishop of Mainz, who had authorized the particular sale of indulgences.— ED.

answer that it is of more than minor importance. For October 31 was a day on which the castle church was crowded with pilgrims taking advantage of the titular feast of All Saints. Luther's theses on the door would have constituted a public protest. If Luther made such a scene on the same day that he composed his letter to Archbishop Albrecht, then his letter loses its credibility, even when we take into account its excessive protestations of submissiveness and humility as conventions of the time.

Above all, if Luther did post his theses, then for the rest of his life he knowingly gave a false account of these events by asserting that he only circulated his theses after the bishops failed to act.

If the theses were not posted on October 31, 1517, then it becomes all the more clear that Luther did not rush headlong toward a break with the church. Rather, as Joseph Lortz has never tired of repeating, and as Luther himself stressed, he started the Reformation quite unintentionally. In the preface to an edition of his theses in 1538 Luther gave a detailed picture of the situation in 1517. It is as if he wanted to warn the Protestant world against dramatizing the start of the Reformation with false heroics. First he stresses how weak, reticent, and unsure he was; then he tells of his efforts to contact church authorities. This is something he knows his readers cannot appreciate, since they have grown used to impudent attacks on the broken authority of the pope. . . .

If Luther did turn first to the competent bishops with his protest, or better, with his earnest plea for reform, and if he did give them time to react as their pastoral responsibilities called for, then it is the bishops who clearly were more responsible for the consequences. If Luther did allow the bishops time to answer his request then he was sincere in begging the archbishop to remove the scandal before disgrace came upon him and upon the church.

Further, there was clearly a real opportunity that Luther's challenge could be directed to the reform of the church, instead of leading to a break with the church. But such reform would have demanded of the bishops far greater religious substance and a far more lively priestly spirit than they showed. The deficiencies that come to light here, precisely when the bishops were called on to act as theologians and pastors, cannot be rated too highly when we seek to determine the causes of the Reformation. These deficiencies had far more serious consequences than did the failures in personal morality that we usually connect with the "bad popes" and concubinous priests on the eve of the Reformation. Archbishop Albrecht showed on other occasions as well how indifferent he was to theological questions, and how fully incapable he was of comprehending their often wideranging religious significance. For example, he expressed his displeasure over the momentous

Leipzig debate of 1519 where famous professors were, as he saw it, crossing swords over minor points of no interest for true Christian men. This same Albrecht sent sizable gifts of money to Luther on the occasion of his marriage in 1525 and to Melanchthon after the latter had sent him a copy of his commentary on Romans in 1532.

A whole series of objections might arise here: Do not the indulgence theses themselves mark the break with the church? Do they not attack the very foundations of the church of that day? Or, as Heinrich Bornkamm wrote, do they not decisively pull the ground from under the Catholic conception of penance? Was a reform of the church of that day at all possible by renewal from within? Is not the Luther of the ninety-five theses already a revolutionary on his way inevitably to the Reformation as a division of the church?

Our first question must be whether Luther's indulgence theses deny any binding doctrines of the church in his day. And even if this be true, we cannot immediately brand the Luther of late 1517 a heretic. This would be justified only if he became aware of holding something opposed to the teaching of the church and then remained adamant in the face of correction. It is especially important to recall this in view of Luther's repeated assertions that the theses do not express his own position, but that much in them is doubtful, that some points he would reject, and no single one out of all of them would he stubbornly maintain. . . .

Still, a truly historical judgment on the theses will not consider their precise wording only. We must further ask in what direction they are tending and what development is already immanent in them. Luther's theses can only be understood in the context of late medieval nominalism. This theology had already made a broad separation of divine and human activity in the church. For God, actions in the church were only occasions for his saving action, with no true involvement of the latter in the former. Regarding penance and the remission of punishment, Luther simply carries the nominalist separation of the ecclesiastical and the divine to the extreme in that he denies that ecclesiastical penances and their remission even have an interpretive relation to the penance required by or remitted by God. I see here one root of Luther's impending denial of the hierarchical priesthood established by God in the church.

The theological consequences of the ninety-five theses were not immediately effective. The secret of their wide circulation and their electrifying effect was that they voiced a popular polemic. Here Luther touched on questions, complaints, and resentments that had long been smouldering and had often been expressed already. Luther made himself the spokesman for those whose hopes for reform had often been disappointed in a period of widespread dissatisfaction.

Theses 81–90 list the pointed questions the laity ask about indulgences. If the pope can, as he claims, free souls from purgatory, why then does he not do this out of Christian charity, instead of demanding money as a condition? Why does he not forget his building project and simply empty purgatory? (82) If indulgences are so salutary for the living, why does the pope grant them to the faithful but once a day and not a hundred times? (88) If the pope is more intent on helping souls toward salvation than in obtaining money, why is it that he makes new grants and suspends earlier confessional letters and indulgences which are just as effective? (89) If indulgences are so certain, and if it is wrong to pray for people already saved, why are anniversary masses for the dead still celebrated? Why is the money set aside for these masses not returned? (83) Why does the pope not build St. Peter's out of his own huge wealth, instead of with the money of the poor? (86) These are serious and conscientious questions posed by laymen. If they are merely beaten down by authority, instead of being met with good reasons, then the church and the pope will be open to the ridicule of their enemies. This will only increase the misery of the Christian people. (90)

Here Luther's theses brought thoughts out into the open that all had more or less consciously found troublesome. . . .

The rapid dissemination of his theses was for Luther proof that he had written what many were thinking but, as in John 7:13, they would not speak out openly "out of fear of the Jews" (WBr 1, 152, 17).

Luther regretted the spread of the theses, since they were not meant for the public, but only for a few learned men. Furthermore, the theses contained a number of doubtful points. Therefore he rushed the "Sermon on Indulgences and Grace" into print in March 1518 (W 1, 239–46) as a popular presentation of his basic point on indulgences, and he wrote the *Resolutiones* (W 1, 526–628 and LW 31, 83–252) as an extensive theological explanation of the theses. . . .

[The] prefatory statements accompanying the explanations of the theses have been singled out for a remarkable combination of loyal submissiveness, prophetic sense of mission, and an almost arrogant conviction of their cause. Meissinger saw here the maneuverings of a chess expert. This does not strike me as an adequate analysis. I see rather the genuine possibility of keeping Luther within the church. But for this to have happened the bishops who were involved, and the pope himself, would have to have matched Luther in religious substance and in pastoral earnestness. It was not just a cheap evasion when Luther repeated again and again in 1517 and 1518 that he felt bound only by teachings of the church and not by theological opinions, even if these came from St. Thomas or St. Bonaventure. The binding declaration Luther sought from the church came in Leo X's doctrinal constitution on indulgences, *"Cum postquam"* (DS 1447ff.), on November 9, 1518. . . .

The papal constitution declares that the pope by reason of the power of the keys can through indulgences remit punishments for sin by applying the merits of Christ and the saints. The living receive this remission as an absolution and the departed by way of intercession. The constitution was quite reticent and sparing in laying down binding doctrine. This contrasts notably with the manner of the indulgence preachers and Luther's attackers. . . .

Silvester Prierias, the papal court theologian, exceeded his fellow Dominican Tetzel in frivolity. For him, a preacher maintaining the doctrines attacked by Luther is much like a cook adding seasoning to make a dish more appealing. Here we see the same lack of religious earnestness and pastoral awareness that marked the bishops' reaction to the theses.

This lack of theological competence and of apostolic concern was all the more freighted with consequences, in the face of Martin Luther's zeal for the glory of God and the salvation of souls in 1517–18. There was a real chance to channel his zeal toward renewal of the church from within.

In this context it does seem important whether Luther actually posted his theses for the benefit of the crowds streaming into the Church of All Saints in Wittenberg. It is important whether he made such a scene or whether he simply presented his ninety-five theses to the bishops and to some learned friends. From the former he sought the suppression of practical abuses, and from the latter the clarification of open theological questions.

I, for one, feel compelled to judge Luther's posting of the ninety-five theses a legend. With this legend removed it is much clearer to what a great extent the theological and pastoral failures of the bishops set the scene for Luther to begin the divisive Reformation we know, instead of bringing reform from within the church.

Review and Study Questions

1. Did Luther set out to found a new religious sect? Explain.
2. How did Luther formulate his important concept of justification by faith?
3. How did the indulgence scandal of 1517 contribute to the Reformation?
4. How did Luther move from being an obedient rebel to being an enemy of the established church?

Suggestions for Further Reading

Luther was himself a voluminous and powerful writer, and students should sample his writings beyond the brief excerpt from the *Tabletalk* presented in this chapter. The standard English edition of his works is in many volumes and sets of volumes, each edited by several scholars, elaborately cross-indexed and with analytical contents so that individual works are easy to find. Of particular interest should be the set *Martin Luther, Career of the Reformer,* vols. 31–34 (Philadelphia: Muhlenberg Press, 1957–1960). Some of the same works will be found in another edition, Martin Luther, *Reformation Writings,* tr. Bertram L. Woolf, 2 vols. (New York: Philosophical Library, 1953–1956).

The career of the young Luther, which is emphasized in this chapter, has been of particular interest to Luther scholars. Heinrich Boehmer, *Road to Reformation: Martin Luther to the Year 1521,* tr. John W. Doberstein and Theodore S. Tappert (Philadelphia: Muhlenberg Press, 1946), is the standard work by a great German authority. The same ground is covered by Robert H. Fife, *The Revolt of Martin Luther* (New York: Columbia University Press, 1957). DeLamar Jensen, *Confrontation at Worms: Martin Luther and the Diet of Worms. With a Complete English Translation of the Edict of Worms* (Provo, Utah: Brigham Young University Press, 1973), gives a detailed look at the terminal event in young Luther's career. Erik H. Erikson, *Young Man Luther: A Study in Psychoanalysis and History* (New York: Norton, 1958), is a famous and controversial book that students find provocative.

Of the many works on Luther's theology and thought, two especially are recommended. Heinrich Bornkamm, *Luther's World of Thought,* tr. Martin H. Bertram (St. Louis: Concordia, 1958), is one of the most influential works of modern Luther literature. It is fundamentally a theological rather than a historical work and is difficult but also important. Of particular interest to the background of the young Luther is Bengt R. Hoffman, *Luther and the Mystics: A Re-examination of Luther's Spiritual Experiences and His Relationship to the Mystics* (Minneapolis: Augsburg Press, 1976).

Of the many general biographical works, James Atkinson, *Luther and the Birth of Protestantism* (Baltimore: Penguin, 1968), places emphasis on his theological development. Probably the best and most readable of all the Luther biographies is Roland H. Bainton, *Here I Stand: A Life of Martin Luther* (Nashville: Abingdon Press, 1950). Three books are recommended for the broader topic of Luther and his age. Two are very large and comprehensive: Ernest G. Schwiebert, *Luther and His Times: The Reformation from a New Perspective* (St. Louis: Concordia, 1950), and Richard Friedenthal, *Luther: His Life and Times,* tr. John Nowell (New York: Harcourt, Brace, 1970). The third, A. G.

Dickens, *The German Nation and Martin Luther* (New York: Harper & Row, 1974), is really an attractive, authoritative extended essay. Eric W. Gritach, *Martin—God's Court Jester: Luther in Retrospect* (Philadelphia: Fortress Press, 1983), while not a connected biography, is a study of aspects of Luther's life, personality, work, and influence by a great European authority. It is scrupulously based on Luther's own writings but reviews in a knowledgeable way the best modern scholarship. An attractive, up-to-date biography is Walther von Loewenich, *Martin Luther, The Man and His Work*, tr. Lawrence W. Denef (Minneapolis: Augsburg Publishing House, 1986).

For the still larger topic of Luther in relation to the Reformation, see A. G. Dickens, *Reformation and Society in Sixteenth-Century Europe* (New York: Harcourt, Brace, 1966); Lewis W. Spitz, *The Renaissance and Reformation Movements*, vol. 2 (Chicago: Rand McNally, 1971); and Harold J. Grimm, *The Reformation Era*, 2nd ed. (New York: Macmillan, 1973). The new social history intrudes into Lutheran-Reformation studies with Steven Ozment, *When Fathers Ruled: Family Life in Reformation Europe* (Cambridge: Harvard University Press, 1983). A short book by R. W. Scribner, *The German Reformation* (Atlantic Highlands, N.J.: Humanities Press International, 1986), surveys the recent trends of Lutheran and Reformation scholarship and has an excellent annotated bibliography.

MONTEZUMA: THE LAST GREAT SPEAKER OF THE AZTECS

1467	Born
1480	Succession of Montezuma's uncle Tizoc as Great Speaker
1480–84	Montezuma trained as priest and warrior
1485	Succession of another uncle, the war leader Axayacatl
1497	Appointed commander of the Aztec army
1502	Elected Great Speaker
1519	First meeting with Cortés
1520	Died

The Spaniards who flocked to the New World in the wake of Columbus's discoveries were after not only land but the gold that was persistently rumored to be had there in such abundance. Among the seekers was an impoverished *hidalgo*[1] named Hernan Cortés. He made himself useful to Don Diego Velásquez, the Deputy Admiral of the Islands and Governor of Cuba, and was entrusted with an expedition to the mainland of Mexico. With only a bare handful of men and horses and a few cannon and shotguns, this man, who would shortly become the greatest of the *conquistadores*, set out on an incredible journey of conquest. He won the support of native people near the coast, including an invaluable woman, Doña Marina, who became his interpreter and mistress. And he began to hear of the great and wealthy empire of the Aztecs, the Mexica. He allied himself with the

---

[1]A *hidalgo* was a Spanish nobleman of secondary rank, below that of a grandee.—ED.

Tlaxcalans, another native people, who were bitter enemies of the Aztecs, and with some Tlaxcalan support and his own small force Cortés pressed inland toward the Aztec capital of Tenochtitlan, the later site of Mexico City, entering the city on November 8, 1519. He was met by a large delegation of high officials sent out by the Emperor Moctezuma—or Montezuma as he was more commonly called by the Spaniards—and at last by the emperor himself.

What sort of man was Montezuma and what sort of state and culture did he represent? He was in his early fifties. He had been Great Speaker, the ruler of the Aztec empire, for nearly twenty years, having been elected to succeed his uncle as Great Speaker in 1502. Long before that he had been a powerful figure in the ruling Mexica nobility. As he is characterized by one of his modern biographers, "In his own world Montezuma was considered a wise man and one with prophetic gifts which were of great value to his nation. One may say that he was regarded as the ideal of a noble ruler by his own people and that in their fear and reverence for the Great Speaker there was mingled not a little love."[2]

His state comprised the Aztec empire, which had been put together over the past two centuries by the conquests of his aggressive, warlike people. The Aztecs had subjugated the many indigenous peoples of central Mexico in a closely controlled imperial state that claimed between a million and a million and a half people, ruled from the capital city of Tenochtitlan. Tenochtitlan itself had some 400,000 people and spread out from its central temple, with its towering twin pyramids and spacious temple compound, to cover more than five square miles. It included religious structures, government buildings, and residences of the nobility, all built of stone and coated in glistening white and painted stucco, and the more modest homes of craftsmen and artisans. It had an enormous market where all the products of Meso-America were available for purchase. It was supplied with fresh water by aqueducts from Chapultapec and surrounded by the waters of Lake Texcoco, entered by an elaborate system of elevated causeways that also acted as dikes and breakwaters.

But the Aztec state was also a religious community. The Aztecs worshipped many gods, but the all-powerful "Lord of the World" was the sun god Huitzilopochtli, the Blue Hummingbird. It was mainly this god whose worship accounted for the most arresting feature of Aztec religion—mass human sacrifice and cannibalism. The practice of human sacrifice had grown over recent years until by the time of Montezuma thousands of persons were sacrificed every year—their

---

[2]C. A. Burland, *Montezuma, Lord of the Aztecs* (New York: Putnam, 1973), p. 144.

chests slashed open by priests in ceremonies that took place atop the temple pyramids, their blood and still-beating hearts consecrated to the god and their flesh cooked and eaten by the priests and the people. One of the main motives of Aztec wars was to capture prisoners to serve as sacrifices; they were called, ironically, "flower wars." Montezuma, as Great Speaker, was the chief priest of Huitzilopochtli, the servant of the god on behalf of his subjects.

But conquest tradition claimed that Montezuma was also devoted to the god Quetzalcoatl, the Feathered Serpent, the special deity of an earlier warrior people, the Toltecs, to whom the Aztec nobility traced their own ancestry. This tradition also recounted how Quetzalcoatl had returned to find his people so contented with their way of life and so intermingled with the native inhabitants that they refused to follow him. So he returned to the East once more, whence he had come. But the Aztecs were convinced that he would come again to reclaim their loyalty or that he would send someone in his stead.

On that November day of 1519 the stage was set for the most important confrontation in the entire story of the Spanish conquest of the New World.

The Second Letter to Emperor Charles V

HERNAN CORTÉS

There are several contemporary Spanish accounts of the first meeting and subsequent relations between Cortés and Montezuma. The most interesting and authoritative is that of Cortés himself, in the form of one of several detailed dispatch letters that he sent to Spain, to the Emperor Charles V, in whose name he claimed his conquests. The Second Letter, describing his dealings with Montezuma, was written less than a year after the events, and was dated October 30, 1520.

When we had passed this bridge Muteczuma himself came out to meet us with some two hundred nobles, all barefoot and dressed in some kind of uniform also very rich, in fact more so than the others. They came forward in two long lines keeping close to the walls of the street, which is very broad and fine and so straight that one can see from one end of it to the other, though it is some two-thirds of a league in length and lined on both sides with very beautiful, large houses, both private dwellings and temples. Muteczuma himself was borne along in the middle of the street with two lords one on his right hand and one on his left, being respectively the chief whom I described as coming out to meet me in a litter and the other, Muteczuma's brother, ruler of Iztapalapa, from which only that day we had set out. All three were dressed in similar fashion except that Muteczuma wore shoes whereas the others were barefoot. The two lords bore him along each by an arm, and as he drew near I dismounted and advanced alone to embrace, but the two lords prevented me from touching him, and they themselves made me the same obeisance as did their comrades, kissing the earth: which done, he commanded his brother who accompanied him to stay with me and take me by the arm, while he with the other lord went on a little way in front. After he had spoken to me all the other lords who were in the two long lines came up likewise in order one after the other, and then re-formed in line again. And while speaking to Muteczuma I took off a necklace of pearls and crystals which I was wearing and threw it round his neck;

whereupon having proceeded some little way up the street a servant of his came back to me with two necklaces wrapped up in a napkin, made from the shells of sea snails, which are much prized by them; and from each necklace hung eight prawns fashioned very beautifully in gold some six inches in length. The messenger who brought them put them round my neck and we then continued up the street in the manner described until we came to a large and very handsome house which Muteczuma had prepared for our lodging. There he took me by the hand and led me to a large room opposite the patio by which we had entered, and seating me on a daïs very richly worked, for it was intended for royal use, he bade me await him there, and took his departure. After a short time, when all my company had found lodging, he returned with many various ornaments of gold, silver and featherwork, and some five or six thousand cotton clothes, richly dyed and embroidered in various ways, and having made me a present of them he seated himself on another low bench which was placed next to mine, and addressed me in this manner:

"Long time have we been informed by the writings of our ancestors that neither myself nor any of those who inhabit this land are natives of it, but rather strangers who have come to it from foreign parts. We likewise know that from those parts our nation was led by a certain lord (to whom all were subject), and who then went back to his native land, where he remained so long delaying his return that at his coming those whom he had left had married the women of the land and had many children by them and had built themselves cities in which they lived, so that they would in no wise return to their own land nor acknowledge him as lord; upon which he left them. And we have always believed that among his descendants one would surely come to subject this land and us as rightful vassals. Now seeing the regions from which you say you come, which is from where the sun rises, and the news you tell of this great king and ruler who sent you hither, we believe and hold it certain that he is our natural lord: especially in that you say he has long had knowledge of us.[3] Wherefore be certain that we will obey you and hold you as lord in place of that great lord of whom you speak, in which service there shall be neither slackness nor deceit: and throughout all the land, that is to say all that I rule, you may command anything you desire, and it shall be obeyed and done, and all that we have is at your will and pleasure. And since you are in your own land and house, rejoice and take your leisure from

---

[3]This "knowledge" on the part of the Spanish emperor was, of course, simply made up by Cortés.—ED.

the fatigues of your journey and the battles you have fought; for I am well informed of all those that you have been forced to engage in on your way here from Potonchan, as also that the natives of Cempoal and Tlascala have told you many evil things of me; but believe no more than what you see with your own eyes, and especially not words from the lips of those who are my enemies, who were formerly my vassals and on your coming rebelled against me and said these things in order to find favour with you: I am aware, moreover, that they have told you that the walls of my houses were of gold as was the matting on my floors and other household articles, even that I was a god and claimed to be so, and other like matters. As for the houses, you see that they are of wood, stones and earth." Upon this he lifted his clothes showing me his body, and said: "and you see that I am of flesh and blood like yourself and everyone else, mortal and tangible."

Grasping with his hands his arms and other parts of his body, he continued: "You see plainly how they have lied. True I have a few articles of gold which have remained to me from my forefathers, and all that I have is yours at any time that you may desire it. I am now going to my palace where I live. Here you will be provided with all things necessary for you and your men, and let nothing be done amiss seeing that you are in your own house and land."

I replied to all that he said, satisfying him in those things which seemed expedient, especially in having him believe that your Majesty was he whom they had long expected, and with that he bade farewell. On his departure we were very well regaled with great store of chickens, bread, fruit, and other necessities, particularly household ones. And in this wise I continued six days very well provided with all that was necessary and visited by many of the principal men of the city. . . .

Having passed six days, then, in the great city of Tenochtitlan, invincible Prince, and having seen something of its marvels, though little in comparison with what there was to be seen and examined, I considered it essential both from my observation of the city and the rest of the land that its ruler should be in my power and no longer entirely free; to the end that he might in nowise change his will and intent to serve your Majesty, more especially as we Spaniards are somewhat intolerant and stiff-necked, and should he get across with us he would be powerful enough to do us great damage, even to blot out all memory of us in the land; and in the second place, could I once get him in my power all the other provinces subject to him would come more promptly to the knowledge and service of your Majesty, as indeed afterwards happened. I decided to capture him and place him in the lodging where I was, which was extremely strong. . . .

Cortés's stratagem was to accuse Montezuma of an attack on his men that had occurred earlier, along the way, at the hands of some of his subject chiefs. Montezuma immediately summoned those chiefs to account for themselves, but in the meantime, Cortés insisted that Montezuma accompany him to the quarters provided for him, under house arrest. Amazingly, Montezuma agreed! A few days later the guilty chiefs were taken and executed.

Muteczuma proclaimed an assembly of all the chiefs of the neighbouring towns and districts; and on their coming together he sent for me to mount to the platform where he already was and proceeded to address them in this manner: "Brothers and friends, you know well that for many years you, your fathers and your grandfathers have been subjects and vassals to me and to my forefathers, and have ever been well treated and held in due esteem both by them and me, as likewise you yourselves have done what it behoves good and loyal vassals to do for their lords; moreover I believe you will recollect hearing from your ancestors that we are not natives of this land, but that they came to it from another land far off, being led hither by a powerful lord whose vassals they all were; after many years he returned to find our forefathers already settled in the land married to native wives and with many children by them in such wise that they never wished to go back with him nor acknowledge him as lord of the land, and upon this he returned saying that he would come again himself or send another with such power as to force them to re-enter his service. And you know well that we have always looked to this and from what the captain has told us of the king and lord who sent him hither, and the direction from which he came I hold it certain as ye also must hold it, that he is the lord whom we have looked to, especially in that he declares he already had knowledge of us in his own land. Therefore while our ancestors did not that which was due to their lord, let us not so offend now, but rather give praise to the gods that in our times that which was long expected is come to pass. And I earnestly beg of you, since all that I have said is notorious to everyone of you, that as you have up till now obeyed and held me as your sovereign lord, so from henceforth you will obey and hold this great king as your natural lord, for such he is, and in particular this captain in his place: and all those tributes and services which up to this time you have paid to me, do you now pay to him, for I also hold myself bound to do him service in all that he shall require me: and over and above doing that which is right and necessary you will be doing me great pleasure."

All this he spoke to them weeping, with such sighs and tears as no man ever wept more, and likewise all those chieftains who heard him wept so that for a long space of time they could make no reply. And I can assure your Majesty that there was not one among the Spaniards who on hearing this speech was not filled with compassion. After some time when their tears were somewhat dried they replied that they held him as their lord and had promised to do whatever he should bid them, and hence that for that reason and the one he had given them they were content to do what he said, and from that time offered themselves as vassals to your royal Majesty, promising severally and collectively to carry out whatever should be required of them in your Majesty's royal name as loyal and obedient vassals, and duly to render him all such tributes and services as were formerly rendered to Muteczuma, with all other things whatsoever that may be commanded them in your Majesty's name. All this took place in the presence of the public notary and was duly drawn up by him in legal form and witnessed in the presence of many Spaniards. . . .

From this point, however, the situation began to deteriorate. The Spaniards had discovered vast treasuries of gold in the city. There was an incident in which they attacked the Aztecs during a religious festival and killed a large number of priests and nobles. The Aztec nobility, now led by Montezuma's brother, turned against the Spaniards and besieged them in their quarters.

Muteczuma, who was still a prisoner together with his son and many other nobles who had been taken on our first entering the city, requested to be taken out on to the flat roof of the fortress, where he would speak to the leader of the people and make them stop fighting. I ordered him to be brought forth and as he mounted a breastwork that extended beyond the fortress, wishing to speak to the people who were fighting there, a stone from one of their slings struck him on the head so severely that he died three days later: when this happened I ordered two of the other Indian prisoners to take out his dead body on their shields to the people, and I know not what became of it; save only this that the fighting did not cease but rather increased in intensity every day.

Cortés and his men at this point were forced to withdraw from the city with many casualties, but he recovered and, against impossible odds, defeated the Aztec army sent after him. After enlisting more Tlaxcalan allies he returned and besieged the city of Tenochtitlan, which finally surrendered on August 13, 1521. There was never again to be serious native resistance to Spanish rule.

The Aztec Account

The incredible events of the Spanish conquest, including the incredible be-
havior of Montezuma, are described in the surviving Aztec documents as
well as in Spanish sources, and in suspiciously similar terms. The most
comprehensive Aztec account is that contained in the so-called Codex
Florentino. *It was written in Nahuatl, the Aztec language, by native stu-*
dents in the school founded by the Franciscan missionary Bernardino de
Sahagún. He had worked out a way of writing Nahuatl in Latin characters
with Spanish sound values and taught the method to his native pupils.
They used it to record much of their Aztec culture and to describe historical
events, such as the conquest. For their account they depended on the recollec-
tions of aged natives who had witnessed the events, on traditional songs
and orations transmitted orally, and on contemporary Spanish sources. The
first version of the account was done in about 1555 but does not survive.
Brother Bernardino made a resumé of it in Spanish and later, about 1585,
reconstructed the original text in Nahuatl.

Our excerpt begins after the first reports of the Spaniards' arrival have
reached Montezuma. He has sent messengers to them and anxiously awaits
their return.

While the messengers were away, Motecuhzoma could neither sleep
nor eat, and no one could speak with him. He thought that everything
he did was in vain, and he sighed almost every moment. He was lost in
despair, in the deepest gloom and sorrow. Nothing could comfort him,
nothing could calm him, nothing could give him any pleasure.

He said: "What will happen to us? Who will outlive it? Ah, in other
times I was contented, but now I have death in my heart! My heart
burns and suffers, as if it were drowned in spices . . . ! But will our
lord come here?"

Then he gave orders to the watchmen, to the men who guarded the
palace: "Tell me, even if I am sleeping: 'The messengers have come
back from the sea.' " But when they went to tell him, he immediately
said: "They are not to report to me here. I will receive them in the
House of the Serpent. Tell them to go there." And he gave this order:
"Two captives are to be painted with chalk."

The messengers went to the House of the Serpent, and Motecuhzoma arrived. The two captives were then sacrificed before his eyes: their breasts were torn open, and the messengers were sprinkled with their blood. This was done because the messengers had completed a difficult mission: they had seen the gods, their eyes had looked on their faces. They had even conversed with the gods!

When the sacrifice was finished, the messengers reported to the king. They told him how they had made the journey, and what they had seen, and what food the strangers ate. Motecuhzoma was astonished and terrified by their report, and the description of the strangers' food astonished him above all else.

He was also terrified to learn how the cannon roared, how its noise resounded, how it caused one to faint and grow deaf. The messengers told him: "A thing like a ball of stone comes out of its entrails: it comes out shooting sparks and raining fire. The smoke that comes out with it has a pestilent odor, like that of rotten mud. This odor penetrates even to the brain and causes the greatest discomfort. If the cannon is aimed against a mountain, the mountain splits and cracks open. If it is aimed against a tree, it shatters the tree into splinters. This is a most unnatural sight, as if the tree had exploded from within."

The messengers also said: "Their trappings and arms are all made of iron. They dress in iron and wear iron casques on their heads. Their swords are iron; their bows are iron; their shields are iron; their spears are iron. Their deer carry them on their backs wherever they wish to go. These deer, our lord, are as tall as the roof of a house.

"The strangers' bodies are completely covered, so that only their faces can be seen. Their skin is white, as if it were made of lime. They have yellow hair, though some of them have black. Their beards are long and yellow, and their moustaches are also yellow. Their hair is curly, with very fine strands. . . .

When Motecuhzoma heard this report, he was filled with terror. It was as if his heart had fainted, as if it had shriveled. It was as if he were conquered by despair. . . . Motecuhzoma listened to their report and then bowed his head without speaking a word. For a long time he remained thus, with his head bent down. And when he spoke at last, it was only to say: "What help is there now, my friends? Is there a mountain for us to climb? Should we run away? We are Mexicanos: would this bring any glory to the Mexican nation?

"Pity the old men, and the old women, and the innocent little children. How can they save themselves? But there is no help. What can we do? Is there nothing left us?

"We will be judged and punished. And however it may be, and whenever it may be, we can do nothing but wait." . . .

The Spaniards arrived in Xoloco, near the entrance to Tenochtitlan. That was the end of the march, for they had reached their goal.

Motecuhzoma now arrayed himself in his finery, preparing to go out to meet them. The other great princes also adorned their persons, as did the nobles and their chieftains and knights. They all went out together to meet the strangers. . . .

Thus Motecuhzoma went out to meet them, there in Huitzillan. He presented many gifts to the Captain and his commanders, those who had come to make war. He showered gifts upon them and hung flowers around their necks; he gave them necklaces of flowers and bands of flowers to adorn their breasts; he set garlands of flowers upon their heads. Then he hung the gold necklaces around their necks and gave them presents of every sort as gifts of welcome.

When Motecuhzoma had given necklaces to each one, Cortes asked him: "Are you Motecuhzoma? Are you the king? Is it true that you are the king Motecuhzoma?"

And the king said: "Yes, I am Motecuhzoma." Then he stood up to welcome Cortes; he came forward, bowed his head low and addressed him in these words: "Our lord, you are weary. The journey has tired you, but now you have arrived on the earth. You have come to your city, Mexico. You have come here to sit on your throne, to sit under its canopy.

"The kings who have gone before, your representatives, guarded it and preserved it for your coming. The kings Itzcoatl, Motecuhzoma the Elder, Axayacatl, Tizoc and Ahuitzol ruled for you in the City of Mexico. The people were protected by their swords and sheltered by their shields.

"Do the kings know the destiny of those they left behind, their posterity? If only they are watching! If only they can see what I see!

"No, it is not a dream. I am not walking in my sleep. I am not seeing you in my dreams. . . . I have seen you at last! I have met you face to face! I was in agony for five days, for ten days, with my eyes fixed on the Region of the Mystery. And now you have come out of the clouds and mists to sit on your throne again.

"This was foretold by the kings who governed your city, and now it has taken place. You have come back to us; you have come down from the sky. Rest now, and take possession of your royal houses. Welcome to your land, my lords!"

When Motecuhzoma had finished, La Malinche[4] translated his address into Spanish so that the Captain could understand it. Cortes replied in his strange and savage tongue, speaking first to La Malinche: "Tell Motecuhzoma that we are his friends. There is nothing to fear. We have wanted to see him for a long time, and now we

---

[4]Another name for Cortés's translator, Doña Marina.—ED.

have seen his face and heard his words. Tell him that we love him well and that our hearts are contented."

Then he said to Motecuhzoma: "We have come to your house in Mexico as friends. There is nothing to fear."

La Malinche translated this speech and the Spaniards grasped Motecuhzoma's hands and patted his back to show their affection for him. . . .

When the Spaniards entered the Royal House, they placed Motecuhzoma under guard and kept him under their vigilance. . . .

Then the Spaniards fired one of their cannons, and this caused great confusion in the city. The people scattered in every direction; they fled without rhyme or reason; they ran off as if they were being pursued. It was as if they had eaten the mushrooms that confuse the mind, or had seen some dreadful apparition. They were all overcome by terror, as if their hearts had fainted. And when night fell, the panic spread through the city and their fears would not let them sleep. . . .

When the Spaniards were installed in the palace, they asked Motecuhzoma about the city's resources and reserves and about the warriors' ensigns and shields. They questioned him closely and then demanded gold.

Motecuhzoma guided them to it. They surrounded him and crowded close with their weapons. He walked in the center, while they formed a circle around him.

When they arrived at the treasure house called Teucalco, the riches of gold and feathers were brought out to them: ornaments made of quetzal feathers, richly worked shields, disks of gold, the necklaces of the idols, gold nose plugs, gold greaves and bracelets and crowns.

The Spaniards immediately stripped the feathers from the gold shields and ensigns. They gathered all the gold into a great mound and set fire to everything else, regardless of its value. Then they melted down the gold into ingots. As for the precious green stones, they took only the best of them; the rest were snatched up by the Tlaxcaltecas. The Spaniards searched through the whole treasure house, questioning and quarreling, and seized every object they thought was beautiful. . . .

The Aztec sources, like the Spanish, then tell of the massacre of the Aztec priests and nobles by the Spaniards—but in greater detail.

When the news of this massacre was heard outside the Sacred Patio, a great cry went up: "Mexicanos, come running! Bring your spears and shields! The strangers have murdered our warriors!"

This cry was answered with a roar of grief and anger: the people shouted and wailed and beat their palms against their mouths. The captains assembled at once, as if the hour had been determined in advance. They all carried their spears and shields.

Then the battle began. The Aztecs attacked with javelins and arrows, even with the light spears that are used for hunting birds. They hurled their javelins with all their strength, and the cloud of missiles spread out over the Spaniards like a yellow cloak.

The Spaniards immediately took refuge in the palace. They began to shoot at the Mexicans with their iron arrows and to fire their cannons and arquebuses. And they shackled Motecuhzoma in chains. . . .

On the third day, Motecuhzoma climbed onto the rooftop and tried to admonish his people, but they cursed him and shouted that he was a coward and a traitor to his country. They even threatened him with their weapons. It is said that an Indian killed him with a stone from his sling, but the palace servants declared that the Spaniards put him to death by stabbing him in the abdomen with their swords.

On the seventh day, the Spaniards abandoned the city along with the Tlaxcaltecas, the Huexotzincas and their other allies. They fled down the causeway that leads out to Tlacopan. But before they left, they murdered King Cacama of Tezcoco, his three sisters and two of his brothers.

A New Explanation

J. H. ELLIOTT AND ANTHONY PAGDEN

In the whole account of the conquest of Mexico nothing is more puzzling than the behavior of Montezuma. He was in the prime of life, in secure and undisputed control of an aggressive, warlike empire that could field hundreds of thousands of soldiers on his order alone. He had a considerable reputation for military leadership himself. Yet he was virtually paralyzed by the course of events.

The explanation that is presented both in the Spanish and the Aztec sources—as we have seen—is that Montezuma profoundly believed that Cortés was the agent of the Aztec god Quetzalcoatl and that Cortés acted on behalf of the god, incarnate in the person of his sovereign Charles V.

But was this the case? In the critical notes to the latest and best edition of the Cortés letters, the editor, Anthony Pagden, and the author of the introduction, J. H. Elliott, offer an alternative explanation. Elliott argues that Cortés's letters were not only reports on the events of the conquest but carefully crafted political apologies as well. He notes, quite correctly, that Cortés was operating without any real official authorization. He had been sent by Don Diego Velásquez, the Governor of Cuba, to investigate the loss of a small exploration fleet and to rescue any Spaniards being held captive in Yucatan. He was also authorized to explore and trade—but he had no permission to colonize. Yet he had founded the town-settlement of Vera Cruz, in large part so that he could be authorized by the town government (which was himself) to undertake an expedition to the interior. He had set out on that expedition on the basis of this contrived and specious authority.

Cortés had therefore defied his own immediate superior, Velázquez, and had potentially antagonized Velázquez's powerful friends at Court. He knew well enough the grave risks he was running. But to Cortés and his friends . . . the risks paled before the attractions of the anticipated prize. Nothing could more quickly obliterate the stigma of treachery and rebellion than a brilliant military success and the acquisition of fabulous riches. If new peoples were won for the Faith, and rich new lands won for the Crown, there was reason to hope that the original defiance of Velázquez would be regarded as no more than a peccadillo, and that Velázquez's friends and protectors would be silenced by a *fait accompli.* . . .

Success in arms, and resort to the highest authority of all, that of the king himself—these were the aims of Cortés and his fellow conspirators as they prepared in April, 1519, to compound their defiance of Velázquez by a landing which would mark the real beginning of their attempt to conquer an empire. They were concerned, like all conquistadors, with fame, riches and honor. But behind the willful defiance of the governor of Cuba there existed, at least in Cortés's mind, a philosophy of conquest and colonization which made his action something more than an attempt at self-aggrandizement at the expense of Velázquez. He entertained, like so many Castilians of his generation, an exalted view of the royal service, and of Castile's divinely appointed mission. Both the divine and the royal favor would shine on those who cast down idols, extirpated pagan superstitions, and won new lands and peoples for God and Castile. . . .

But what seemed plausible enough in Mexico was bound to seem highly implausible in Cuba and at the Spanish Court. Clearly it was essential to win support in Spain for an action which Fonseca[5] and his friends would certainly represent to the king as an act of open rebellion. . . .

---

[5]Juan Rodríguez de Fonseca, Bishop of Burgos, was Velásquez's relative and patron at the Spanish court and the royal councilor principally responsible for the affairs of the Indies during the previous reign.—ED.

Everything now depended on the successful presentation of his case at Court, where the Fonseca group would certainly do all in its power to destroy him. If possible, Charles and his advisers must be reached and won over before they had time to learn from Velázquez himself of Cortés's act of rebellion. . . .

The first letter from Mexico, then, was essentially a political document, speaking for Cortés in the name of his army, and designed to appeal directly to the Crown over the heads of Velázquez and his friends in the Council of the Indies. Cortés was now involved in a desperate race against time. Montejo and Puertocarrero[6] left for Spain on July 26, 1519, with their bundle of letters and the gold; and unless, or until, they could persuade Charles to sanction retrospectively the behavior of Cortés and his men, Cortés was technically a traitor, liable to arrest and persecution at the hands of an irate governor of Cuba, fully empowered to act in the royal name. The danger was acute, and the blow could fall at any time, perhaps even from within Mexico itself. For there was still a strong group of Velázquez partisans in the expedition, and these men would do all they could to sabotage Cortés's plans. But Cortés, who had his spies posted, was well aware of the dangers. The friends of the governor of Cuba appear to have been plotting to send him warning of the mission of Montejo and Puertocarrero, so that he could intercept their ship. The plot was discovered, the conspirators arrested, and two of them, Juan Escudero and Diego Cermeño, put to death. . . . As long as Cortés could command the loyalties of his army—and this would ultimately depend on his ability to capture and distribute the fabulous riches of Motecuçoma's empire—he was now reasonably safe from subversion within the ranks. . . .

Velázquez began to organize an army to be sent to Mexico against Cortés. . . . At a time when a smallpox epidemic was raging in Cuba, Velázquez felt unable to lead his army in person, and handed over the command to one of his more reliable but less intelligent friends, Pánfilo de Narváez. The army, twice the size of that of Cortés, set sail from Cuba on March 5, 1520. . . . During the autumn and winter of 1519, therefore, at the time when Cortés was securing the submission of Motecuçoma and had established himself precariously in Tenochtitlan, he was faced with the prospect of a military confrontation with his immediate superior, the governor of Cuba. . . .

The outcome was likely to be determined on the battlefield, in an internecine struggle of Spaniard against Spaniard, which could well jeopardize and even destroy Cortés's uncertain hold over the Aztec empire. But in the Spanish monarchy of the sixteenth century a

---

[6]Cortés's agents.—ED.

military solution could never be final. Legality was paramount, and the key to legality lay with the king.

Everything therefore turned on the success of Montejo and Puerto-carrero in Spain. They duly reached Seville at the beginning of November, 1519, only to find their country on the verge of revolt. Charles had been elected Holy Roman Emperor on June 28. Once elected, his immediate aim was to extract the largest possible subsidies from the Cortes[7] of the various Spanish kingdoms, and then to leave for Germany. When the procuradores[8] arrived in Seville, the emperor was still in Barcelona, heavily preoccupied with plans for his departure; and the Castilian cities were beginning to voice their dissatisfaction at the prospect of heavy new fiscal demands and an absentee king.

At this particular moment the chances of winning the emperor's support for a still-unknown adventurer on the other side of the world hardly looked very promising. . . . From Barcelona they [Montejo and Puertocarrero] moved across Spain in the tracks of the emperor, finally catching up with him at Tordesillas, near Valladolid, early in March. Here, seven months after leaving Vera Cruz, they could at last petition the emperor in person to confirm Cortés in his position as captain general and *justicia mayor.* . . .

Meanwhile, in Mexico, Cortés had seized the initiative, divided his forces, and moved to intercept Narváez's army. This was his situation at the time of the massacre of the Aztec lords at the religious festival. He defeated Narváez, conscripted the bulk of Narváez's men to his own cause, and returned to Tenochtitlan.

Narváez's defeat left the governor of Cuba a ruined and broken man. Cortés had defeated Velázquez—geographically his nearest enemy— but he was still without news from the Spanish Court. Moreover, his march to the coast to defeat Narváez had fatally weakened the Spanish position in Tenochtitlan. When Cortés got back to the capital on June 25 it was already too late. The behavior of Alvarado and his men in Tenochtitlan during Cortés's absence had precipitated an Indian uprising, and neither Cortés's troops, nor the diminished authority of Motecuçoma, proved sufficient to quell the revolt. Motecuçoma, rejected by his own subjects, died his strange death on June 30. During

---

[7]The *Cortes* were the legislative bodies of the Spanish kingdoms.—Ed.

[8]The *procuradores* were the "agents" whom Cortés had sent from Mexico to the Spanish court.—Ed.

the course of the same night, the *noche triste,* the Spaniards made their famous retreat from Tenochtitlan. Cortés might have defeated the governor of Cuba, but he had also lost the empire he had promised to Charles.

It was during the autumn months of 1520, while Cortés was preparing for the siege and reconquest of Tenochtitlan, that he wrote the Second Letter. This letter, like its predecessor from Vera Cruz, is both more and less than a straightforward narrative of events, for it, too, has an essentially political purpose. Cortés, when writing it, was influenced by three major considerations. In the first place, he still did not know what decision, if any, had been reached in Spain on his plea for retrospective authorization of his unconventional proceedings. In the second place, he had by now heard the news of Charles's election to the imperial throne. Finally, he had won a new empire for Charles and had proceeded to lose it. His letter, therefore, had to be so angled as to suggest that, at the most, he had suffered no more than a temporary setback . . . and that he would soon be in a position to render the most signal new services to a king who had now become the mightiest monarch in the world.

With these considerations in mind, Cortés carefully contrived his letter to convey a predominantly "imperial" theme. Its opening paragraph contained a graceful allusion to Charles's new empire in Germany, which was skillfully coupled with a reference to a second empire across the Atlantic, to which he could claim an equal title. This reference set the tone for the document as a whole. The fact that Cortés was no longer at this moment the effective master of the Mexican empire was no doubt inconvenient, but could be played down as far as possible. For the thesis of the letter was that Charles was already the *legal* emperor of this great new empire, and that Cortés would soon recover for him what was rightfully his.

The entire story of the march to Tenochtitlan and the imprisonment of Motecuçoma was related in such a way as to support this general thesis. Motecuçoma, by his speeches and his actions, was portrayed as a man who voluntarily recognized the sovereignty of Charles V, and voluntarily surrendered his empire into his hands. Whether Motecuçoma did indeed speak anything like the words which Cortés attributes to him will probably never be known for certain. Some passages in his two speeches contain so many Christian overtones as to be unbelievable coming from a pagan Aztec. Others, and in particular the identification of the Spaniards with the former rulers of Mexico wrongly banished from their land, may be an ingenious fabrication by Cortés, or may conceivably reflect certain beliefs and legends, which Motecuçoma himself may or may not have accepted. Whatever its origins, the story of the expected return of lords from the east was essential to Cortés's grand design, for it enabled him to allege and explain a "voluntary" submission of Motecuçoma, and the "legal" transfer of his empire—an empire far removed from the jurisdiction of the Audiencia of Santo Domingo and from the Caribbean world of Diego Colón[9] and Velázquez—to its rightful ruler, Charles V.

Motecuçoma's death at the hands of his own subjects left Charles the undisputed master of the field. It was unfortunate that the Mexicans were now in open rebellion—a situation which could only be ascribed to the nefarious activities of the governor of Cuba, acting through his agent Pánfilo de Narváez. But although Narváez's invasion had nearly brought disaster, the tide had now been turned, because God was on the emperor's side. With divine help, and through the agency of that most loyal of lieutenants, Hernán Cortés, the land would soon be recovered; and what better name could be bestowed upon it than that of New Spain?

Anthony Pagden, the editor of the text, turns more specifically to the inexplicable behavior of Montezuma. He begins with the speech that Montezuma made as soon as Cortés and his men had been settled in their quarters in Tenochtitlan.

Both this speech and the one that follows . . . would seem to be apocryphal. Motecuçoma could never have held the views with which Cortés accredits him. Eulalia Guzmán (*Relaciones de Hernán Cortés,* I: 279 ff.) has pointed out the Biblical tone of both these passages and how their phraseology reflects the language of the *Siete Partidas.*[10] Cortés is casting Motecuçoma into the role of a sixteenth-century Spaniard welcoming his "natural lord," who in this case has been accredited with a vaguely Messianic past. Indeed the whole setting has a mythopoeic ring: Motecuçoma is made to raise his garments and to declare, "See that I am flesh and blood like you and all other men, and I am mortal and substantial," words reminiscent of those of Jesus to his disciples, "A spirit hath not flesh and bones as ye see me have" and of Paul and Barnabas to Lystra, "We also are men of like passions with you." (J. H. Elliott, "The Mental World of Hernán Cortés," pp. 51–53). There is evidence, however, that Motecuçoma

---

[9]The son of Christopher Columbus, who had inherited the title of Admiral from his father.—ED.

[10]This is a thirteenth-century compilation of Castilian law.—ED.

did believe himself to be the living incarnation of Huitzilopochtli (see Durán, chaps. LIII–LIV; and Sahagún, bk. IV, chap. 10), and certainly such an identification would not have been alien to Mexica religious thought. Despite the absurdity of attributing such words and gestures to an Amerindian, it seems likely that Cortés's account of the events is based on partially understood information about the native mythologies. A number of modern commentators seem to believe the thesis of Motecuçoma's speeches, namely, that the Mexica lived in fear of a vengeful Messiah, who would one day return from the east, and mistook Cortés for his captain. Later this Messiah, who in the words attributed to Motecuçoma is only a legendary tribal chieftain, becomes Quetzalcoatl, the "Plumed Serpent" lord of Tula, whose story as told by Sahagún bears some resemblance to the Cortés-Motecuçoma version of Mexica prehistory. There is, however, no preconquest tradition which places Quetzalcoatl in this role and it seems possible therefore that it was elaborated by Sahagún . . . from informants who themselves had partially lost contact with their traditional tribal histories.

The identification of Cortés with Quetzalcoatl is also the work of Sahagún (see bk. XII, chap. 4, pp. 11 ff.). Don Antonio de Mendoza, first viceroy of New Spain, however, said that Cortés was mistaken for Huitzilopochtli (Elliott, *op cit.,* p. 53), traditionally associated with the south, and about whom no Messianic legend is known to exist. It is possible that Mendoza was told this by Cortés himself, and "Uchilobos" was the only Mexica deity Cortés could name.

Cortés may have picked up a local legend and embellished it in an attempt to prove that Motecuçoma was himself an usurper and therefore had no right to the lands he ruled (cf. the Third Letter, n. 3). . . .

Where Cortés first heard the story is uncertain. Cervantes de Salazar (bk. 111, chap. 49) and Bernal Díaz (chap. 79) both say that it was in Tlaxcala but both are very vague (see also Muñoz Camargo, pp. 184–185). Professor Guzmán says that a similar legend was common in the Antilles. But perhaps the first contact was made in Yucatán, where a foliated cross appears on a number of Mayan buildings and seems to have been associated with Quetzalcoatl, called Kukulcan in Maya. . . . If it is unlikely that Motecuçoma took the Spaniards to be the vicars-on-earth of the "Plumed Serpent," it is even more unlikely that it would have in any way affected his attitude toward Cortés. Besides the improbability of any leader acting on a prophecy, Quetzalcoatl's cult was largely confined to the lowland regions beyond Popocatepetl and Iztaccihuatl and appears to have held little sway in central Mexico itself (*Códice Borgia,* 1: 67). Its cult center was Cholula, which, when it came under Mexica rule, was granted no special respect and even forced to venerate Huitzilopochtli. Nor, it might be added, did Cholula accord to Cortés the welcome he might be expected to receive as Quetzalcoatl's lieutenant. Motecuçoma was himself a priest of Huitzilopochtli; and, secure in the power of the tutelary deity of his race, it does not seem likely that he would have resigned his powers to the supposed avatars of an apotheosized Toltec chieftain.

The attitude of the Mexica toward the Spaniards can best be explained by the traditional immunity from harm enjoyed by all ambassadors—and Cortés claimed to be an ambassador albeit without an embassy. It is also possible that once Motecuçoma had realized Cortés's intentions, he deliberately drew him inland, not understanding that the sea could be a supply route for the Spaniards. . . . Motecuçoma may well have underestimated the Spanish powers of diplomacy and the state of unrest within his own empire. It was unfortunate for him . . . that the Spaniards were in a position to play one Indian against another. . . .

Pagden next turns to the puzzle of Montezuma's death.

There are two versions of Motecuçoma's death. The first, that given by Cortés, is corroborated by most of the Spanish writers. Bernal Díaz (chap. 126) and Vázquez de Tapia, both witnesses, say that there were a large number of Spanish soldiers on the roof guarding the *Uei Tlatoani;*[11] if this was so, it is possible that the Mexica were aiming at them rather than at Motecuçoma. Gómara (p. 365) suggests that the Mexica did not see him, and Juan Cano told Oviedo (bk. XXXIII, chap. 54) that "Motezuma died from a stone which those outside threw at him, which they would not have done had not a buckler been placed in front of him, for once they had seen him they would not have thrown." Bernal Díaz says that Motecuçoma died because he refused to eat or to have his wound attended, a story repeated by Herrera (dec. 11, bk. X, chap. 10). If the Mexica did attack him on the roof, this might be true. Bernal Díaz then goes on to say that Cortés and the other soldiers wept at Motecuçoma's death as though they had lost a father, which seems somewhat unlikely.

The second theory is that Motecuçoma was stabbed to death shortly before the Spaniards fled the city. This idea is advanced by most of the native writers, though some of them agree that Motecuçoma had been discredited and would therefore be open to attack if he ap-

---

[11]"The Great Speaker."—ED.

peared in public. The *Anales Tolteca-Chichimeca* (quoted by Orozco y Berra, IV: 425) even say that it was Cuauhtemoc who threw the stone. Durán (chap. LXXVI) also mentioned the wound but says that when Motecuçoma was found it was almost healed, and that he had been stabbed five times in the chest. Ixtlilxóchitl (I:341), who is largely pro-Spanish, repeats the Spanish version of the killing but adds, "his vassals say that the Spaniards killed him by stabbing him in the bowels." The *Codex Ramirez* (p. 144) also says that he was killed by a sword thrust in the bowels. Torquemada (bk. IV, chap. 70), following Sahagún, says that Motecuçoma and Itzquauhtzin, lord of Tlatelolco, were found garroted. There is little evidence to support this: garroting was for formal executions, not assassination.

Review and Study Questions

1. What were the hidden motives of Cortés in his letter to Charles V detailing his conquest of Montezuma's empire?

2. How much credence do you place in the story that Montezuma and the Aztecs believed Cortés to be the agent of the god Quetzalcoatl? Explain.

3. How do you account for the submissive tone of the Aztec account of the conquest?

4. Regardless of the motives of Montezuma himself, how do you account for the surprising ease with which Cortés accomplished the conquest of Mexico?

Suggestions for Further Reading

In addition to *Hernando Cortés: Five Letters,* tr. and ed. J. Bayard Morris (New York: Norton, 1960), excerpted for this chapter, there are two other editions: *Conquest: Dispatches of Cortéz from the New World,* intro. and commentary Irwin R. Blacker, ed. Harry M. Rosen (New York: Grosset and Dunlap, 1962) and *Hernán Cortés: Letters from Mexico,* tr. and ed. A. R. Pagden, intro. J. H. Elliott (New York: Grossman, 1971), also excerpted for this chapter. There are two more contemporary Spanish accounts of the conquest. One is Francisco López de Gómara, *Cortés: The Life of the Conqueror by His Secretary,* tr. and ed. Lesley Byrd Simpson (Berkeley, Los Angeles, London: University of California Press, 1964). Although Gómara never actually visited the New World, he had access to Cortés's own papers and recollections.

The other account is by one of the soldiers on the expedition, written many years later from his recollections: *The Bernal Díaz Chronicles: The True Story of the Conquest of Mexico,* tr. and ed. Albert Idell (Garden City, N.Y.: Doubleday, 1957) and another edition, Bernal Díaz del Castillo, *The Discovery and Conquest of Mexico, 1517–1521,* ed. and tr. A. P. Maudslay, intro. Irving A. Leonard (New York: Farrar, Straus and Cudahy, 1956). In addition to *The Broken Spears: The Aztec Account of the Conquest of Mexico,* ed. and intro. Miguel Leon-Portilla (Boston: Beacon Press, 1962), excerpted for this chapter, another contemporary Indian work is Fray Bernardino de Sahagún, *1547–1577, A History of Ancient Mexico,* tr. Fanny R. Bandelier (Glorieta, N. M.: The Rio Grande Press, Inc., 1976). This is actually not a history but an account of the Aztec religion; it is, furthermore, largely a series of selections from the much more comprehensive edition of Fray Bernardino de Sahagún, *Florentine Codex: General History of the Things of New Spain,* ed. Arthur J. O. Anderson and Charles E. Dibble (Santa Fe, N. M. and Salt Lake City, Utah: The School of American Research and The University of Utah, 1955–1982), a massive work in thirteen parts. The account of Cortés and Montezuma occurs in No. 14, Part XIII.

Of the modern accounts of the dramatic confrontation between Aztec and Spaniard, Cortés and Montezuma, the best is R. C. Padden, *The Hummingbird and the Hawk: Conquest and Sovereignty in the Valley of Mexico, 1503–1541* (Columbus: Ohio State University Press, 1967). A much less substantial and analytical popular work is Maurice Collis, *Cortés and Montezuma* (New York: Harcourt, Brace and Co., 1954). An earlier work that tried to make some of the same analyses that Padden did is Charles S. Braden, *Religious Aspects of the Conquest of Mexico* (Durham: Duke University Press, 1930).

The standard modern biography of Cortés is Salvador de Madariaga, *Hernán Cortés, Conqueror of Mexico* (New York: Macmillan, 1941). There is also a 1955 edition of this work, published by Henry Regnery Co., Chicago. A brief, popular, but competent biography is William Weber Johnson, *Cortés* (Boston–Toronto: Little, Brown and Co., 1975). The only substantial modern biography of Montezuma is C. A. Burland, *Montezuma, Lord of the Aztecs* (New York: Putnam, 1973); this is a brilliantly written if somewhat fictionalized account, but solidly based on the standard sources. The masterwork on the entire history of the period is William H. Prescott, *History of the Conquest of Mexico,* 3 vols. (Philadelphia: Lippincott, 1843 and five later editions). There is a one-volume abridgement of this work, dealing only with the career of Cortés: *A History of the Conquest of Mexico,* ed. Harry Block (New York: Heritage Press, 1949).

Of the many works on the Aztecs themselves, probably the best general history is Nigel Davies, *The Aztecs: A History* (London: Macmillan, 1973). Rudolf A. M. van Zantwijk, *The Aztec Arrangement: The Social History of Pre-Spanish Mexico* (Norman: University of Oklahoma Press, 1985) is a detailed but somewhat difficult book on Aztec social organization by a great European anthropologist.

SULEIMAN THE MAGNIFICENT: GOD'S SLAVE AND SULTAN OF THIS WORLD

1494	Born
1520	Became Ottoman sultan
1521	Turks take Belgrade
1522	Surrender of Rhodes
1526	Battle of Mohács
1529	Siege of Vienna
1534–55	Campaigns against Persia
1560	Naval victory of Djerba
1566	Died

In the year 1520 Suleiman came to the throne of the Ottoman Empire, the only surviving son and successor of the Sultan Selim I. Thus began a reign that would last for forty-six years, during the course of which the Ottomans would reach the apex of their history. The accomplishments of Suleiman would outweigh even those of Muhammad II, the conqueror of Constantinople. To his Turkish subjects Suleiman was known as Kanuni, the Lawgiver, the second Solomon. To the West he was known as the Magnificent. This latter title, so ruefully granted to the sultan by his western contemporaries, reflects his great military career, particularly his campaigns and conquests in Europe. Those conquests were to establish the Turks as a presence in Europe for the next three hundred years, intruding "the Turkish question" into virtually every matter of international politics until the twentieth century.

Suleiman's two predecessors, Bayazid II (1481–1512) and his father Selim I (1512–1520) had been concerned mainly with the Asiatic portions of the Ottoman Empire. But Suleiman was to be preoccupied with the conquest of the West.

One of his first acts was to mount a campaign against the Balkan

279

fortress city of Belgrade, which fell to his armies in 1521. At nearly the same time, his naval forces blockaded the island of Rhodes, the last crusading stronghold in the Near East, held by the Knights of St. John. In 1522 it fell. In 1526 he mounted another massive campaign in the Balkans that culminated in the decisive defeat of the Hungarians at Mohács and the death of their king, Louis II. Three years later his armies stood before Vienna. The siege of Vienna was to be the high-water mark of Suleiman's conquests in Europe.

That the main line of Suleiman's imperial policy was the conquest of Europe was the conclusion of the greatest of all European authorities on the Ottoman Empire, the nineteenth-century Austrian historian Josef von Hammer-Purgsdahl. "We recall," he wrote, "the thirteen campaigns that he conducted in person, his numerous battles and conquests: Rhodes and Belgrade, those two roads to empire on land and sea, opened at the beginning of his reign," and "the Ottoman banners planted before the walls of Vienna. . . . He extended the frontier of his empire" to the fortress of Gran, "to the foot of Mount Semmering and the mountains of Styria. . . . In the Mediterranean the fleets, led by Khäreddin-Barbarossa and Torghoud, carried their conquests and their depredations to the Greek islands, Apulia and Calabria, Sicily and Corsica, making Rome tremble, and advancing to the mouth of the Rhone where they besieged Marseille. . . . The designation of a great ruler incontestably belongs to him."[1]

---

[1]The translation of this passage is made from the superior, updated French edition of the work, J. De Hammer, *Histoire de l'Empire Ottoman*, tr. J.-J. Hellert (Paris: Bellizard, 1836), VI, pp. 287–89.

Suleiman: The Last Years

OGIER GHISELIN DE BUSBECQ

*There are many contemporary accounts of the Sultan Suleiman. He himself
kept a detailed diary; there are accounts and descriptions by court figures
and official Turkish historians; and there are reports of European diplomats at the Porte.[2] For the purpose of revealing the character and motives
of the sultan the Turkish sources are limited. Suleiman's diary is prosaic
and factual and not very revealing of the man who wrote it. The accounts
of courtiers and official chroniclers are marred by excessive adulation of the
sultan and hence unreliable. Western diplomats' accounts, while sometimes
useful, are more often too closely related to their own policy ends. An exception is the account of Ogier Ghiselin de Busbecq.*

*Busbecq was a noble Fleming, born in 1522, who spent most of his life
as a professional diplomat, much of it in the service of King Ferdinand, the
brother of the Hapsburg Emperor Charles V, Charles's regent for the eastern
Hapsburg lands and his successor as Holy Roman Emperor. Busbecq was
hastily summoned back to Vienna in 1554 from London, where he had
represented Ferdinand at the marriage of Queen Mary Tudor and Prince
Philip of Spain. Relations with the Turks had taken a turn for the worse.
Since the Turkish siege of Vienna had failed in 1529, Turkish relations
with the Hungarians and Hapsburgs had swung between truce and open
warfare, with first one and then the other gaining a momentary advantage,
the preponderance usually on the side of the Turks. Ferdinand had succeeded in 1551 in taking Transylvania. Suleiman was furious, accusing
Ferdinand of bad faith and duplicity, and threatened full-scale war. The
only hope Ferdinand had of preserving the precarious position he held in
Hungary lay in the skill and tact of his diplomats. He asked Busbecq to go
to Constantinople as his ambassador; Busbecq agreed. It was not an envi-
able assignment. His immediate predecessor, Giovanni Maria Malvezzi,
had spent the last two years locked in a Turkish prison, under threat of
torture and mutilation in punishment for his king's perfidy.*

*Busbecq went to Constantinople, where he was to spend most of the next
eight years, with occasional journeys back to Vienna to consult with his
government. The substance of his mission and the account of the sights and*

---

[2]The seat of Ottoman government, "The Sublime Porte" was the sultan's palace in
Constantinople, named after its gate (port).—Ed.

people he saw—including the sultan—are all contained in a series of
"Turkish Letters" that he wrote to an old friend, fellow diplomat, and fellow
Fleming Nicolas Michault, Lord of Indeveldt. Busbecq's account is ex-
tremely candid and perceptive. It reveals that Suleiman saw himself not
only as a participant in European affairs but as the prime participant, the
arbiter of Europe's destiny, as of Asia's. It also reveals a man used to the
exercise of absolute power, impatient with the delays and disappointments of
diplomacy and the deceitfulness of diplomats and their political masters—a
man nearing the end of his reign and his life, and uncertain about his
place in history.

In his account Busbecq has already described the long and harrowing
trip to the East. Now he has arrived and been summoned to see the sultan
at Amasia, the capital of Cappadocia.

On our arrival at Amasia we were taken to call on Achmet Pasha (the chief Vizier) and the other pashas—for the Sultan himself was not then in the town—and commenced our negotiations with them touching the business entrusted to us by King Ferdinand. The Pashas, on their part, apparently wishing to avoid any semblance of being prejudiced with regard to these questions, did not offer any strong opposition to the views we expressed, and told us that the whole matter depended on the Sultan's pleasure. On his arrival we were admitted to an audience; but the manner and spirit in which he listened to our address, our arguments, and our message, was by no means favourable.

The Sultan was seated on a very low ottoman, not more than a foot from the ground, which was covered with a quantity of costly rugs and cushions of exquisite workmanship; near him lay his bow and arrows. His air, as I said, was by no means gracious, and his face wore a stern, though dignified, expression.

On entering we were separately conducted into the royal presence by the chamberlains, who grasped our arms. This has been the Turkish fashion of admitting people to the Sovereign ever since a Croat, in order to avenge the death of his master, Marcus, Despot of Servia, asked Amurath[3] for an audience, and took advantage of it to slay him. After having gone through a pretence of kissing his hand, we were conducted backwards to the wall opposite his seat, care being taken that we should never turn our backs on him. The Sultan then listened to what I had to say; but the language I held was not at all to his taste, for the demands of his Majesty breathed a spirit of independence and dignity, which was by no means acceptable to one who deemed that

---

[3]Amurath is a variant spelling of Murad I (1360–1389). The incident referred to never actually occurred.—ED.

his wish was law; and so he made no answer beyond saying in a tetchy way, 'Giusel, giusel,' i.e. well, well. After this we were dismissed to our quarters. . . .

By May 10 the Persian Ambassador had arrived, bringing with him a number of handsome presents, carpets from famous looms, Babylonian tents, the inner sides of which were covered with coloured tapestries, trappings and housings of exquisite workmanship, jewelled scimitars from Damascus, and shields most tastefully designed; but the chief present of all was a copy of the Koran, a gift highly prized among the Turks; it is a book containing the laws and rites enacted by Mahomet, which they suppose to be inspired.

Terms of peace were immediately granted to the Persian Ambassador with the intention of putting greater pressure on us, who seemed likely to be the more troublesome of the two; and in order to convince us of the reality of the peace, honours were showered on the representative of the Shah. . . .

Peace having been concluded with the Persian, as I have already told you, it was impossible for us to obtain any decent terms from the Turk; all we could accomplish was to arrange a six months' truce to give time for a reply to reach Vienna, and for the answer to come back.

I had come to fill the position of ambassador in ordinary; but inasmuch as nothing had been as yet settled as to a peace, the Pashas determined that I should return to my master with Solyman's letter, and bring back an answer, if it pleased the King to send one. Accordingly I had another interview with the Sultan. . . . Having received the Sultan's letter, which was sealed up in a wrapper of cloth of gold, I took my leave; the gentlemen among my attendants were also allowed to enter and make their bow to him. Then having paid my respects in the same way to the Pashas I left Amasia with my colleagues on June 2. . . .

You will probably wish me to give you my impressions of Solyman.

His years are just beginning to tell on him, but his majestic bearing and indeed his whole demeanour are such as beseem the lord of so vast an empire. He has always had the character of being a careful and temperate man; even in his early days, when, according to the Turkish rule, sin would have been venial, his life was blameless; for not even in youth did he either indulge in wine or commit those unnatural crimes which are common among the Turks; nor could those who were disposed to put the most unfavourable construction on his acts bring anything worse against him than his excessive devotion to his wife, and the precipitate way in which, by her influence, he was induced to put Mustapha to death; for it is commonly believed that it was by her philtres and witchcraft that he was led to commit this act. As regards herself, it is a well-known fact that from the time he made her his lawful wife he has been perfectly faithful to her, although there was nothing in the laws to prevent his having mistresses as well.[4] As an upholder of his religion and its rites he is most strict, being quite as anxious to extend his faith as to extend his empire. Considering his years (for he is now getting on for sixty) he enjoys good health, though it may be that his bad complexion arises from some lurking malady. There is a notion current that he has an incurable ulcer or cancer on his thigh. When he is anxious to impress an ambassador, who is leaving, with a favourable idea of the state of his health, he conceals the bad complexion of his face under a coat of rouge, his notion being that foreign powers will fear him more if they think that he is strong and well. I detected unmistakable signs of this practice of his; for I observed his face when he gave me a farewell audience, and found it was much altered from what it was when he received me on my arrival. . . .

This was only the first of several journeys back to Vienna between 1554 and 1562. Busbecq finally departed Constantinople for good in August of 1562.

I commenced my wished-for journey, bringing with me as the fruit of eight years' exertions a truce for eight years, which however it will be easy to get extended for as long as we wish, unless some remarkable change should occur. . . .

The truce Busbecq had negotiated entailed, on Austria's part, the recognition of all Ottoman conquests and the independence of Translyvania under Ottoman suzerainty. Ferdinand was also obliged to continue to pay tribute. But it was a peace that spared Hungary the agony of yet another Turkish invasion and spared the strapped Austrian monarchy the need to mount yet another expensive military defense. Busbecq's account of his successful negotiation is followed by his judicious assessment of the situation between Suleiman and Ferdinand.

Against us stands Solyman, that foe whom his own and his ancestors' exploits have made so terrible; he tramples the soil of Hungary

---

[4]Suleiman was indeed devoted to Roxelana, who enjoyed the unusual status of his lawful wife and lived not in the harem but in the imperial palace. She did exercise a baneful influence over the sultan and may even have influenced his decision to execute his eldest son Mustapha, who had rebelled against him. However, deep suspicion of a sultan's sons and even their murder by their father was a common occurrence among the Ottoman rulers. All of Suleiman's brothers, for example, had been killed by Selim.—ED.

with 200,000 horse, he is at the very gates of Austria, threatens the rest of Germany, and brings in his train all the nations that extend from our borders to those of Persia. The army he leads is equipped with the wealth of many kingdoms. Of the three regions, into which the world is divided, there is not one that does not contribute its share towards our destruction. Like a thunderbolt he strikes, shivers, and destroys everything in his way. The troops he leads are trained veterans, accustomed to his command; he fills the world with the terror of his name. . . . Nevertheless, the heroic Ferdinand with undaunted courage keeps his stand on the same spot, does not desert his post, and stirs not an inch from the position he has taken up. He would desire to have such strength that he could, without being charged with madness and only at his own personal risk, stake everything on the chance of a battle; but his generous impulses are moderated by prudence. He sees what ruin to his own most faithful subjects and, indeed, to the whole of Christendom would attend any failure in so important an enterprise, and thinks it wrong to gratify his private inclination at the price of a disaster ruinous to the state. He reflects what an unequal contest it would be, if 25,000 or 30,000 infantry with the addition of a small body of cavalry should be pitted against 200,000 cavalry supported by veteran infantry. The result to be expected from such a contest is shown him only too plainly by the examples of former times, the routs of Nicopolis and Varna, and the plains of Mohacz, still white with the bones of slaughtered Christians. . . .

It is forty years, more or less, since Solyman at the beginning of his reign, after taking Belgrade, crushing Hungary, and slaying King Louis, made sure of obtaining not only that province but also those beyond; in this hope he besieged Vienna, and renewing the war reduced Güns, and threatened Vienna again, but that time from a distance. Yet what has he accomplished with his mighty array of arms, his boundless resources and innumerable soldiery? Why, he has not made one single step in Hungary in advance of his original conquest. He, who used to make an end of powerful kingdoms in a single campaign, has won, as the reward of his invasions, ill-fortified castles or inconsiderable villages, and has paid a heavy price for whatever fragments he has gradually torn off from the vast bulk of Hungary. Vienna he has certainly seen once, but as it was for the first, so it was for the last time.

Three things Solyman is said to have set his heart on, namely, to see the building of his mosque finished (which is indeed a costly and beautiful work), by restoring the ancient aqueducts to give Constantinople an abundant supply of water, and to take Vienna. In two of these things his wishes have been accomplished, in the third he has been stopped, and I hope will be stopped. Vienna he is wont to call by no other name than his disgrace and shame.

The Young Suleiman

ROGER B. MERRIMAN

From the foregoing account of an ailing and world-weary Suleiman at the end of his reign, with his ambitions for the conquest of Europe thwarted, we turn back to the beginning of his reign and the bright promise which that conquest seemed to hold. The account is by the American scholar Roger B. Merriman.

Merriman is best known for his massive four-volume work The Rise of the Spanish Empire in the Old World and in the New, *published between 1911 and 1934. It remains the preeminent work on its subject. In the course of his research for that book, Merriman became interested in not only the Spanish but the Austrian Hapsburgs, and their imperial problems, not the least of which was the Turks. Then, in the early 1940s, he undertook to finish a book on Suleiman the Magnificent that had been left unfinished by a close friend and Harvard colleague, Archibald Coolidge, on his death. Merriman updated the research, reworked parts of the manuscript, and rewrote other parts entirely. The result is his* Suleiman the Magnificent 1520–1566, *which appeared in 1944 and which is still the most comprehensive and authoritative biography of Suleiman in English.*

After sketching in the background of Suleiman's reign, dealing with his boyhood, youth, and accession to the throne, and his first two major campaigns against Belgrade and Rhodes, Merriman takes up the story of the campaign of Mohács and Vienna, between 1526 and 1529, the culminating events of Suleiman's assault on Europe.

On Monday (reckoned a lucky day) the twenty-third of April, 1526, Suleiman, accompanied by Ibrahim[5] and two other vizirs, left Constantinople at the head of more than 100,000 men with 300 cannon. The Sultan's diary gives many details of the advance, which contin-

---

[5]Ibrahim Pasha was an early favorite of Suleiman whom he had rapidly advanced to the office of Grand Vizier and to whom he granted extraordinary powers. Ibrahim's personal ambition, however, finally became a threat even to the sultan and, encouraged by Roxelana, Suleiman had him put to death in 1536.—ED.

ued for more than eighty days before contact was established with the enemy. . . .

The two middle weeks of August were the really critical period of the campaign. The Hungarian king, council, magnates, and generals had been wrangling at Buda and Tolna over the question of the defence of the realm; while Tömöri,[6] from across the Danube, kept sending them messages of the continued advance of the Turks which he was impotent to impede. The obvious thing for the Hungarians to do was, of course, to move southward and defend the strong line of the Drave, but petty jealousies prevented this. The most they would consent to do was to advance to the plain of Mohács, on the west side of the Danube, some thirty miles to the north of the point where the Drave unites with it. The inhabitants of Esseg, on the south bank of the Drave, realized that they had been abandoned, and made haste to send the keys of their town to the Sultan, in token of submission, as he slowly approached in a driving rain. When Suleiman reached the Drave, he could scarcely believe his eyes when he found that its northern bank had been left undefended, but he was prompt to avail himself of a God-given opportunity. On August 15 he "gave orders to throw a bridge of boats across this river and personally supervised the work." As the Turkish historian Kemal Pasha Zadeh rapturously declares, "They set to work without delay to get together the materials necessary for this enterprise. All the people expert in such matters thought that the construction of such a bridge would take at least three months, but yet, thanks to the skilful arrangements and the intelligent zeal of the Grand Vizir, it was finished in the space of three days." (The Sultan's diary makes it five.) After the army had crossed over, Esseg was burned and the bridge destroyed. It was a bold step to take; for though the invaders were thereby partially protected from the arrival of Hungarian reënforcements from Croatia, they were also deprived of all means of escape in case of defeat by their Christian foes. . . .

Meantime the Hungarians were slowly assembling on the plain of Mohács. King Louis had a bare 4,000 men with him when he arrived there; but fresh detachments came continually dribbling in, and others were known to be rapidly approaching. But they were a motley host, whose mutual jealousies made it wellnigh impossible for them effectively to combine. There was much difficulty over the choice of a commander-in-chief. King Louis was obviously unequal to the task;

---

[6]Paul Tömöri, the Archbishop of Kalocsa, was a warlike cleric who had been assigned the task of defending the Turkish frontier and who was the most experienced of the Hungarian commanders.—ED.

the Palatine Stephen Báthory had the gout; and so it was finally decided to give the place to Archbishop Tömöri, the memory of whose past successes in border warfare against the Moslems was enough to stifle his own protestations that he was not the man for the task. Soon after his appointment, and when the Turks had already crossed the Drave, the Hungarians held a council of war to determine the strategy most expedient for them to adopt. The more cautious of them advocated a retreat toward Buda-Pesth; then the Turks would have no choice but to follow, for Buda was their announced objective and they were staking everything on success. Every day's march forward would take them further from their base, while the Hungarians if they retired would be sure to be joined by reënforcements. John Zápolya[7] was but a few days distant with 15,000 to 20,000 men; John Frangipani was coming up from Croatia; the Bohemian contingent, 16,000 strong, was already on the western frontier of the realm. But unfortunately the bulk of the Hungarians, including Tömöri himself, refused to listen to such reasoning as this. They were filled with an insane overconfidence. The gallant but rash and turbulent Magyar nobility clamored for an immediate fight. They distrusted the king. Many of them were hostile to Zápolya, and unwilling to have him share in the glory of the victory which they believed certain. It was accordingly decided to give battle at once; and the Hungarians, who could choose their own ground, elected to remain on the plain of Mohács, in a place which would give them full play for their cavalry. Apparently they forgot that the enemy, whose horsemen were much more numerous than their own, would derive even greater advantage from the position they had chosen.

The relative size of the two armies which were about to encounter one another has been a fertile source of discussion ever since. One thing only is certain; the contemporaneous estimates on both sides are ridiculously exaggerated. Tömöri told King Louis, on the eve of the battle, that the Sultan had perhaps 300,000 men; but that there was no reason to be frightened by this figure, since most of the Turks were cowardly rabble, and their picked fighting-men numbered only 70,000! Even if we accept the statement that Suleiman left Constantinople at the head of 100,000 men, we must remember that less than one-half of them were troops of the line. It seems likely that his losses through skirmishing and bad weather, as he advanced, must have more than counterbalanced his gains through reënforcements re-

---

[7]John Zápolya was the ruler of Transylvania and sometime claimant to the Hungarian throne.—ED.

ceived along the route. If we put the Janissaries[8] at 8,000, the regular cavalry of the bodyguard at 7,000, the Asiatic feudal cavalry at 10,000, the European at 15,000, and the miscellaneous levies at 5,000, we get a total of 45,000 Turkish fighting troops, besides the irregular and lightly armed akinji,[9] possibly 10,000 to 20,000, who hovered about the battlefield but were never expected to stand the charge of regular soldiers. It is also very doubtful if Suleiman still had anywhere near the 300 cannon with which he is said to have left Constantinople in the previous April.

The actual size of the Hungarian army is almost equally difficult to estimate—principally because of the reënforcements which continued to arrive until the day of the fight. In the grandiloquent letter which the Sultan despatched a few days after the battle to announce his victory to the heads of his different provinces, he puts the number of his Christian foes at approximately 150,000, but it seems probable that the true figures were less than one-fifth as large: perhaps 25,000 to 28,000 men, about equally divided between cavalry and infantry, and 80 guns. Part of these troops were well drilled professional soldiers, many of them Germans, Poles, and Bohemians; there was also the Hungarian national cavalry, made up of the brave but utterly undisciplined nobles. And they had, besides, large numbers of heavy-armored wagons, which could be chained together to make rough fortifications, or even pushed forward, like the modern tank, to pave the way for an infantry or a cavalry charge. . . .

The plain of Mohács, some six miles in length, is bounded on the east by the Danube. At the northern end is the town, while to the south and west there is a line of low hills, then covered with woods, which furnished an admirable screen for the Turkish advance. Apparently neither side expected a combat till well after noon of the day on which it occurred, and actual fighting did not begin till after three. The story of the details of the battle itself varies widely in the different contemporaneous accounts that have come down to us, but the main outlines seem reasonably clear. The combat opened with a tremendous charge of the heavy-armed Hungarian cavalry against the centre of the Turkish line emerging from the woods. It pierced the opposing ranks, and soon after appeared to be so decisively successful that orders were given for a general advance of all the Hungarian forces. But the Turkish centre had been withdrawn on purpose, in

---

[8]The Janissaries were the primary infantry force of the Ottomans, made up of Christian boys raised as Moslems in strict military discipline.—ED.

[9]Akinji were irregular cavalry forces.—ED.

order to lure their enemies on to their destruction. By the time they had reached the Janissaries and the Sultan's standard, they were held up. There were furious hand-to-hand combats between the Christian leaders and the members of Suleiman's bodyguard; at one moment Suleiman himself was in grave danger. But the Turkish artillery was far more skilfully handled than that of their opponents; the Hungarians were mowed down in droves; most important of all, the concentration of the Christians in the centre gave their numerous foes a splendid opportunity, of which they were prompt to take advantage, to outflank their enemies, particularly on the westward. Within an hour and a half, the fate of the battle had been decided. The Hungarians fled in wild disorder to the north and east. Such, apparently, are the principal facts. But as we are following the story of the battle from the Turkish standpoint, it will be worth while to supplement these data by a few passages from the history of Kemal Pasha. He gives Ibrahim all the credit for the feint by which the Christians were enticed to disaster. "The young lion," he declares, "no matter how brave, should remember the wisdom and experience of the old wolf. . . . When the Grand Vizir seized his redoubtable sword, ready to enter the lists, he looked like the sun, which sheds its rays on the universe. In combat, he was a youth, ardent as the springtime: in council, he was an old man, as experienced as Fortune in numerous vicissitudes." When the battle began, he continues, "the air was rent with the wind of the fury of the combatants; the standards shone forth in the distance; the drums sounded like thunder, and swords flashed like the lightning. . . . While the faces of the miserable infidels grew pale and withered before they felt the flame of the blades . . . the cheeks of our heroes, drunk with lust for combat, were tinged with the color of roses. . . . With all these murderous swords stretched out to lay hold on the garment of life, the plain seemed like a fiend with a thousand arms; with all these pointed lances, eager to catch the bird of life in the midst of slaughter, the battlefield resembled a dragon with a thousand heads." And then, when the rout began, he concludes: "At the order of the Sultan the fusiliers of the Janissaries, directing their blows against the cruel panthers who opposed us, caused hundreds, or rather thousands of them, in the space of a moment, to descend into the depths of Hell."

The slaughter which followed the battle was indeed fearful. The Turks took no prisoners, and few of the defeated escaped. The Sultan's diary is even more than usually laconic. For August 31 it reads "The Emperor, seated on a golden throne, receives the homage of the vizirs and the beys: massacre of 2000 prisoners: the rain falls in torrents"; and for September 2; "Rest at Mohács; 20,000 Hungarian infantry and 4000 of their cavalry are buried." On this occasion his figures seem to be corroborated, in round numbers at least, by the Christian accounts of the disaster. Mohács indeed was the "tombeau de la nation hongroise";[10] never has a single battle proved so fatal to the life of a people. In addition to the annihilation of its army, almost all of its leaders had perished. King Louis, after fighting bravely, turned to flee when all was lost, but his horse, in trying to climb the steep bank of a small stream, fell backwards into the waters below and buried his rider under him. Tömöri and his second in command were also killed, together with two archbishops, five bishops, many magnates, and the greater part of the Hungarian aristocracy; the flower of the nation, both lay and clerical, had been sacrificed on the fatal day. Suleiman's announcement of his victory to his governors is couched in more expansive language than is his diary, but the impression conveyed in the following sentences from it is substantially correct, as seen from the standpoint of the Turks. "Thanks be to the Most High! The banners of Islam have been victorious, and the enemies of the doctrine of the Lord of Mankind have been driven from their country and overwhelmed. Thus God's grace has granted my glorious armies a triumph, such as was never equalled by any illustrious Sultan, all-powerful Khan, or even by the companions of the Prophet. What was left of the nation of impious men has been extirpated! Praise be to God, the Master of Worlds!"

After Mohács organized resistance practically ceased. On the day following the battle John Zápolya with his army reached the left bank of the Danube; but he made haste to withdraw as soon as he learned of the catastrophe. On September third the Ottoman army resumed its advance; on the tenth it entered Buda. Apparently the keys of the town had been sent out in advance to Suleiman in token of submission by those who had been unable to flee (Kemal Pasha assures us that only "humble folk" had remained within the walls), and the Sultan, in return promised them that they should be spared the horrors of a sack. But his troops got out of hand, and he was unable to keep his word. As his diary tersely puts it (September 14), "A fire breaks out in Buda, despite the efforts of the Sultan: the Grand Vizir seeks in vain to extinguish it": as a matter of fact the entire city was burnt to the ground with the exception of the royal castle, where Suleiman himself had taken up his residence. There the Sultan found many treasures which he carried back with him to Constantinople. . . .

In the midst of the celebrations of his victory he was seriously considering the question of the disposition he should make of the prize that he had won. . . . On the whole it seemed wiser to be satis-

---

[10]"Tomb of the Hungarian nation."—ED.

fied with what had already been achieved. To quote Kemal again, "The time when this province should be annexed to the possessions of Islam had not yet arrived, nor the day come when the heroes of the Holy War should honor the rebel plains with their presence. The matter was therefore postponed to a more suitable occasion, and heed was given to the sage advice; 'When thou wouldst enter, think first how thou wilt get out again.'"

On September 13, accordingly, the Sultan ordered the construction of a bridge of boats across the Danube from Buda to Pesth, and seven days later the vanguard of the Turkish army passed across it. On the night of the twenty-third the bridge apparently broke into three parts, two of which were swept away, so that the last detachments had to be ferried over in boats. The next day Pesth was burnt, and on the morrow the Ottoman army started homeward. . . .

In the year following his return from Mohács, his chief immediate care was the suppression of two insurrections in Asia Minor. The first, in Cilicia, was put down by the local authorities. The second, in Karamania and the districts to the east of it, was more serious; and Ibrahim had to be despatched with a force of Janissaries to insure the final defeat of the rebels in June, 1527. Meantime the Sultan had remained at Constantinople; partly, perhaps, because he did not wish to lower his own prestige in the eyes of his subjects by seeming to be obliged to deal personally with revolts; but more probably because he was principally interested in the course of events in Hungary. . . .

By midsummer of 1528 . . . it must have been reasonably clear that Suleiman soon intended to launch a third great expedition up the Danube, this time as the ally, or perhaps better the protector, of Zápolya, against Ferdinand and the power of the House of Hapsburg. There is no reason to be surprised that he delayed his departure until the following year. The season was already too late to embark on an enterprise whose ultimate goal, Vienna, was so remote. Moreover the Sultan fully realized that in challenging Ferdinand he was also indirectly bidding defiance to the Emperor Charles V. On May 10, 1529, however, he left Constantinople, at the head of a much larger army than that of 1526. The Christian chroniclers talk vaguely of 250,000 to 300,000, though it is doubtful if there were more than 75,000 fighting men, and it seems clear that four-fifths of them were cavalry. Ibrahim was again seraskier,[11] and the artillery is given, as before, at 300 guns. The rains, which in the preceding campaign had been a nuisance, were this year so continuous and torrential that they seri-

---

[11]The title of the Turkish Minister of War, who was also the army commander.—Ed.

ously affected the outcome of the campaign. Suleiman did not reach Vienna till a month later than he expected, and that month may well have made just the difference between failure and success. The Sultan's comments on the bad weather in his diary are constant and bitter. At Mohács, on August 18, he had been joined by Zápolya, whose prospects had speedily revived when it became known that he had won the favor of Suleiman. He brought with him 6,000 men. The Sultan recieved him with great pomp, and presented him with four robes of honor and three horses caparisoned with gold. But Suleiman, in his diary, takes great pains to point out that he regarded him merely as a vassal. He explains that the gifts were only bestowed in recognition of the voivode's[12] homage; and he emphasizes the fact that Zápolya twice kissed his hand. At Buda a feeble resistance was offered by a few hundred Austrian mercenaries; but they soon surrendered after a promise of good treatment, which was shamefully violated by the Janissaries. Zápolya was permitted to make a royal entrance there on September 14; but he was obviously dominated and controlled by the Turkish soldiers and officials who escorted him. . . . September 18 the akinji swarmed across the Austrian frontier, and swept like a hurricane through the open country. On the twenty-seventh the Sultan himself arrived before Vienna. Two days later the investment was complete.

The siege of Vienna appeals strongly to the imagination. Never since the battle of Tours, almost precisely eight centuries before, had Christian Europe been so direfully threatened by Mohammedan Asia and Africa. Had the verdict on either occasion been reversed, the whole history of the world might have been changed. And the cause of the Moslem defeat in both cases was fundamentally the same; the invaders had outrun their communications. This is well demonstrated in the case of Vienna by the fact that the long distances and heavy rains had forced the Turks to leave behind them the bulk of their heavy artillery, which had been such a decisive factor in the siege of Rhodes. The lighter cannon, which was almost all that they succeeded in bringing with them, could make little impression on the city walls. Only by mining operations could they hope to open a breach for a general assault. . . .

The Sultan's headquarters were his splendid red tent, pitched on a hill, three or four miles away. Mining and countermining operations were vigorously pushed during the early days of October. Several times the besiegers were encouraged to launch assaults, which were invariably repulsed. On the other hand, the constant sorties of the

---

[12]A Slavic word denoting the military commander or governor of a territory.—ED.

garrison were generally unsuccessful. October 12 was the critical day of the siege. On that morning the walls had been breached by mines, and the Turks had delivered the most furious of their attacks. Only with great difficulty had it been beaten off, and the garrison was deeply discouraged; that very afternoon it despatched the most pressing of its messages to hasten the arrival of relief. But the Turks were in even worse case. At the Divan which they held that same day, the preponderance of opinion was in favor of withdrawal. The season was ominously late; supplies were getting short; the Janissaries were murmuring; powerful Christian reënforcements were known to be at hand. Ibrahim besought his master to go home. One more last attack was launched on October 14; but despite the unprecedented rewards that had been offered in case it should be successful, it was delivered in such half-hearted fashion that it was foredoomed to failure from the first. That night the Turks massacred some 2000 of the prisoners that they had taken from the Austrian countryside; they burnt their own encampment; on the fifteenth they began to retire. Their retreat was cruelly harassed by enemy cavalry, and truly horrible weather pursued them all the way to Constantinople. It was cold comfort that Zápolya came out from Buda as the Sultan passed by to compliment his master on his "successful campaign." All that the Sultan had "succeeded" in doing was to expel Ferdinand from his Hungarian dominions; and we need not take too seriously the statement in his diary that since he had learned that the archduke was not in Vienna, he had lost all interest in capturing the place! The fundamental fact remained that Suleiman had been beaten back before the walls of the Austrian capital by a force a third the size of his own, or perhaps less. His prestige, about which, like all Orientals, he was abnormally sensitive, had suffered a serious blow.

Suleiman the Statesman: An Overview

HALIL INALCIK

Despite the best efforts of Merriman, in the previous selection, to write his account "from the Turkish standpoint," it is inescapably Eurocentric, as was that of Busbecq. Fortunately, we have an assessment of Suleiman and

his achievements by "the leading Turkish historian of the Balkans today,"[13]
Halil Inalcik, from his The Ottoman Empire, The Classical Age
1300–1600. *Inalcik is not only familiar with the works of Turkish histori-*
ans and what he calls the "unusually rich" Ottoman archives, but with the
standard western accounts of the wars and politics of the Reformation. For
the first time, he weaves together the two traditions and shows us the extent
to which Suleiman was regarded not only as a dangerous scourge by the
West but as a counter in the western concept of the balance of power. He
also shows us the extent to which Suleiman himself was aware of western
politics and how that awareness affected his policies. It is a brilliant achieve-
ment of historical synthesis.

In 1519 the Habsburg Charles V and Francis I of France were candi-
dates for the crown of the Holy Roman Empire, and both promised to
mobilize all the forces of Europe against the Ottomans. The Electors
considered Charles V more suited to the task, and shortly after the
election, in March 1521, these two European rulers were at war with
each other. Europe, to the great advantage of the Ottomans, was
divided, and Süleymân I chose this time to march against Belgrade,
the gateway to central Europe. Belgrade fell on 29 August 1521. On
21 January 1522 he captured Rhodes, the key to the eastern Mediterranean, from the Knights of St. John.

When Charles V took Francis prisoner at Pavia in 1525, the French,
as a last resort, sought aid from the Ottomans. Francis later informed
the Venetian ambassador that he considered the Ottoman Empire the
only power capable of guaranteeing the existence of the European
states against Charles V. The Ottomans too saw the French alliance as
a means of preventing a single power dominating Europe. Francis I's
ambassador told the sultan in February 1526 that if Francis accepted
Charles' conditions, the Holy Roman Emperor would become 'ruler
of the world'.

In the following year Süleymân advanced against Hungary with a
large army. The Ottoman victory at Mohács on 28 August 1526, and
the occupation of Buda, threatened the Habsburgs from the rear. The
Ottomans withdrew from Hungary, occupying only Srem, and the
Hungarian Diet elected John Zapolya as King. At first the Ottomans
wished to make Hungary a vassal state, like Moldavia, since it was
considered too difficult and too expensive to establish direct Ottoman
rule in a completely foreign country on the far side of the Danube. But
the Hungarian partisans of the Habsburgs elected Charles V's brother,

---

[13]Peter F. Sugar, *Southeastern Europe under Ottoman Rule, 1354–1804* (Seattle and London: University of Washington Press, 1977), p. 305.

Archduke Ferdinand, King of Hungary, and in the following year he occupied Buda and expelled Zapolya. Süleymân again invaded Hungary, and on 8 September 1529 again enthroned Zapolya in Buda as an Ottoman vassal. Zapolya agreed to pay an annual tribute and accepted a Janissary garrison in the citadel. Although the campaigning season was over, Süleymân continued his advance as far as Vienna, the Habsburg capital. After a three-week siege, he withdrew.

In 1531 Ferdinand again entered Hungary and besieged Buda. In the following year Süleymân replied by leading a large army into Hungary and advancing to the fortress of Güns, some sixty miles from Vienna, where he hoped to force Charles V to fight a pitched battle. At this moment Charles' admiral, Andrea Doria, took Coron in the Morea from the Ottomans. Realizing that he now had to open a second front in the Mediterranean, the sultan placed all Ottoman naval forces under the command of the famous Turkish corsair and conqueror of Algiers, Hayreddîn Barbarossa, appointing him *kapudan-i deryâ*— grand admiral—with orders to cooperate with the French. Since 1531 the French had been trying to persuade the sultan to attack Italy and now they sought a formal alliance. In 1536 this alliance was concluded. The sultan was ready to grant the French, as a friendly nation, freedom of trade within the empire. The ambassadors concluded orally the political and military details of the alliance and both parties kept them secret. Francis' Ottoman alliance provided his rival with abundant material for propaganda in the western Christian world. French insistence convinced Süleymân that he could bring the war to a successful conclusion only by attacking Charles V in Italy. The French were to invade northern Italy and the Ottomans the south. In 1537 Süleymân brought his army to Valona in Albania and besieged Venetian ports in Albania and the island of Corfu, where a French fleet assisted the Ottomans. In the following year, however, the French made peace with Charles. Francis had wished to profit from the Ottoman pressure by taking Milan, and when the emperor broke his promise he reverted to his 'secret' policy of alliance with the Ottomans.

In the Mediterranean Charles captured Tunis in 1535, but in 1538 Barbarossa defeated a crusader fleet under the command of Andrea Doria at Préveza, leaving him undisputed master of the Mediterranean.

When Francis again approached the sultan in 1540 he told Charles' ambassadors, come to arrange a peace treaty, that he was unable to conclude a peace unless Charles returned French territory. There was close cooperation between the Ottomans and the French between 1541 and 1544, when France realized that peaceful negotiations would not procure Milan.

In 1541 Zapolya died, and Ferdinanad again invaded Hungary.

Süleymân once again came to Hungary with his army, this time bringing the country under direct Ottoman rule as an Ottoman province under a beylerbeyi.[14] He sent Zapolya's widow and infant son to Transylvania, which was then an Ottoman vassal state. Since 1526 Ferdinand had possessed a thin strip of Hungarian territory in the west and north, to which the Ottomans, as heirs to the Hungarian throne, now laid claim. In 1543 Süleymân again marched into Hungary with the intention of conquering the area, and at the same time sent a fleet of 110 galleys, under the command of Barbarossa, to assist Francis. The Franco-Ottoman fleet besieged Nice and the Ottoman fleet wintered in the French port of Toulon. In return, a small French artillery unit joined the Ottoman army in Hungary. This cooperation, however, was not particularly effective. With the worsening of relations with Iran Süleymân wanted peace on his western front. As in 1533, he concluded an armistice with Ferdinand, which included Charles. According to this treaty, signed on 1 August 1547, and to which Süleymân made France a party, Ferdinand was to keep the part of Hungary already in his possession in return for a yearly tribute of thirty thousand ducats.

Three years later war with the Habsburgs broke out again when Ferdinand tried to gain control of Transylvania. The Ottomans repulsed him, and in 1552 established the new *beylerbeyilik* of Temesvár in southern Transylvania.

When the new king, Henry II, came to the throne in France he realized the need of maintaining the Ottoman alliance in the struggle against Charles V. The French alliance was the cornerstone of Ottoman policy in Europe. The Ottomans also found a natural ally in the Schmalkalden League of German Protestant princes fighting Charles V. At the instigation of the French, Süleymân approached the Lutheran princes, urging in a letter that they continue to cooperate with France against the pope and emperor. He assured them that if the Ottoman armies entered Europe he would grant the princes amnesty. Recent research has shown that Ottoman pressure between 1521 and 1555 forced the Habsburgs to grant concessions to the Protestants and was a factor in the final official recognition of Protestantism. In his letter to the Protestants, Süleymân intimated that he considered the Protestants close to the Muslims, since they too had destroyed idols and risen against the Pope. Support and protection of the Lutherans and Calvinists against Catholicism would be a keystone of Ottoman policy in Europe. Ottoman policy was thus intended to maintain the political disunity in Europe, weaken the Habsburgs and pre-

---

[14]A governor of a Turkish province.—ED.

vent a united crusade. Hungary, under Ottoman protection, was to become a stronghold of Calvinism, to the extent that Europe began to speak of 'Calvino-turcismus'. In the second half of the sixteenth century the French Calvinist party maintained that the Ottoman alliance should be used against Catholic Spain, and the St. Bartholomew's Day Massacre of the Calvinists infuriated the Ottoman government.

It should be added that at first Luther and his adherents followed a passive course, maintaining that the Ottoman threat was a punishment from God, but when the Turkish peril began to endanger Germany the Lutherans did not hesitate to support Ferdinand with military and financial aid; in return they always obtained concessions for Lutheranism. Ottoman intervention was thus an important factor not only in the rise of national monarchies, such as in France, but also in the rise of Protestantism in Europe.

Charles V, following the example of the Venetians, entered into diplomatic relations with the Safavids of Iran, forcing Süleymân to avoid a conflict with the Safavids, in order not to have to fight simultaneously in the east and west. . . .

When the Ottomans renewed the war in central Europe, the Persians counterattacked, and in 1548 Süleymân, for the second time, marched against Iran. This war lasted intermittently for seven years. By the Treaty of Amasya, signed on 29 May 1555, Baghdad was left to the Ottomans.

These Ottoman enterprises resulted, in the mid-sixteenth century, in a new system of alliances between the states occupying an area stretching from the Atlantic, through central Asia, to the Indian Ocean. In this way the European system of balance of power was greatly enlarged. . . . In an inscription dating from 1538 on the citadel of Bender;[15] Süleymân the Magnificent gave expression to his world-embracing power:

> I am God's slave and sultan of this world. By the grace of God I am head of Muhammad's community. God's might and Muhammad's miracles are my companions. I am Süleymân, in whose name the *hutbe*[16] is read in Mecca and Medina. In Baghdad I am the shah, in Byzantine realms the Caesar, and in Egypt the sultan; who sends his fleets to the seas of Europe, the Maghrib[17] and India. I am the sultan who took the crown and throne of Hungary and granted them to a humble slave.

---

[15]A Turkish fortress in Moldavia.—ED.

[16]The sermon following the Friday prayer in which the sultan's name was mentioned.—ED.

[17]An Arabic term for North Africa, from Egypt to the Atlantic.—ED.

The voivoda Petru[18] raised his head in revolt, but my horse's hoofs ground him into the dust, and I conquered the land of Moldavia.

But in his final years international conditions became unfavourable to the Ottomans and Süleymân's attempt at world-wide domination met its first decisive failures.

The Peace of Cateau-Cambrésis in 1559 established Spanish hegemony in Europe, and as France was drawn into civil war she ceased to be the Ottomans' main ally in European politics. The withdrawal from Malta in 1565 and Süleymân's last Hungarian campaign in 1566 marked the beginning of a halt in the Ottoman advance into central Europe and the Mediterranean.

Review and Study Questions

1. From these selections, what sort of picture do you derive of Suleiman?
2. In the face of the overwhelming superiority of the Turks, how do you account for Suleiman's failure to conquer Europe?
3. Why were the Christian forces so disastrously defeated at the battle of Mohács?
4. Why did Suleiman fail in his siege of Vienna?
5. What role did Suleiman play in European diplomacy?

Suggestions for Further Reading

There are no Turkish sources for Suleiman available in English. See two bibliographical articles by Bernard Lewis, "The Ottoman Archives," *Journal of the Royal Asiatic Society* (1951), 139–55, and "The Ottoman Archives," *Report on Current Research* (Washington, 1956), 17–25. Halil Inalcik, *The Ottoman Empire: The Classical Age 1300–1600*, tr. Norman Itzkowitz and Colin Imber (New York and Washington: Praeger, 1973), excerpted for this chapter, is the only narrative history in English based on Turkish sources. Of some value, however, are the relevant chapters in L. S. Stavrianos, *The Balkans since 1453* (New York: Rinehart, 1958), the standard work on the subject. Also useful is Peter F. Sugar, *Southeastern Europe under Ottoman Rule, 1354–1804* (Seattle and London: University of Washington Press, 1977),

---

[18]The last independent ruler of Moldavia, more commonly known as the pretender Jacob Basilicus.—ED.

although it is organized topically and geographically and is of limited value as a historical work. A classic work of the same sort is A. H. Lybyer, *The Government of the Ottoman Empire in the Time of Suleiman the Magnificent* (Cambridge: Harvard University Press, 1913). Norman Itzkowitz, *Ottoman Empire and Islamic Tradition* (New York: Knopf, 1972) is a useful brief general survey of Ottoman history and culture. A useful and interesting article is Merle Severy, "The World of Suleyman the Magnificent," *National Geographic Magazine*, 172, No. 5 (November 1987), 552–601. Another interesting source, excerpted in this chapter, is C. T. Forster and F. H. B. Daniell, *The Life and Letters of Ghiselin de Busbecq* (Geneva: Slatkine Reprints, 1971 [1881]); it contains an account on Suleiman by a Western diplomat.

Of the biographies of Suleiman, the best, even though it is a generation old, is still Roger B. Merriman, *Suleiman the Magnificent 1520–1566* (New York: Cooper Square, 1966 [1944]), excerpted for this chapter. Of considerable value is a popular work by Antony Bridge, *Suleiman the Magnificent, Scourge of Heaven* (New York: Franklin Watts, 1983), mainly because it focuses on the role of Suleiman in Europe; unfortunately, it has no critical apparatus and only a perfunctory bibliography. Less valuable are the relevant chapters in Noel Barber, *The Lords of the Golden Horn: From Suleiman the Magnificent to Kamal Ataturk* (London: Macmillan, 1973). This work is simplistic and journalistic, emphasizing the most sensational episodes in Turkish domestic history.

Because of this chapter's emphasis on Suleiman's European ambitions, the standard histories of Europe in the Age of the Reformation are of some value. Two of the best are Harold J. Grimm, *The Reformation Era*, 2nd ed. (New York: Macmillan, 1973) and A. G. Dickens, *Reformation and Society in Sixteenth-Century Europe* (New York: Harcourt, Brace, 1966). Two topical works are also recommended: Sir Charles Oman, *A History of the Art of War in the Sixteenth Century* (London: Methuen, 1937) and S. A. Fischer-Galati, *Ottoman Imperialism and German Protestanism 1521–1555* (Cambridge: Harvard University Press, 1959).

Acknowledgments (continued from p. iv)

From *India: A Modern History,* New Revised Edition, by Sir Percival Spear, 1972. Reprinted by permission of the University of Michigan Press.

Confucius: "Confucius and Confucianism," trans. George Danton and Annian Periam Danton. Reprinted by kind permission of Routledge, Kegan, and Paul, 11 New Fetter Lane London EC4P 4EE.

Reprinted by permission of Macmillan Publishing company from *The Analects of Confucius* translated and edited by Arthur Waley. Copyright © 1938 by George Allen and Unwin, Ltd. Reproduced by kind permission of Unwin Hyman, Ltd.

Excerpt from *Confucius: The Man and the Myth* by Herrlee Glessner Creel. Copyright © 1949 by Herrlee Glessner Creel. Reprinted by permission of HarperCollins Publishers.

Socrates: From *The Clouds* by Aristophanes, translated by William Arrowsmith. Translation copyright © 1962 by William Arrowsmith. Reprinted by permission of the publisher, New American Library, a division of Penguin Books USA Inc.

Plato, "The Apology" from *The Dialogues of Plato,* trans. Benjamen Jowett, 1939. Clarendon Press (Oxford University Press).

Excerpts from *Heroes and Gods* by Moses Hadas and Morton Smith. Reprinted by permission of HarperCollins Publishers.

Alexander the Great: *The Campaigns of Alexander by Arrian,* translated by Aubrey De Selincourt (Penguin Classics, 1958). Copyright © the Estate of Aubrey de Selincourt, 1958. Reprinted by permission of Penguin Books, Ltd.

"Alexander the Great and the Unity of Mankind," by W. W. Tarn. Reprinted by permission of the British Academy. *Proceedings of the British Academy, Volume XIX,* 1933.

N. G. L. Hammond, *Alexander the Great: King, Commander, and Statesman,* Second Revised Edition. Reprinted by permission of Bristol Classic Press.

Asoka: From *Asoka and the Decline of the Mauryas* by Romila Thapar, 1961. Reprinted by permission of Oxford University Press.

John Strong, *Legend of King Asoka: A Study and Translation of the Asokavadana.* Copyright © 1984 Princeton University Press. Excerpt, pp. 204–212, 215–220, reprinted with permission of Princeton University Press.

From *A Short History of India,* Fourth Edition, by W. H. Moreland and Atul Chatterjee, 1969, pages 53–56. Reprinted by permission of Longman Group UK Limited.

Julius Caesar: From *The Lives of the Twelve Caesars* by Suetonius, edited and translated by Joseph Gavorse. Copyright 1931 and reviewed 1959 by Modern Library, Inc. Reprinted by permission of Random House, Inc.

From *Provinces of the Roman Empire* by Theodor Mommsen, 1968. Reprinted by permission of the University of Chicago.

From *The Roman Revolution* by Ronald Syme, 1939. Reprinted by permission of Oxford University.

Muhammad: Reprinted by permission from *The Life of Muhammad: A Translation of Ibn Ishaq's Sirat Rasul Allah* with Introduction and Notes by A. Guillame, published by Oxford University Press, Karachi.

From *The Spirit of Islam: A History of The Evolution and Ideals of Islam, With a Life of the Prophet,* Revised Edition by Sayed Ameer Ali, 1978. Reprinted by permission of the publisher, Chatto and Windus.

Reprinted from *Muhammad at Medina* by W. Montgomery Watt (1956) by permission of Oxford University Press. Copyright © 1956 Oxford University Press.

Murasaki Shikibu: From *The Tale of Genji* by Murasaki Shikibu, translated by Edward G. Seidensticker. Copyright © 1976 By Edward Seidensticker. Reprinted by permission of Alfred A. Knopf, Inc.

R. Bowling, editor, *Murasaki Shikibu: Her Diary and Poetic Memoirs*. Copyright © 1982 Princeton University Press. Excerpt, pp. 129–131, 133–135, 137–141 reprinted by permission of Princeton University Press.

From *The World of the Shining Prince: Court Life in Ancient Japan* by Ivan Morris. Copyright © 1964 by Ivan Morris. Reprinted by permission of Alfred A. Knopf, Inc. Reprinted by permission of Oxford University Press.

Eleanor of Aquitaine: From *The Historia Pontificalis of John Salisbury*, edited and translated by Marjorie Chinball (1956). Reprinted by permission of Oxford University Press.

E. A. Babcock, A. C. Krey, *William Archbishop of Tyre: A History of Deeds Done beyond the Sea*, Volume II. Copyright © 1943, Columbia University Press. Reprinted by permission of Columbia University Press, New York.

Reprinted by permission of the publisher from *Eleanor of Aquitaine and the Four Kings* by Amy Kelly, Cambridge, Mass.: Harvard University Press. Copyright © 1950 by the President and the Fellows of Harvard College.

From *Eleanor of Aquitaine* by Marion Meade. Copyright © 1977 by Marion Meade. Reprinted by the permission of the publisher, Dutton, an imprint of New American Library, a division of Penguin Books, USA, Inc.

Leonardo da Vinci: From *Lives of the Most Eminent Painters, Sculptors, and Architects*, Volume IV, Giorgio Vasari, Translation Gaston deVere, The Medici Society, London, NI 9HG.

"The Place of Leonardo da Vinci in the Emergence of Modern Science" by John Herman Randall, Jr., from *Journal of the History of Ideas* 14, 1953. Copyright © Journal of the History of Ideas. Reprinted by permission.

From *Leonardo's Legacy: An International Symposium* edited by C. D. O'Malley. Published by the University of California Press. Pages 69–81, 83–84, 99–100. Copyright 1969 The Regents of the University of California.

Martin Luther: Reprinted from *Luther's Works*, Volume 54, edited and translated by Theodore G. Tappert. Copyright © 1967 Fortress Press. Used by permission of Augsburg Fortress.

Martin Luther: His Life and Work by Hartmann Grisar, adapted from the German by F. J. Eble, Ed. A. Pruess, pp. 58–64.

From *These Theses Were Not Posted* by Erwin Iserloh. Copyright © 1968 by Erwin Iserloh. Reprinted by permission of Beacon Press.

Montezuma: From *Hernando Cortes: Letters from Mexico* edited and translated by Anthony Pagden. Copyright © 1968 Yale University Press. Reprinted by permission of Yale University Press.

Hernando Cortes, *Five Letters, 1519–1526*, translated and edited by J. Bayard Morris, 1960. Reprinted by kind permission of Routledge and Kegan Paul, Ltd.

Texts from *Codex Florentino* taken from *The Broken Spears* by Miguel Leon Portilla. Copyright © 1962 by Beacon Press. Reprinted by permission of Beacon Press.

Suleiman the Magnificent: From *The Life and Letters of Ogier Ghiselin de Busbecq* by C. T. Forster and F. A. B. Daniell, 1971. Reprinted by permission of Editions Slatkine, Publishers.

From *The Ottoman Empire: The Classical Age 1300–1804* by Halil Inalcik, translated by Norman Itzkowitz and Colin Imber, 1973. Reprinted by permission of George Weidenfeld and Nicolson.